P9-ELO-028

PRAISE FOR *FULLY CONNECTED*

"I thoroughly enjoyed *Fully Connected*. Amazing insights on a subject critical to modern working and living. I wholly endorse it, not just as a must-read but also as a much-needed compass to navigating the 21st century workplace."
Dambisa Moyo, Economist and Author

"Julia Hobsbawm is the unofficial UK Queen of Networking, but she understands that networking is about much more than lunches and parties. As a student of networks in history, I read *Fully Connected* with great pleasure and profit."
Niall Ferguson, senior fellow, the Hoover Institution, Stanford University

"Julia cares passionately about relationships and networks – and it shows. With loving precision and insight, she examines, describes and waxes lyrical about their power. She shows how our networks create or destroy our social health, distract us or support our creativity. She brings her whole authentic self to her narrative, and through her reflections and thoughts we learn more about her story, reflect on our own story, and think more deeply about the world we live in. Brimming with ideas and insights – fascinating, intriguing, thoughtful."
Lynda Gratton, Professor of Management Practice, London Business School

"I am buzzing about this book. Really outstanding."
William Eccleshare, President and CEO, Clear Channel International

"This is one of those brilliantly insightful books everyone has to read to understand the zeitgeist."
Baroness Helena Kennedy QC, Principal, Mansfield College Oxford

"*Fully Connected* is the most profound book about connectivity published this century. Hobsbawm nails it. She's the Marshall McLuhan of our always-on age."
Andrew Keen, author of Digital Vertigo *and* The Internet is Not The Answer

"Julia Hobsbawm reminds us that social media and social networks are about human connections not technology. She wants us to see that stilling the shrill voices of tech will connect us better. *Fully Connected* is a very good read."
Stephan Chambers, The Marshall Institute, London School of Economics

"Our social networks are both huge opportunities and lurking dangers, depending on how we manage them. Julia Hobsbawm's stellar new book, *Fully Connected*, pinpoints their pervasive effects on what and who we know, what jobs we get, our political views, our health and wellbeing, and more – and then tells us to improve our social health. A must-read for individuals and policy makers alike."
Professor Herminia Ibarra, INSEAD

"A great read, which provides fascinating insights into how connectivity is changing our lives and how we can thrive in a Fully Connected world."
Ian Goldin, Professor of Globalisation and Development at the University of Oxford

FULLY CONNECTED

FULLY CONNECTED

*Surviving and Thriving in
an Age of Overload*

JULIA HOBSBAWM

Bloomsbury Business
An imprint of Bloomsbury Publishing Plc

B L O O M S B U R Y
LONDON · OXFORD · NEW YORK · NEW DELHI · SYDNEY

Bloomsbury Business

An imprint of Bloomsbury Publishing Plc

50 Bedford Square	1385 Broadway
London	New York
WC1B 3DP	NY 10018
UK	USA

www.bloomsbury.com

BLOOMSBURY and the Diana logo are trademarks of Bloomsbury Publishing Plc

First published 2017

© Julia Hobsbawm, 2017

Julia Hobsbawm has asserted her right under the Copyright, Designs and Patents Act, 1988, to be identified as Author of this work.

All rights reserved. No part of this publication may be reproduced or transmitted in any form or by any means, electronic or mechanical, including photocopying, recording, or any information storage or retrieval system, without prior permission in writing from the publishers.

No responsibility for loss caused to any individual or organization acting on or refraining from action as a result of the material in this publication can be accepted by Bloomsbury or the author.

British Library Cataloguing-in-Publication Data
A catalogue record for this book is available from the British Library.

ISBN:	HB:	978-1-4729-2684-5
	ePDF:	978-1-4729-2686-9
	ePub:	978-1-4729-2685-2

Library of Congress Cataloging-in-Publication Data
Names: Hobsbawm, Julia, author.
Title: Fully connected : surviving and thriving in an age of overload / by Julia Hobsbawm.
Description: New York : Bloomsbury Publishing Plc, [2017] | Includes bibliographical references and index.
Identifiers: LCCN 2016050058 (print) | LCCN 2017009608 (ebook) |
ISBN 9781472926845 (hardback) | ISBN 9781472926869 (ePDF) |
ISBN 9781472926852 (ePub)
Subjects: LCSH: Information society.
Classification: LCC HM851 .H62 2017 (print) | LCC HM851 (ebook) | DDC 303.48/33–dc23
LC record available at https://lccn.loc.gov/2016050058

Cover design by Eleanor Rose
Cover image © Getty Images

Typeset by RefineCatch Limited, Bungay, Suffolk
Printed and bound in Great Britain

For my husband Alaric and our beloved family:
Roman, Anoushka, Wolfie and their big siblings Rachael and Max.
And for my great Sister-Friend, Jessica Morris.

I am OK but have too much to do –
crazy things I said I'd do long ago seem to be crowding around . . .
I can't get those long calm necessary pieces of time.

IRIS MURDOCH

CONTENTS

PREFACE

The spreading rate

One spring day in 2014, a young woman called Louise Kamano walked to the river from her home near the town of Guēckēdou in a corner of Guinea, in equatorial West Africa. Bad things were happening to people around her and she was scared. She crossed the river Moa by water taxi. No-one stopped her at the border. This land was full of crocodiles and AK47s, but Louise had something more dangerous to contend with. Although she had no visible possessions with her, something was concealed within her body – something she did not realise or understand. As she stepped out of her dugout canoe and onto dry land in neighbouring Sierra Leone, she unwittingly brought one of the deadliest communicable diseases known to humankind into a nation with a population of six million people. Louise Kamano was infected with Ebola.

From one nation to another: in total six West African countries would lose 11,000 people between them in the space of a single year to Ebola.[1] The disease carried across connected borders by people just like Louise. A local blog in Guinea put it like this: 'The muddy streets and shoddy buildings should not obscure the fact that towns like Guēckēdou are cosmopolitan, where people from all over the region plug into the global economy. Traders from a mosaic of ethnic groups and nationalities shuttle back and forth across borders'.[2]

---

[1] PBS, Frontline, 'Outbreak', 5 May 2015 and BBC, This World 'Outbreak: The truth about Ebola', 2015.
[2] 'The Toxic Politics of Ebola' – *Foreign Policy* by Peter Tinti, October 6, 2014.

Society is underpinned and connected by a mosaic of networks. We do not even notice them most of the time. Networks are the structures – animal, plant, machine and human – that carry everything from gossip to megabytes, timber to telecommunications. And illness. Some networks are weak and fizzle out – this happened with the original outbreak of Ebola in 1976 because it was in a remote area which was contained. All networks spread faster with an accelerant. In the case of HIV, it is unprotected sex. In the case of the Zika virus, it is the water on which mosquitoes breed. The accelerant is often social: poverty, for instance, such as people with no choice but to drink infected water. With Ebola, the accelerant was people – just people being alive and connecting with each other.

The network physicist Albert-László Barabási analyses the components and characteristics of different types of networks. He calls the kind which begins to replicate exponentially from many hubs and nodes simultaneously, quickly spiralling out of control as a 'scale-free network'. Ebola operates like this. So does another kind of network altogether – the internet.[3] For physical and virtual epidemics, as Barabási puts it, 'in scale-free networks, even if a virus is not very contagious, it spreads and persists'.[4]

In close-up, a highly-magnified picture of EVD, or Ebola virus disease, looks strangely beautiful. The diseased cells form clusters of blue and pink, tightly wound together in overlapping, porous, sticky clumps. These cells give rise to high fever, intense vomiting, diarrhoea, bleeding and damage to the central nervous system. The body reaches peak contagion in the final days before, during and immediately after death. The incubation period is up to 21 days. Epidemiologists refer to what happens to others during this incubation period as the 'diffusion' or 'spreading rate'. Roughly half of the people infected with Ebola survived. Louise Kamano was one of them. But in surviving, she wreaked havoc on those around her.

---

[3] Albert-László Barabási, *Linked: The New Science of Networks*.
[4] Ibid.

Criss-crossing home and rejoining her family network, Loui
thought to have passed the illness to the respected local healer,
who succumbed and later died. The funeral was very well attended. ...
came from far and wide. The ritual in West African communities such as those
in Guinea is to wrap and caress the body, to touch and kiss it, and send it safely
on to the afterlife. Rituals, as sociologist Richard Sennett reminds us, 'transform
objects, bodily movements or bland words into symbols'.[5] Funerals, the most
potent symbol of connection, lit the touchpaper for Ebola's spread and are a
reminder of what fully connects us in life and at death: love.

Human networks survive and thrive on information spread. Bad
communication and miscommunication can prove deadly. The World Health
Organization was famously slow to heed the warning bells being rung
repeatedly and bravely by the smaller, more agile charity Médecins Sans
Frontières, which urgently called for field hospitals, quarantine, soap and
hydration (there was no vaccine). Their early warnings were all but ignored.
WHO later tried to catch up but for many it was too little, too late.

Regional politicians also fatally mismanaged and miscommunicated with
others – and with themselves. It is believed that Louise was on a list of people
exposed to Ebola but that the authorities did not quarantine her. They were
looking at the bigger picture – how would it look to the outside world if they
shut themselves off? These were some of the world's poorest countries,
desperate to show an 'open for business' face to the world. Not understanding
that some who appeared well were in fact incubating the virus, they reasoned
wrongly. They decided not to count her at all. Louise herself was running away
because everyone in her village mistook the Médecins Sans Frontières
volunteers in their protective clothing as white witchcraft. This falsehood
accelerated through the community as fast as Ebola itself.

---

[5] Richard Sennett, *Together: The Rituals, Pleasures and Politics of Co-operation*.

Network effects and lessons apply everywhere. While Louise Kamano was superspreading Ebola, over 5,000 kilometres away in England the iconic British singer Kate Bush was doing something structurally similar – with music. The famous but reclusive singer put tickets for 'Before the Dawn', her first shows in thirty-five years, on the internet. Every single ticket had sold out in fifteen minutes. The effects of a scale-free network spread the word of these rare tickets like wildfire. Kate Bush said, unironically, 'I'm completely overwhelmed'.[6] There are other connections to be made about network behaviour and spread. In Belgium and France, a network of terrorist instruction began to move through a prison system and out into society with a force that erupted on the streets of Paris and Brussels in 2015 and 2016, overpowering authorities with its scale and depth. Barely visible to the naked eye, almost undetectable by political institutions, they are lethal if they are not tracked or stopped.

Culture, disease, ideas: they all operate on networks. The connective tissue is spookily similar. When they reach epidemic or endemic levels, we call this, thanks to social observer Malcolm Gladwell, 'the tipping point'. But how do we un-tip the wrong kind of spread? How do we to recognise connection and its discontents and know what to do? How can we have more of healthy connectedness and less of what harms us?

This book takes health itself as a metaphor for how we manage the spread and containment of modern connectedness. Putting the right kind of behaviour around what we do on networks, using our knowledge, and acting fast enough or slow enough, makes a big difference. In our bodies, in our societies, in our social systems.

The practices that enable us to connect the right knowledge with the right people at the right time I have called 'Social Health'. There was undoubtedly poor physical health in West Africa in 2014, but we can easily see how this was

---

[6] 'Stampede as Kate Bush tickets sellout in 15 minutes', Keith Perry, 28 March 2014, *The Telegraph*.

exacerbated and inflamed by poor Social Health too. What made Ebola spread from the relative confines of a remote village to the populous towns and cities is not just a cautionary tale about contagion. Ebola is the metaphor for our times: we are connected by social ties, by travel, by politics, by ritual and custom, by fear and by love. We are fully connected. What next?

Introduction
Peak connection

What does it mean to shift overnight from a society in which people walk down the street looking around to one in which people walk down the street looking at machines?

JACOB WEISBERG[1]

The very first cables of contemporary connectedness were laid in 1857, underwater between Newfoundland and Ireland: a core of copper wire, encased in gutta percha and 'wrapped in jute yarn which had been soaked in a composition consisting of $5/12$ Stockholm tar, $5/12$ pitch, $1/12$ boiled linseed oil and $1/12$ common beeswax'.[2] These early telegraph cables were the start of an era that led ultimately to all modern connected life: the telephone, the car, the railroad, the electric lightbulb, the aeroplane, the refrigerator and, of course, the computer. The global technology giants that we now rely on to connect people or objects with each other – Google, Facebook, China Mobile, Delta Air Lines, Samsung, Amazon web services, AliBaba, LinkedIn, Twitter – are all direct descendants of the nineteenth century, not newly born in the twentieth or twenty-first.

---

[1] Jacob Weisberg, 'Hopelessly Hooked', *New York Review of Books*, 25 February–9 March 2016.
[2] Bill Glover, 'Cabot Strait Cable and 1857–58 Atlantic Cables', *History of The Atlantic Cable & submarine Telegraphy*. www.atlantic-cable.com. See also *The transatlantic cables built in the mid-19th century shrank time and space* Frank Trentmann, *History Today*.

Ever aware, 24/7

Today we have more opportunity to be connected than at any time in human history. Mobile, social media and the internet – what the social scientists Barry Wellman and Lee Rainie call 'The Triple Revolution'[3] – make up the background hum in every corner of the planet. Today they are faster and more continuous than ever before, via an exploding mix of platforms and mediums. The World Economic Forum notes that, by 2020, there will be fifty billion connected devices in circulation.[4] Welcome to the fully connected era.

On one level, we connect with each other in the modern world in much the same way as we ever did, with language, images and stories. 'Our stories', asserts the writer Elif Shafak, 'and therefore our destinies, are interconnected'.[5]

When Facebook officially reached over a billion users on a single day in 2015, its founder Mark Zuckerberg posted online, 'It's just the beginning of connecting the whole world'.[6] But how healthy or desirable is this, really? In *May We Be Forgiven*, a contemporary novel, the character of George, a TV Network executive who commits mayhem and murder announces 'I am ever aware, 24/7'.[7] There's an edge of madness creeping in to all of this connection and it is called something: Overload.

Connection is like early industrialisation: the sweep of progress (from smartphone banking in Africa to wholesale revolutionary farm-to-table apps in China) nevertheless has its own belching factory smoke, its own unhealthy consequences. Humanity is beginning to choke on the fumes of excess. Most of

---

[3] Rainie and Wellman coined this phrase in *Networked. The New Operating System*.
[4] World Economic Forum article, 'The Internet of Things is Here', January 2016, https://www.weforum.org/events/world-economic-forum-annual-meeting-2016/sessions/the-internet-of-things-is-here/.
[5] Elif Shafak, 'As Storytellers, We Speak for Pluralism and Democracy', *The Guardian*, 21 March 2015.
[6] Zuckerberg initially posted on Facebook in August 2015 and then produced a series of media posts including the article 'To Unite the World, Connect It', co-authored with Bono and published in the *New York Times* on 26 September 2015.
[7] A. M. Holmes, *May We Be Forgiven*, 2012.

us lack a coping strategy or tangible tactics. We fall upon the idea of 'digital detox' or of temporary disconnection as if it is some kind of novelty, like being coated in seaweed at a health spa, and not an everyday routine. It is almost impossible *not* to be fully connected in society today. Emails, texts, 'feeds' of news, mobile phones that are not 'smart' . . . the list goes on and on.

We can no longer bank or board a plane or pay a bill without using connected technology. We have entered an eery virtual era when almost everything exists electronically first: we pay with our 'cashless' card, are tracked via embedded apps, and absorb adverts that use algorithms which are beginning to second guess us far more accurately than we might like (although there are always comic and irritating exceptions). Humans have been around a long time but we are now living cheek by jowl with another species entirely: technology.

The teeming brain

While Sir Tim Berners-Lee is the godfather of the current connected world having invented the worldwide web, the birth father of connectivity as we know it was Thomas Alva Edison, who, just 150 years ago, ushered in mass connection. He was the pioneering inventor of devices ranging from the phonograph to the electric lightbulb. Edison, who had studied the cable telegraph system extensively and had written about it at length,[8] devised the original carbon transmitter, the basis for that most common form of connected technology we still know today – the telephone network – for the Bell Telephone Company.

The digital telephone made its appearance in the 1980s but evolutionary echoes of Edison are with us in today's network technology. There is surprisingly

---

[8] Extensive papers for *Appleton's Cylopaedia of Applied Mechanics* (1849) cite Thomas Edison as co-author, and much of the material matches his own manuscripts.

little change from the days of manual carbon-filled glass tubes and using magnets and batteries in small batches, to those Elon Musk is using to design his subsonic Hyperloop transit system using passive magnetic sources to create levitation.[9] However, there is one crucial difference between then and now: human behaviour. Where we were once users of networks – travellers on trains, boats and in cars, people picking up a telephone (cautiously initially; no-one ever thought the telephone would catch on, and it was originally designed exclusively for business use) – now our lives are so embedded in and on networks that we behave as if we have actually *become* them.

Where does all of this connectedness lead us? The advances and benefits of networked technology in the advanced and developing worlds cannot be overstated. Of course, I love being connected. I take it for granted. Don't we all all? Skyped medical consultations. Webinars. Conference calls. Sharing and posting clips from YouTube, or uploading documents to cloud-based document sharing apps such as Dropbox or Slack. Email, LinkedIn, Instagram, Twitter, Facebook, FaceTime, WhatsApp, Snapchat . . . the list is endless; so are the possibilities.

Life can be spent in a series of windows within windows, opening and widening onto yet more. Connection comes before conversation via iPad or laptop. The mobile phone is used less to speak into than to text on or to scroll through. If I want to know something, of course I turn first to Google or Wikipedia, BuzzFeed or the BBC. Getting our information and relaying it to others in this way has become second nature. Connection is movement, mobile. Nothing stands still, and nor do we. Technology companies sell us limitless possibility. Finite somehow equates to failure. The blue, blue sky of online storage always beckons.

There may be convenience, the necessary thrill of innovation. There is also a radical reshaping of the way we live and work to factor in. Despite the manifest benefits of this connected age – the medical, mechanical, cultural and

---

[9] Luke Edwards, 'What is Elon Musk's 700mph Hyperloop? The subsonic train explained'. www.pocket-lint.com.

commercial advances – it also exacerbates, complicates, accelerates and infiltrates our lives, creating more problems alongside the many solutions. Our lives today are full of cognitive dissonance, all based around some of the tensions which happen when you put human beings, with their natural limits, in a computerized social world that is literally programmed to be without limit and never switched off. Unlike computers, we do not have limitless storage, nor do we have unlimited time: we still only have 168 hours in the week, a number that has not changed fundamentally since the Sumerian calendar first began to express time in terms of cycles.[10]

The twenty per cent of my time per week that is spent 'managing' my inbox, including having to look at the 'clutter' folder (which still manages to swallow emails I need; algorithms are actually no substitute for the human mind), feels like a necessary cost of modern living, even if the mind feels, as the nineteenth-century romantic poet John Keats described his 'teeming brain', too full of things to express and too time-poor to get them all out, before 'I cease to be'.[11]

Find me anyone working in an office, a school, a call centre, a warehouse, a parliamentary chamber, a public state frontline service, an NGO or a university who does not struggle with overload, who does not admit that much of daily life is not working well or indeed properly. Individuals and institutions share many of the same problems: we are already full to capacity.

Degrees of connectedness

I was born in 1964, in London's Bloomsbury, around the time that Gordon E. Moore, the founder of Intel, framed 'Moore's Law' – that computing capacity

---

[10] The Sumerians of Babylon are thought to be the first people to make a calendar. They used the phases of the moon, counting twelve lunar months a year and twelve hours between the dawn and sunset.
[11] John Keats, *'When I have Fears'*. Originally written in 1818 and published posthumously in 1848.

would double every two years.[12] This was also just a handful of years before the psychologist Stanley Milgram undertook a landmark study looking at just how short the social connection paths were between people. The answer, famously, was six – hence the phrase 'six degrees of separation', which we all instinctively know and understand to mean, ironically, its opposite. Rather than how separate or disconnected we are, the experiment showed just how *connected* we are to everyone, by only six removes. In a small world – and this experiment has indeed been dubbed 'Small World Theory' – connections are limited. Now they are not: Twitter, Ebola, airlines ... take your pick. We may still live and work and operate in small clusters, but we reach many, many others. And nowadays we can reach them very, very quickly indeed.

Moore's law sits inside two other movements: the death of distance and the rise of what I call 'peak connection'. First, distance. I was five in 1969 when the supersonic airliner Concorde took its maiden flight and Neil Armstrong took his first steps on the Moon, 370,300 km away from Earth. Just under a generation later, in 1997, the same year that the space station Atlantis docked with the Mir space station, the management thinker Frances Cairncross coined the phrase 'the death of distance', to convey how the new connecting technologies were blowing away not just timeframes but mere miles.[13] My working life has coincided with the death of distance. During the early 1990s – after twenty years of mass consumerism, television, the computer, all being connected by cables to a wall, at vast expense, some distance away – the distance changed. It moved right in and up close. First to our desks; now to our hands.

Second, peak connection. Back in the 1960s, I was far less interested in walking on the moon than I was in holding close my most prized possession: the Sindy doll. Sindy has long gone but I can remember exactly how she felt in

---

[12] See '50 Years of Moore's Law', www.intel.com
[13] Frances Cairncross, *The Death of Distance: How the Communications Revolution will Change our Lives.*

my arms and exactly what she meant to me. I could dress her and play with her; she was like a friend. The little girls of today still play with their dolls but their favourite characters are often an infinite distance away, up in the cosmos of the internet. As I write, the current game of choice for children is Pokémon Go, which involves the global toy of choice: a smart mobile phone. The world began its ascent a very short time ago, just half a century or less, to where we are now. Fully connected – and not always in a good way.

Origins of the stressed species

We may tell ourselves that it is technology that connects us most, which makes us somehow more human ('better enabled'), yet technology is the amplifier for the instrument that makes the music: it is still us, the person or group of people, who remain the most successful transmitters. The series of computing code and algorithms that gave birth to the connected social age were just an evolutionary echo of something fundamental: how everything from species development to ideas spread is done by people. The spreading rate of human society has, in evolutionary terms, been very rapid indeed.

The historian Yuval Noah Harari believes that the speed with which humans have evolved has meant that, as a species, we are immature at dealing with stress. He notes that for a worker in Jericho's wheat settlements of 8,500 BC, the newly flourishing farming communities of the ancient world 'revved up the treadmill of life to ten times its former speed and made our days more anxious and agitated'.[14] I often feel anxious and agitated, just like our Jericho forebears. Middle Eastern bakers back then could never have imagined that today I can download a 'breadmaking basics' app[15] on Apple or Android for £1.49, or that

---

[14] Yuval Noah Harari, *Sapiens: A Brief History of Humankind*.

[15] *'Bread Baking Basics'*, app, Ruhlman Enterprises Inc, October 2011.

'artisan bread' would become an in-store staple at the most mass-produced emporiums in the world: supermarkets. Could our Neolithic forbears, domesticating einkorn wheat in a world with fewer than five million people living in it, have imagined the possibilities of global exports of bread itself in a world of seven billion people, where cereal production will soon exceed 2,500 million tonnes?[16] So it is not just speed to which the fully connected life must adapt: it is scale, too.

We do not see life in the fully connected living as a crisis, especially not a health crisis, in particular, but we should. We think nothing of going to the gym and working out, but have not yet seemed to realise that our new connectedness has many discontents too. Take 'Generation Z', the social group that has followed the 'Millennials' and which is, according to Goldman Sachs, 'the first generation to be born in a post-internet world, truly device-in-hand'.[17] They can spend up to eighteen hours a day looking at their screens, more comfortable on social media than in many face-to-face settings. AI will soon give them computers that can 'talk' to them. Is this socially healthy? It is socially here. Now.

The attention span of students is changing fundamentally; some universities are being built without lecture theatres, catering for shorter attention spans and embracing their new desire to continually share rather than soak up learning from 'on high'.[18] Cinemas struggle to adhere to a 'mobiles off' rule, as customers seem unable to stop fidgeting with their phones. If we think about the staggering *Lancet* study statistic that twenty per cent of the global

---

[16] See Food and Agriculture Organization of the United Nations, '*World Food Situation: FAO Cereal Supply and Demand Brief*', December 2015.

[17] Christopher Wolf, '*What if I told You ... Gen-Z Matters More Than Millennials*', Emerging Theme Radar report, 2 December 2015, Goldman Sachs.

[18] The *Northampton Chronicle* reported in November 2013 that lecture theatres 'may not be included' in the new University of Northampton campus, while Frank Gehry's design for Sydney's Dr Chau Chak Wing Building School of Technology, which opened in 2015, features a '120 seat collaborative lecture theatre' and rooms 'designed for flexible configurations with moveable furniture to support group activities' see: www.uts.edu.au.

population will soon be clinically obese,[19] what might be the measurements for over-connectedness, bloated connection or discontented connection?

There is not nearly enough measurement or monitoring of the impact of the fully connected world because, until recently, we have been in love with, and in thrall to, its very existence and blind to its social consequences. Perhaps blind is not the right word. *Distracted.* It is true that parents have worried about 'sexting', and that Wikileaks, and subsequently Edward Snowden, have expressed deep public unease about invasions of privacy. But the culture of this new technology is addictive, and technology companies deliver us beautifully packaged, marketed products that have taken hold. Like cigarettes and sugar, such products can be highly addictive. We may be only just waking up to the disadvantages, but the commercial advantages are all too clear. The American media commentator Michael Wolff, writing about television, notes a similar trend. He likens the general speed, access and costs of connected technology to those of canned, frozen and processed foods following the Second World War. His prediction is that, like the rise in all things 'foodie', a refined sensibility around content might ultimately become desirable as a counterbalance to information obesity.[20] For now, everyone wants more. More information. More choice. More personalisation. More platforms. Our addictive appetites have been well and truly unleashed. And we are overfeeding them.

A new operating system

If we really were computers, we could do with a new operating system. Cars have them. Mobile phones have them. When could we humans have a new,

---

[19] 'Trends in Adult Body-mass Index in 200 Countries from 1975 to 2014: A Pooled Analysis of 1698 Population-based Measurement Studies with 19.2 Million Participants'. *The Lancet*, 387: 1377–96.
[20] Michael Wolff, *Television Is the New Television: The Unexpected Triumph of Old Media in the New Digital Age*, p. 195.

fresh way of looking at the tangle that fully connected living has become? It would help, would it not, to feel that our bodies, both the physical and the organisational, were clean and lean and uncluttered, that we had ways to 'defrag' and correct the blockages and stoppages?

Medicine invents new solutions all the time. In the space of months, cancer treatment leapt from being all about blasting tumours with broad-brush, one-size-fits-all surgery and drug regimes, to highly personalised procedures being carried out on patients.[21] When time is of the essence – and it is for every one of us – there is no reason not to be radical, and focus on what will extend time (life) or improve the quality of it (often how we spend our time). The good news is that the innovations are often not reliant on very new and expensive techniques. New thinking in health is informing new practice. For instance, very precise surgery, such as that required for bowel cancer, is being transformed by simple procedures aimed at making techniques simpler and less invasive. They are re-routing the way this surgery is conducted and it is having as radical an effect as a new drug – but it is actually just a change in technique.[22] All of this seems obvious the minute it happens, but it is due to trial and error, which, when it works, we call innovation.

The modern mass connectivity that began 150 years ago, and which accelerated at the turn of this century with email and the internet, is full of answers to its own problems – just like health and medicine. Some of these answers are ancient and some are modern. We would do well to look at them – it might make the difference between being a society that feels sick or one that behaves and feels as if it is actually well.

---

[21] This is even called 'personalised medicine'. See Elizabeth Mendes, *'Personalised Medicine: Redefining Cancer and Its Treatment'*.

[22] *'Life-threatening bowel ischemia can often be treated by balloon angioplasty.'* Medical Xpress, February 2016, reported that this relatively straightforward intervention provides 'a clear improvement compared to earlier treatment outcomes', one of a wave of new ways medicine is asking what constitutes good treatment techniques which are not always high tech.

The kingdom of the well

I have aggressive brain cancer. It's a gargantuan task but my diagnosis comes with a licence to be outrageously ambitious in my thinking. Uncertainty has moved from being my literal nightmare to my new best friend.

JESSICA MORRIS[23]

Most of us in developed economies have a basic literacy about physical and mental fitness. We know to smoke less, drink less, exercise more, and appreciate the difference between a carb and a calorie. Gym membership and the wellness market is so buoyant that it is not completely fanciful to suggest that tourist health spas in some parts of the Middle East may significantly make up for lost oil revenue. We know the value of both hydration and sleep; calming techniques ranging from yoga to mindfulness are booming business models of their own, culturally normalised. We cannot influence where we are born and we are only just beginning to influence how long we can live. We do know that we are going to live longer, whether we live with illness or without it.

My friend Jessica's approach to her aggressive brain tumour, which catapulted her at a moment's notice to that middle distance between what the writer Susan Sontag called 'the kingdom of the well and the kingdom of the sick'[24] has everything to do with health and very little to do with sickness. She is joining up as much patient-led information with the latest medical research and treatment data as possible and synthesising it to create a new pattern in understanding what does and does not work. Far from being daunted by it, she is energised, and with it she is breaking new ground.

We know that good health comes from individual action, but with collective support from culture around us: when everyone around us stops smoking, so

---

[23] Jessica Morris, *'Living with Uncertainty'*. www.jessicamorrisnyc.wordpress.com.
[24] Susan Sontag's *Illness as Metaphor*, published in 1978, was a groundbreaking treatise on the social customs and attitudes towards cancer, based on her own personal experience.

do we. On the other hand, we know that obesity likes a friend: you are more likely to 'catch it' from someone with whom you socialise.[25] So, in order to change behaviour, you need to have 'social proof'[26] that others are doing it too. Social proof theory teaches us something that network science and psychology can too: that behaviour is catching. Healthy behaviour – or misbehaviour – can be determined partly by others. Or by us. We just need to know what to aim for.

Health is a useful metaphor precisely because, at some level, it resonates with everyone, and we can identify with the idea that modern life is simply not that healthy. Perhaps a better word is *functional*. More often than not, modern life, working and personal, does not function well. Aside from bureaucracy (the most inefficient kind of network), other old cables of connectedness, particularly transport networks, can also vary hugely in their efficiencies. The more connected they are to giant hubs, the greater the risk of them being compromised or causing substantial chaos when they 'go down'.

When Sony experienced a catastrophic and malicious hack in 2015, their global electronic system failed to function for a period of weeks. Over and above the embarrassment of celebrity correspondence with executives being made public, now part of the 'TMI' (too much information) aspect of being fully connected, something far more systemic attacked Sony. I am told that pretty much every email, every record, every invoice and every order was lost, and for a period of time the production of movies and TV went into freefall. What got the system back up to a functioning state was something no-one had ever imagined: the manual, verbal, face-to-face calling in of favours. One executive told me, 'I had to call up a guy I know and say, "Look, we need this stuff printed and we need it now but we have no order systems or means of processing payment. Will you trust me?"' The healthy state of their relationship

---

[25] See Nicholas A. Christakis's study on connected behaviour around obesity, '*The Spread of Obesity in a Large Social Network over 32 Years*'.

[26] See *Influence: The Psychology of Persuasion* by Robert B. Cialdini.

kept Sony up and running in a crucial period; this kind of mending was happening all over the company.

Personally, no-one can fail to notice how far we have come in the literacy and practice of core health principles; diet, exercise and mental wellbeing are all factors that can determine the difference between an obese, sedentary, stressed life and an active, mobile and agile one. We have scores of diets, exercise programmes, apps, and above all considerable cultural push towards achieving wellness. However, we do not yet have a system of any meaningful kind around good connectedness, and nor are we yet acknowledging the scale of the problem of what happens to the health of a society when overload is unchecked. It is for this reason that this book takes health as its metaphor for social connectedness and argues that we can successfully transform how we function in a hyperconnected digital world by looking to the most ancient of all technologies – the human body and the human psyche.

Hardware, software

When my grandchildren are born, they may marvel that we ever survived without the hologram or the robot. They may only work in the 'Second Machine Age',[27] which will be intermediated by computerised, simulated 'humans' who are artificially programmed to mimic us. 'Wearable tech' may even become 'wearable human'. Why does this matter? Well, quite simply because we have a high degree of intelligence, which sets us significantly apart from and ahead of other animals. We err as humans, we forgive as humans, we connect as humans. Our signals to each other are very visible and audible, and drive our progress as a species. The authors of *The Second Machine Age* concede that, despite the doom

---

[27] Erik Brynjolfsson and Andrew McAfee, *The Second Machine Age: Work, Progress, and Prosperity in a Time of Brilliant Technologies.*

and gloom about jobs being lost, the one area that cannot be taken away from humans is in fact the service sector around social life.[28] So there is something not entirely positive about so much energy being directed to teach computers to think for us and to anticipate us, let alone replace us. Machines have an animal simplicity. 'Sensor' is usually without language, without the connective tissue and cognitive complexity that makes humans so . . . well, human. The efforts to teach a prototype driverless car to use its 'senses', as well as its sensors, baffle and annoy me. What kind of ambition for society is that? Quite apart from the politics of it (millions of people rely on cars for jobs and these will go if driverless cars actually happen in a mainstream way), it speaks of something else: an obsession with peak connection more for its own sake than for anything else.

So, we need healthy perspectives in this brave new machine-filled era and healthy behaviours based on a concept of health itself. Perspective to know that we embrace too much outsourced technology at our peril, and perspective to know that it surrounds us like an incoming tide whether we like it or not. We need perspective to judge the speed and pace of this tide, and to know when, if not to put on lifebuoys, to swim like crazy to reach dry land – at least some of the time. The psychology professor Sherry Turkle of MIT tells the incredible story of a young twentysomething called Trevor who is, 'a master of phubbing – the art of talking to other people but with your eyes on your phone. When I tell him I'm working on a book on conversation, his reaction is close to a snort. "Conversation? It died in 2009."'[29] Or as the trader-turned-philosopher Nassim Nicholas Taleb puts it, 'We are victims of the post-Enlightenment view that the world functions like a sophisticated machine, to be understood like a textbook engineering problem and run by wonks. In other words, like an appliance, not like the human body.'[30]

---

[28] Erik Brynjolfsson and Andrew McAfee, 'Will Humans Go the Way of Horses? Labor in the Second Machine Age', *Foreign Affairs*, July/August 2015.
[29] Sherry Turkle, *Reclaiming Conversation: The Power of Talk in A Digital Age.*
[30] Nassim Nicholas Taleb, *Antifragile: Things That Gain from Disorder.*

We overlook at our peril the benefits of social customs laid down precisely at the moment when *Homo sapiens* became, literally, the king of the jungle over all of our animal competitors: family gatherings, small groups of face-to-face trusted connections, and social intimacy associated with the five senses of touch, taste, sight, hearing and smell. And stories. Communication. Humans communicate naturally and instinctively. Why do we want a social future where that somehow plays a secondary role to machines, especially when we have some kind of choice? No matter how much of a march AI makes, there remain choices, much of the time. Without making those choices, why do we imagine our complicated world is going to feel functional and healthy?

Given how technology-dependent we are, perhaps we should look at the 'health' of a person and where they live and work in connected/integrated terms as being both 'hardware' and 'software'. They can, after all, be integrated rather than in opposition to each other, as 'mind plus body' is now accepted as more of a winning health combination than merely one or the other. Patterns of behaviour in networked technology, physics and the 'hard' sciences can be looked at alongside the structure of relationships, and the 'soft power' and 'social ties' of the social sciences, particularly in sociology, organisational behaviour, social network science, neuroscience and psychology. We have seen the start of this view in the research that marries neuroscience with economics, and the rise of new behavioural economics or 'nudge' theories, regularly deployed to inch attitudes and behaviour metrics upwards using simple but effective techniques based largely on social psychology.[31]

It is time to connect the academic literature of networks and the wealth of studies and papers stretching across the academic canon, which often lie deeply buried in journals like artefacts stored in a museum basement, known to few and ignored by many; rediscovering this archive of ideas helps us to

---

[31] See, variously, the works of Daniel Kahneman, Richard Thaler, Cass Sunstein, Rory Sutherland and David Halpern.

know the unique moment in which our society finds itself. This is because many of the solutions lie here, in unconnected strands that simply need joining together and looking at from a freshly ordered perspective. Management and wellbeing, sociology and behavioural economics, social networks analysis and the new social study which interests me – behaviours in networking itself.

The antidote I propose is Social Health. It is a way of drawing together different existing disciplines into a new, single, joined-up mindset and practice: a healthiness around connectedness. This is the beginning of a long road. In time I hope to see mass medical studies aggregating millions of examples of activities around personal and professional connectedness, in the way that we now can look at obesity trends. I am sure my friend Jessica aspires to the same about the deficit of cancer data when it comes to patient experiences.

As you'll see, the beating heart of Social Health is just that: not dry data but its main driving force; a person's learned and shared experience and how fully connected (or not) they really are.

Social Health

Health is a state of complete physical, mental and social well-being and not merely the absence of disease or infirmity.

WORLD HEALTH ORGANISATION DEFINITION, 1946[32]

It is now seventy years since the World Health Organization was formed and defined 'health' for the first time including the word 'social', although in those days it did not mean social media use, of course.

'Social' is one of the most elastic words in the English language. Wikipedia notes that it is a 'fuzzy concept in which the boundaries of application can vary

---

[32] Preamble to the Constitution of the World Health Organization as adopted by the International Health Conference, New York, 1946; entered into force in 1948.

considerably according to context or conditions, instead of being fixed once and for all', while the *Oxford English Dictionary* references both 'a hierarchical system with complex communication' and 'relating to rank and status in society'. It often has other words tagged on to it, to try and sharpen its meaning: social class, social care, social capital and, of course, social networks. Yet, whatever else it may mean, some constants apply; humans who have relationships with each other in some pattern or form are organised in a social way. Sometimes it is helpful, healthy and productive; sometimes it is the opposite. Sometimes people are alone and socially isolated; at other times they are in permanent communication – in groups, gangs, associations or societies.

Being social is both complex and simple. Let us think of it in very modern technical terms. First, there is the hardware of social relationships – the structures and systems. Take class, for example. If you are born in one social class, you never really become a member of another one, even if you might join it through wealth or career. If you are a management consultant, for example, the chances of you hanging out socially with street sweepers is low. The 'social capital' of the street sweeper, what the World Bank terms 'the connectedness of citizens to their community',[33] is equally low unless he or she becomes part of a bigger community project; a network of one is not as powerful as a network of ten. Second, there is the software – the web of relationships and connections that are made by people in more random ways. In network science, 'brokerage' and 'bridging'[34] lie at the heart of understanding what moves knowledge, influence and behaviour between different groups. In a connected age becoming bloated with connection, Social Health is the next step. Instead of merely doing what many of us feel we do most of the time – surviving – Social Health promises another fitter state: thriving in the Age of Overload.

---

[33] See Partha Dasgupta and Ismail Sergaledin (eds), *Social Capital: A Multifaceted Perspective.*
[34] See Ronald Burt's *Brokerage and Closure: An Introduction to Social Capital.*

To be social today, to be connected at home and at work, in your country and in your community, to do so safely and enjoyably but also productively, these are the challenges. Productivity, in its driest economic definition, is 'a measure of output per unit of input',[35] and the idea of it is polarising. It obsesses managers and policymakers, as anything up to twenty-five per cent of productivity in the modern electronic workplace is compromised or lost by not having better coping mechanisms.[36] Global productivity is stuck at around 2.1 per cent, with the phrase 'weakening performance' applied around the world, from the United States to Japan.[37] Not only is the very notion of productivity contested (it can be especially hard in a knowledge economy) but also the idea of productivity antagonises people who do not like to be measured, fed up with decades of inadequate 'performance management' in corporate life. Productivity as an end antagonises too, because the concept can clash. There is confusion about whether productivity is creative or just mechanistic. I believe it is both. I believe that productivity is essential, not just as a complex component of economic success but as a measure of our very creativity and wellbeing. You cannot be productive if you are not motivated, or if you feel stuck, squashed, poorly managed or in a dysfunctional setup. But most of our business lives and political lives are just that: deeply dysfunctional. They lack Social Health.

However, linking the idea of healthy social connectedness to a definition given seventy years ago by a supranational body built for the 1950s may not be sufficient for our argument. It reminds me of the way banking computer systems creak with incremental additions of code, which simply bring more pressure to the system. Outsourcing adds to the problem, as anyone made irate

---

[35] www.investopedia.com.

[36] McKinsey Global Institute, 'The Social Economy: Unlocking Value and Productivity through Social Technologies', www.mckinsey.com.

[37] The Conference Board Productivity Brief 2015, 'Global Productivity Growth Stuck in the Slow Lane with No Signs of Recovery in Sight', www.conference-board.org.

by hanging on the telephone to a faraway call centre knows. Where you really see the absence of healthy connectedness is not around banking systems, although that is a useful illustration. It is out in society.

The social network

The embodiment of the word meaning and activity, which we understand as 'social', happens on networks. Networks are the connective tissue of society. We talk of 'belonging' to networks like we 'belong' to a family. Networks, groups, associations, societies, member organisations, work cultures all create different manifestations of the network.

We live on networks, we mimic them, we depend on them, but we do not always feel comfortable building and using them ourselves. We can embrace them but so too we can feel distaste, ambiguity, shyness, diffidence and hostility to the idea of *networking* and *managing our networks*, all the while loving the physical networks. This is in itself a fatal disconnect because by doing so, we are overlooking one of the central ways to survive and thrive in the Age of Overload.

Perhaps it is easy for me – I am a natural connector. In my daily life, I engage in what in Hebrew is called 'shidduch' ('matchmaking' in English). There exist a couple of lasting marriages that I have 'made' informally between people whom I sensed would be right for each other. At the same time, I have built a business that allows me to be a composite of the three stereotypes identified by Malcolm Gladwell in his seminal book *The Tipping Point*: the Connector, the Salesperson, and the Maven – in other words, the person who bridges knowledge between groups.[38] Another term for this is, of course, the 'networker', the function of someone who net*works*.

---

[38] Malcolm Gladwell, *The Tipping Point: How Little Things Can Make a Big Difference*.

Academic network science may seem far removed from the more vocational, practical story of networking. Certainly, there were some raised eyebrows when I was made the world's first professor in networking, accepting an Honorary Visiting Professorship at London's Cass Business School. Surely networks are something for the physicists and the mathematicians and social scientists; their application in the real working world was less proven.

It is true that the practice of networking, superficially at least, appears to be pretty straightforward. Most of the literature on the subject is of the 'how to work a room' variety. After all, the context in which networking is culturally understood is of a cultivation of some kind, usually for commercial gain, rather than connected to science, data or pattern and, therefore, to prediction. Every business school in the world runs networking classes of one type or another, but it is taught largely as part of career curriculum, not as a core subject in its own right. To make matters worse, networking is seen as something that extroverts do better than introverts. It is associated with vulgarity more than social observation or cultural theory. It always amuses me that plenty of people eschew the idea that they use networks at all; a common fantasy in certain circles is that things like jobs and connections to groundbreaking ideas are from Mars, landing magically around us and with no intervention, no directed behaviour of any kind, and that if there were anything planned this would be too crass for words. This is, of course, news to the many networks of scientists; CERN may be many things but, above all, it operates as a network. And it is not just scientists, of course a lack of strong networks is a key obstacle to social mobility. Criminals or creatives, politicians or police forces, musicians or managers, all depend on networks and their most obvious human manifestation – networking. As the physicist Albert-László Barabási asserts, 'Networks are everywhere. You just have to look for them.'[39]

---

[39] Albert-László Barabási, *Linked: The New Science of Networks*.

Fully connected outcomes

I am outlining the case here for Social Health because I believe it is time to give connectedness, in all its many forms, a defined goal and definition, and in order to do so properly, Social Health obviously needs its own definition. I would like to focus attention on how connected behaviour can have different effects, and explain what the levers might be to improve what policymakers call 'outcomes'.

There are clear principles behind the idea of Social Health:

- We all live lives dominated by, and embedded in, networked technology and social networks.
- We cannot be – and literally are not – the same as machines.
- We lack a management system to enhance connectedness, and struggle on with no real organised process or underlying vision of what it means to be healthy in the Age of Overload.

If I was adding 'Social Health' to the current WHO definition, I might put it like this:

Social Health means balancing face-to-face and electronic connections in a way that manages flows of knowledge, networks and time. Those with good Social Health know who and what to connect with, as well as the value of disconnection as a way of staying healthy. Social Health is a mindset and a behaviour that applies equally to individuals and organisations.

Because the world's language is reducing – from the 140 characters on Twitter to the three words of the geolocation mapping app, *what3words* – let us really shorten it:

Social Health is who, what and when you know. Those with Social Health balance face-to-face and technology, and know where to find the off switch.

How to use this book

You may be reading this book because you have a general interest in what is happening in the fast-moving currents around connectedness and would like some ideas and suggested reading. You may be interested in business, management, change, strategy, communication, psychology or just simply this question: can the complicated connected life be at all simplified? Is there a way to navigate through the Age of Overload? I hope this book gives you context and ideas that you can take away and explore further. I will call you my Tourist, visiting a land I love and want to show you.

The book is in two parts. The first, The Way to Wellville, sets out the full scale of what I think we are all currently up against in the Age of Overload, and how the metaphor of health and the history of health and fitness over the last century can guide us to a blueprint for Social Health. Because my own life has coincided with some of the many technological changes charted here, I hope you will forgive a measure of autobiography in these pages. You can view these sections as being a story of the personal trip I have made, *'from Telex to Twitter'*.

In Part Two, The Blended Self, I look at the personal and the professional span of our lives and how we approach the Age of Overload in these overlapping spheres, from how we connect at work to the world of sex and intimacy – and the role networks play in everything we do. We are, truly, nations of networkers and I hope to persuade you of why this is the case.

At the end of the book is some practical advice, a series of six steps that can be taken if you want to look at changing some behaviours quickly. I am always asked for practical 'tips', and while the body of this book is not where you will find them, the end of the book is for fast flicking if you would like to skip to some 'how to' advice. You can find more on www.juliahobsbawm.com.

I am both an optimist and a pragmatist. Social Health and healthy behaviours can be created through a series of practices, principles, exercises and habits.

The approach must be both physical and mental. This is a human set of skills and it will rely on trial and error, as well as on building shared experiences. It was Aristotle who said 'We are what we repeatedly do. Excellence, then, is not an act, but a habit'.

PART ONE

THE WAY TO WELLVILLE

1

Hostile landscapes

Not waving but drowning

It is a sunny August day at the English seaside. It is 2007 and the first day of my family holiday in the 'picture postcard' eastern coastal town made famous by composer Benjamin Britten's Aldeburgh Festival. Aldeburgh still emulates the 1950s of his day: its town council regularly votes against increasing telephone mobile masts, keeping the area almost without mobile phone reception. People go to Aldeburgh to be cut off from modern life. I am no different.

I decide to go jogging – despite the fact that I am unfit and have had a streaming cold for what, I realise only at this moment, has been many months. A bunched tissue is permanently in my hand. But here I am, moving tentatively along a beach. I'm gasping a bit as I pound heavily and slowly along the shingle shore. I have not shed the extra pregnancy pounds, even though our youngest child is two years old. Everything looks vague and slightly out of focus. I was in my office until midnight the night before this holiday, finishing up work in a state of agitation. My 'to do' list did not seem to be going down. I never got to the 'When to do' part, because I always seemed to have to dive straight into an incoming tsunami of tasks. The 'new normal' for workers like me, those in the 'knowledge worker' businesses, service sector companies, start ups and office-based jobs – where the lights in the office may go off but work is carried home and continued there – was to be 'always on'.

But I have always loved my work and my family. I consider myself one of the lucky ones. I know all about 'good stress'. I swim strongly in the sea of modern life, I think. I don't feel underwater tremors; I do not see or feel any signs that I am about to go under.

I have run perhaps 1,000 yards and am less than halfway to the 'Scallop', the giant Maggi Hambling metal sculpture on the beach between Aldeburgh and the time-warped village of Thorpeness. I love the warm pitted steel and its curve against the elements. People are drawn to the sculpture, rain or shine; me too. I badly want to reach it but realise, dimly, that I won't make it that far. My legs turn to jelly and I stop, shocked at the sense that I am filling slowly with sand. The blue sky above me looks on mildly as I walk myself carefully back along the shingles. 'God, I'm unfit', I tell myself. 'This always happens when I try to do any energetic exercise.' But there is an internal warning bell going off that I can't quite place. There is something more, something wrong.

My husband and our combined five children are all at the holiday house. Arriving back, I feel horribly disconnected from everything. I am surrounded but alone. I mumble 'I think I've overdone it, I'm going to have a quick sleep', and drag myself upstairs to bed. I feel like I'm drifting away. We go to the local cottage hospital late at 8.00pm, the earliest we can break away from family duties. The doctor examines me briefly, picks up the phone to the main general hospital in Ipswich, 30 miles away, and makes a call. She turns and says to my husband, whose face is suddenly grey with realisation, 'They are waiting for you. Drive fast'.

It is ironic that I'm overwhelmed by something so serious, and so sudden: modern life is going through what the writer Robert Colville calls 'the great acceleration'. How apt that I have no time to prepare.

The diagnosis comes at night after an X-ray and blood tests: severe pneumonia, complicated by septacaemia. In the UK, 100,000 people are admitted to hospital with sepsis every year, 37,000 of whom will die. A blood poisoning whose onset is sudden and often undetected or misdiagnosed, it is a global health problem which accounts for 60–80 per cent of lives lost in the developing world each year.[1] My organs, it turns out, are a couple of hours at most from shutting down. The next few days pass in a blur of intravenous antibiotics.

I recover at the same pace as my descent into illness, only in reverse: initially steep (I survive) and then slowly over the coming weeks. It takes months to feel I can thrive again. But I no longer keep a full tissue with me; I stop feeling as if I'm constantly under water. I begin to negotiate and navigate my way back to life, vowing to find a new equilibrium and balance.

The singer-songwriters The Indigo Girls pierce me, singing in 'Ghost' of love and drowning emotionally by what starts with a 'pinprick through the heart'. A decade on, I realise that the initial pinprick of my illness was general overload, not an infection. Having no 'off switch' means exactly the opposite: always on. In 2007 the world was beginning to gorge on new gushes of information oil, and social networks felt like some kind of gold-rush communication discovery. I could not get enough of it: multi-tasking was my middle name. There I was (along with everybody else) hurtling headlng into the Age of Overload whilst holding on to old, unresolved problems: how to pace myself, how to manage time, and how to cope, not just with the benefits of connection, but the limits of them.

Six degrees of overload

We already know how connected we are. We often itch to disconnect but feel so linked to everything and everyone that the thought is seldom acted on. We feel virtuous if we detox for even a single day. Disconnection does not yet have a proper place in the Age of Overload.

So, speaking personally, how does overload feel to you? By personal, I mean in your 'blended self' – the person who has a homelife and a worklife, themselves often seamlessly connected. Instead of six degrees of separation, here are six

---

[1] www.World-sepsis-day.org.

symptoms of connection and its discontents, some of which you may recognise. They set out the scale of the task that Social Health is designed to remedy.

1   **Information obesity.** You find that your life is rife with information overload. You look after what you eat and how you keep fit, but you cannot withstand 'infobesity'.[2] You graze constantly online, on your phone, tablet, on news feeds, Twitter feeds, internal feeds and interminable emails. You can lose yourself for hours and regularly do. TV networks and news media constantly invite your feedback. Choice becomes a stalker, making you over-active, when, really, some passivity every now and then might be welcome. You often want to 'tune out' and can feel fairly close to 'burnout' – or at least you know someone like that. You have an office intranet but it resembles the contents of a house badly in need of a declutter; actually finding what you need is like being in downtown Los Angeles without a map. Yes, you have Google and Wikipedia and the BBC, but the web cannot help with *everything*. You read less, not more. You read shorter, not longer. You watch as your teenagers decline to read books, and you notice that anything over a few hundred words in a newspaper is grandly titled 'long read', as if you might get a gold star at the end for reading it. Your young team seems to know a lot about a little, and they do not know how to focus long enough to hold an in-depth conversation anymore.

2   **Time starvation.** You have more control over what goes into your body than into your diary. More than fifty per cent of your schedule is dependent on other people. Time feels constantly like the egg-timer when the sand has nearly run out. You will work for 10,000 days in

---

[2] First commented on in 2013, 'infobesity' refers to what the consulting house Bain describes as 'the torrent that flows through most organisations today [which] acts like bad cholesterol, clogging arteries and slowing reactions'. Paul Rogers, Rudy Puryear and James Root, 'Infobesity: The Enemy of Good Decision'.

your life, and you can probably count the contacts in your physical and social network in the hundreds or maybe in the corporate thousands, but you do a double-take when you realise that there are only 168 hours in the week. As most humans have to sleep for about a third of those hours, you are left with a tiny amount of time in an otherwise limitless world. You are not sure you can justify the time to meet anyone at work unless there is a distinct and valid reason. You have begun to view the way time is spent as a de facto commercial transaction, even without noticing. Time is money, so seeing people during work time must be about generating some kind of measurable return.

3   **Techno-spread.** We know about 'middle-aged spread' but what about 'techno-spread', when technology expands around us like a ballooning waistline, seeping across all our boundaries? It was when people starting wearing wristbands in bed, connected to their sleep-monitoring apps, that I began to worry. Who is in charge in your life – technology or you? One can never be quite sure. Using your voice and being face-to-face starts to feel like a luxury when compared to email, text, Twitter and other tongues of technology. Everything exorts you to outsource what you do and how you do it to an app, a cloud or to the Internet of Things. How much of you is *you*, and how much of you is *you plus artificial enhancement*? You communicate often on group emails, group chats or in 'broadcast' mode, and rarely send a physical handwritten letter or pick up the phone, not just because it feels too time-consuming but because it is also less comfortable without technology's protective layer in between. Intimacy feels problematic. It is an exposure to meet someone and talk to them, to make and hold eye contact. It carries risk and uncertainty. And yet when you come to think about it, the people you trust and turn to are all people you know face to face, people you opt to spend time with, people with whom you

share a range of valuable information. You find comfort, joy and answers in social sharing. You share jokes on Facebook, pictures on Instagram and articles via news media apps, and it increases your sense of connectedness in a good way. People and personal relationships matter more not less in an increasingly hostile landscape – it is a scary volatile world 'out there' and yet you are not sure you can manage to organise your social scene without help. It is often good to combine our social and professional worlds, but how exactly feels rather strange and new when, surely, it should just be one thing or the other?

The very thing that promises simplicity and solution is a critical and constant source of malaise: connection technology itself. Modern life has been so utterly transformed, and so quickly, that if you are Generation Y, a 'Millennial', or its successor, Generation Z, you will understand why my daughter, who was born with the eyecatching birthdate of 01.01.01, asked me a question with no irony whatsoever: 'Mum, in your day, were there cars ... or just horses?'

4 **Network tangle.** We all live and work on networks without acknowledging that the roads, communication cables, subways and overhead wires are just that. But what about personal networks? Who has designed a system to bring together – and separate – the different tracks of connections? Your networks are probably a disorganised tangle held on different systems. If there is a pattern, it is hard to see. Your connections, if seen from an aerial view, are a traffic jam on a very complex road bypass.

There is a blur between those in and outside work: the people you know very well, plus people you barely know at all. If you went circuit training at the gym, you would move from machine to machine, from exercise to excerise, to give yourself a well-rounded workout. Networks run on circuits but you do not run your networks like a circuit itself.

Some contacts lie dormant for years, others are on 'reply all'. If you had to identify the 150 most important people in your life right now, in any organised and meaningful way, it would take you days, not hours. You do not have a plan for who you connect and communicate with, nor when, except that you prioritise so that those you need most in the short term win over those who might give you help or intelligence in the longer term. The thought of organising your networks – or, worse, 'networking' – fills you with dread. It seems like one more thing on the 'to do' list, plus it feels contrived and competitive. You would rather not do it, thanks. But somehow, you know you must, or at least should. That you will be somehow left behind if you do not. Maybe you have joined the collective casting couch ushered in by the social age: you swipe left or right to be selected on romantic matching dates, selected first by algorithms, and then human subjectivity. Or you experience intense FOMO (fear of missing out) each time you log on; the grass is always greener, or someone is having more friends and fun than you.

5 **Organizational bloat.** Compromise. Bloat. Blockage. *Orgbloat.* Modern life feels increasingly unfit and complex. Yet the pressure to stay competitive and connected is greater than ever. If you work in a large organisation, you'll have endless systems and protocols, training and assessments at work but they do not feel productive or joined up. Most of the people coming up under you never stay more than two years, so institutional knowledge dwindles, while disruption is continuous. Or if you are in the freelance or self-employed world, 'making your own luck' is the new normal. Everyone is on a zero hours contract in this life, you are only as good as your last project, and the rules keep changing. The market in everything from oil to journalism, healthcare to manufacturing, is bucking about unsteadily. It is an effort to stay focused, because the goal posts themselves keep moving. In

Britain close to twelve million working days a year are lost due to stress, accounting in 2015/16 for thirty-seven per cent of all work-related ill health cases and forty-five per cent of all working days lost to ill health.[3] Productivity, however, is falling and continues to confound economists by the rate at which it declines. Then there is anxiety and depression. When Kenneth Koe, co-creator of the anti-depressant Zoloft, died, his obituary in *The New York Times* noted that since the drug's invention, 'more than 100 million people have been treated'.[4] Zoloft went on the market in 1991. It reached an epidemic of distribution to people who, in the same period of time, had access to the very world of full connection that has shackled so many to ill effects. There is nothing worse than telling a sad or depressed person, 'but you have nothing to feel sad or depressed about'. Yet we persist in saying this to ourselves about the times we live in.

6   **Life gridlock**. Gloria Steinem's rallying feminist cry of 'the personal is political', after the essays of the same name by Carol Hanisch, continues to be true.[5] You can bring more of yourself to work than ever before, and yet who you really are, what you feel and what you know, may not be on show all the time. You must still play a game, fit a mould and work in 'the system' around you. You can see that modern life should function well. The global economy, the social web and popular culture are all more connected than ever before. Yet something still feels out of reach. Perhaps something is out of sync, or out of touch. You may be, as

---

[3] The definition of 'stress', rather like 'social' is elastic, but is commonly understood to mean 'a state of mental or emotional strain or tension resulting from adverse or demanding circumstances', www.oxforddictionaries.com. See data from the Labour Force Survey published by UK Health and Safety Executive, 'Work-related Stress, Anxiety and Depression Statistics in Great Britain 2016', www.hse.gov.uk.

[4] New York Times obituary of Kenneth Koe, 2015.

[5] Feminist and writer Carol Hanisch's essay, titled 'The Personal is Political', appeared in the anthology *Notes From the Second Year: Women's Liberation in 1970*. Quoted at www:womenshistory.about.com.

the poet Stevie Smith wrote, 'not waving, but drowning'. You would like to improve your own lot and the lot of those around you. You like teamwork, provided what you are doing really counts. You distrust the term 'leadership' because so many leaders are awful and besides, there is only ever one leader – and then the rest, which may include you. You look around at politicians, business leaders and your own managers, and you think, 'No, all is not well'. Then you remember (or, if you are a Millennial or younger, someone tells you) that less than a generation ago everyone drank and smoked much more (especially in the office), no-one had a literacy about personal health and fitness like they do now, and wellbeing, mental health and wellness were all concepts regarded as very 'out there' and not remotely mainstream. But just look at us now. Something happened to our culture. There is a word for what can happen: change.

Guilty luck

I am a child of the 'émigré' generation of Adolf Hitler's gentrified refugees from Vienna, sponsored to get to England in 1936 before the full horror of 'Kristallnacht' became so cruelly clear. As such, I feel the shiver of a ghost when I see reports of migrants trying to cross the treacherous Mediterranean in order simply to live a life: that could have been me. So I feel lucky; lucky to thrive and live the ordinary healthy life I do when I could so easily have not survived at all. We all do, those of us with safe places to live, free from repression, healthy (I feel lucky to have escaped the worst of pneumonia), with food in our stomachs and paid work.

Except . . . something odd is happening in parallel in the lucky world of work. A hidden sense, guilty even, that we do not feel lucky at all. We feel a different kind of oppression, we are invisibly harassed by too much to do, too little time in which to do it, and broadly inadequate management systems with which to get whatever job we do, done. We are living under duress of a different kind. We are living in an open and free land, but forced to operate in a hostile landscape.

Do I exaggerate? Professional working life today – the managerial, office kind (even if your office is more virtual than static, your inbox is just as large) – puts people constantly under siege from pressure, competition, information, time poverty, excessive choice and a disorganised, chaotic approach to modern networked life. There is no beginning, middle or end to work. It is continuous. All around us. If we were military personnel instead of working mothers, fathers, students, teachers, shelf stackers, office workers, policy wonks or performers, we would recognise our *terrain* as multi-faceted and full of danger, one that is fraught with risk: the threat of losing a job battle, of shadowboxing an invisible competitor in a different timezone, in a different economy which has lower wages and is therefore more 'competitive' than your own; the risk of debt or of escalating costs; the peril of failing to keep up with the multidirectional demands of home and work.

'Work–life balance' was once a promise; now it feels like a taunt. We may go to the gym or plan what we eat or even be 'mindful' a few times a day, but there is little pattern to our management of information; it rushes in torrents through the networks we belong to and which communicate with us. Spam management, clutter management, LinkedIn messages, direct messages, now text messages: the clamour of people who are trying to get through to us (and us to them). What is wrong with this our hostile territory? Where, were we to look to the military analogy again, is the strategy to tackle it?

Ducking and diving

In a hostile landscape you must be properly equipped, flexible, adaptable and able to use tools and systems that are joined up; one mistake and you might fail not just yourself but others too. And you must know your enemy. On the home front, we are at least facing the threats. Anyone with a teenage child trying to manage their consumption of electronic time and relationships will know this feeling.

Our children are so overconnected that asking them to disconnect at all feels to them like a bereavement. Many of us feel the same. We are addicted. We feel shackled to our devices, even as apps and modernity can liberate us. Anyone with an elederly parent knows how complex and confusing the fully connected world can be. Everything modern is ill-designed for people with restricted or failing cognitive abilities, arthritic hands, poor eyesight; and age, let alone rising dementia, will wither mental faculties eventually. So, the age of connection is more for the young, but the very young are then exposed to far more than they or their parents bargained for.

Arguably some of us have the beginnings of a healthy pattern of behaviour in our home life – a regular family meal, or a fitness routine. The family unit's size makes change easier. You can take control of your health or your family's eating habits. It is easier to impose restriction, restraint or disconnection on a small group of people than a large institution or population. So the workplace often remains far harder to make healthy than the home.

It is for this reason that out in the wider context of society, of politics, business and organisational systems that we see the fully connected life starting to grip like an unwelcome vice. From time to time I join a meeting at the Foreign and Commonwonlth Office's sprawling premises on King James's street in the heart of Westminster, London. A member of the external Diplomatic Excellence Council looking at modern diplomacy, I am occasionally given a ringside glimpse into the inner workings of one of the great inventions of government: the Civil Service.

The process of government at its microscopic policy-delivering level is absorbing to witness up close. I always, incidentally, like the look of the professional emissary – the Ambassador's ambassador ('the guy behind the guy', as playwright David Mamet puts it), who scribbles intently during meetings, their laminated security passes tucked purposefully into their top shirts, the lanyward rope swinging loose above it. There is a lot riding on officialdom. The locations of these meetings marry classical with catalogue: the high ceilings and soaring columns of the original George Gilbert Scott design are chopped bluntly in half by ugly, boxy partitions. The jarring physical layout is a metaphor for the classical-to-contemporary struggle within any modern office. How can you do the old stuff, the day job, when you are under unprecedented new pressures, where time is no longer counted in centuries or months but in nanoseconds?

Of all the complex issues facing these 'mandarins', the scale and volume of their tasks today in a fully connected, fully networked world, coupled with the pace and scale of it all is dizzying and worrying. The Foreign Office has no real space or time in which to reflect, regroup and alter the basic configuration of what they do. Instead, 15,000 employees in 225 postings around the world must sift, find and convey a wealth of information, constantly connected to a web of politicians, ground teams and local communities, as well as any Britons visiting in good times or caught up in bad times, while all the time being under the gaze of social media's ruthless spin cycle. They do it, in my view, unbelievably well.

Connecting and communicating with citizens, employees and stakeholders is frankly regarded as a headache for many institutions and organisations – and with good reason. To do so efficiently and effectively, and at the speed we expect (usually instant, or as close to it as possible), requires skills and experience for which all but a handful are ill-equipped. The more that technology is relied upon, often the worse the problem becomes. Try looking on a government website to find what you want, or calling up a government office. Then do the same thing with your mobile phone provider. You will find the same situation. You enter an unhealthy tangle of automation that has nothing to do with good intention and everything to do with an overflow: too much to convey and too little time in which to convey it, and often in too little space (the best website cannot contain that many words).

Many facets of social connection and of basic communication – in politics especially – show the classic symptoms of anxiety and stress, of signals that not everything is working as it should be. Communication breakdown alone is not just rife but responsible for some of the worst side-effects of the age of connection's most egregious disconnections. Terrorist atrocities in recent years – from the Boston Bombings of 2014, to the Paris, Baghdad, Brussels, Tunisian and Turkish attacks of 2015–2017 all suffered from communication failures and massive holes at the centre of the intelligence networks, despite record levels of surveillance and funding for anti-terrorism tracking worldwide.

What else is communication breakdown except a failure of connection? The security services want more surveillance, not less. But they clearly cannot cope with sifting all the information and intelligence they generate. Granted, an extreme example, but good Social Health is about gathering different intelligence – local, trusted information from within those communities that are seen to be at risk. No amount of phone tapping can replace this. Social Health recognises that you often need to make small changes to effect bigger change, to value the granular as well as the grandiose approach. I agree with the anthropologist-journalist Gillian Tett who notes that, 'We can change the formal and informal rules that we use to organize the world. Or we can if we stop and think.'[6]

Look outside our national borders. Our global institutions are creaking at the political seams. All were set up in the middle of the last century and the postwar generation following the Second World War: the United Nations, the European Union, NATO and the World Bank. The World Health Organization itself came out of the UN immediately following the Second World War. It cannot be coincidence that they are out of sync with the new generation, this new momentum. They were not built for this particular era – and it shows.

---

[6] Gillian Tett, *The Silo Effect, Why every organisation needs to disrupt itself to survive.*

Not only are the old establishment systems of government and global governance under stress. The new generation of decision-makers – that is, both leaders of tomorrow and ordinary voters – are reacting not by measured consideration of what to do next, but exactly the opposite. The British commentator Matthew d'Ancona put it well, noting that 'In the Babel of the digital nanosecond, voters are driven less by pristine moral imperatives than by the crushing weight of the immediate and of proximate stimuli.'[7] We are in the teenage years of a new century but somehow cling to a narrative set – such as the WHO definition of health – from the middle-aged years of the last one. Here are two examples of the connected age and how it remains a hostile landscape for society at large.

Lost girls

August, wrote the novelist Edna O'Brien, is a wicked month. During the summer of 2002, the national psyche was haunted by two young girls who had gone missing from Soham in Cambridgeshire. Day after day, their faces shone out terribly from photographs on TV and newspaper front pages. Holly Wells and Jessica Chapman, both aged ten, had vanished from one moment to the next. We knew what they were wearing: in the photograph they stand close to each other, as best friends do, proudly wearing their red and white Manchester United football club strips. One of them beams confidently at the camera while the other smiles more hesitantly. We all searched that photograph for meaning, every time we saw it; perhaps it might contain the mystery of their fate.

The girls disappeared in an English county with borders (and connections) with a total of seven others: Lincolnshire and Norfolk to the north/north-east, Suffolk to the east, Essex and Hertfordshire to the south, and Bedfordshire and

---

[7] Matthew d'Ancona, 'Forget History, in the New Politics Only the Now Matters', The Guardian, August 2015.

Northamptonshire to the west. The landmass of Cambridgeshire is just under 4,000 square miles. The alarm was raised quickly but over the next two weeks there was an escalating sense of dread as the two girls could not be found.

The reason they could not be found was because someone had killed them. That someone was a man called Ian Huntley, the caretaker at the girls' school. He had a string of convictions and near-convictions in his home town of Grimsby, Humberisde, but 'flaws in the system', let him loose to kill and fool the media and families into thinking he was helping to search for the girls. He was so assiduous in his help that it must have alerted the psychological profilers. In fact, he had murdered Holly and Jessica within a few hours of them going missing and within yards of where they were last seen. They had gone out locally for some sweets and Huntley had invited them into his house on a casual pretext. Because they knew him and could not have imagined they were in any danger, the girls went inside. What happened next is unknowable, except for the fact that on 17 August their bodies were found, partially decomposed, across the county border in Norfolk.

In the case of the Soham murders, the Social Health of the police and their inability to spot patterns or to intervene was woeful. Sometimes police forces are accused of covering up. In this case they had already uncovered evidence but failed to connect its significance, to join up the dots. In the public enquiry that followed the murders, it transpired that, three years earlier, in 1999, an internal police intelligence report in Grimsby had said of Huntley: 'It is quite clear that he is a serial sex attacker and is at liberty to continue'. Why were the patterns not recognised? There was no pattern of Social Health, no idea that a procedure which puts connectedness itself at the heart could have been developed or implemented. The national police network failed; knowledge of Huntley's propensity to attack girls was not passed on. At the time he applied to become a school caretaker in Soham, vital information was simply left on a fax machine. Human error allowed an inhumane man to kill two young girls. The police forces involved were fully computerised – fully connected in a technical sense but completely disconnected where it mattered. In the same public enquiry a catalogue of social health errors was laid bare. There was 'organisational bloat', 'techno spread' and 'information obesity' in abundance.[8]

The muddle, chaos and miscommunication in the public agencies, ranging from the police to the local government's Social Services, provide an object lesson in what happens when there is no Social Health at play in public agencies. In the summer of 2016, two women in Fife, Scotland, were convicted of inflicting hideous torture and injuries on several young boys, including the murder of the two-year-old son of one of the women. The Social Services teams involved had simply failed to function with any of the behaviours I outlined in the definition of Social Health or what some might simply called 'joined-up thinking'. Why does this still keep happening? Because the idea that fully connected lives are full of dysfunction and that we need to take specific steps to address this has not happened – yet. Fully connected problems – and solutions – happen everywhere. In small or large bureaucracies, in 'miscoms' between people in a two-way conversation or played out in magnified multi-agency landscapes. The principles of recovery from what are at the very least bad habits and poor practices can be as surprising as they are effective. What political agencies often refer to, after the fact, as 'lessons learned'.

Quarantine

In that same summer of 2002, when Holly Wells and Jessica Chapman were abducted and killed, I took our young daughter Anoushka to a family fair in a

---

[8] Sir Michael Bichard's 'The Bichard Inquiry Report: Safeguarding Children' was published in 2004 following Ian Huntley's conviction for the murders of Jessica Chapman and Holly Wells, reflecting the findings of an independent inquiry into safeguarding procedures, record keeping, vetting and information sharing in Humberside Police and Cambridgeshire Constabulary.

park. Not a funfair but a day out with bouncy castles and stalls. I put her in an enclosed nursery and took out my new toy – a mobile phone. This would have been 'digital cellular' back then, i.e., nothing fancy. If it had been, I would have checked the news – the bulletins were dominated all day by the two girls in Soham. At the back of their minds, everyone must have felt uneasy. I looked up and away for a moment – and when I looked back, my daughter was gone.

The on-site police were wonderful, and immediately swung into action. The first thing they did was lock down the area, effectively putting the park into temporary quarantine. They quickly found my little girl, with her short brown hair and dark brown eyes. I still have a photograph of her from that time, clasping her hands together and wearing the outfit she wore in those agonizing few minutes that seemed to stretch into centuries of desperate fear. She wore a navy blue t-shirt on top of leggings. The t-shirt had a big silver star on it and pink and blue stripey arms. It is amazing how often you can send your children out into the world wearing unmemorable clothing but I regularly thank an invisible God that this day was not one of them, and that I could recount her clothes very clearly.

Recently I told Anoushka, now a teenager, about that day; it turns out she remembers it quite clearly. She says she walked out of the confined nursery area 'because I wanted to, even though I knew I shouldn't, so I went and sat on a bench and then they came and found me'. I had never filled in those hideous long minutes until now. The way in which the police went about finding our daughter showed no connection disorder, and other than the fact that I looked away for a second, nor was there any in losing her. The response to finding Anoushka was a socially healthy one: everything joined up well. Mainly, I believe, she was found because the possible exits and avenues through which she could have walked or been taken out of the park were quickly closed. In effect, the police implemented an immediate quarantine, a disconnection.

The quarantine approach happened in a broader context in West Africa during the Ebola crisis. There, it was not a little girl accidentally breaking out of her enclosure and going wandering off. It was a disease breaking out of the confines of its animal barriers, breaking into humans, and then spreading out through the unlocked gates of poorly managed Social Health. Remember that Louise Kamano (whose story is told in the Preface) simply walked over the border into Sierra Leone. Whilst the politics of policing a single park in London are very different from those of policing a population restless with anxiety and trying to quarantine them, there are distinct parallels. When Ebola was running rampant, and control of its medical and geographical borders was all but lost, there was one critical solution: to quarantine the sick people as soon as they showed symptoms. But local customs and superstitions and fear that the medics in their white suits were practising witchcraft instead of medicine meant that many stayed hidden away at home, pushing the disease deeper into their communities. Only one African leader (the only female leader in Africa) was brave enough to say and do the unthinkable: at the height of the crisis, President Ellen Johnson Sirleaf of Liberia imposed a nationwide curfew from 9.00am to 6.00pm.

Initially the strategy was met with scepticism from the WHO itself and uproar from the community. President Johnson admitted that the move raised tensions. But the quarantine, coupled with the communication of a highly visible public health awareness campaign on the back of it, dramatically shortened the spread of Ebola. *The New York Times* commented that 'the disease has declined drastically in Liberia over the past few months'.[9] But it became obvious that what the President had done was brave and right. She had shut down the network system of transmission when it became the only option. She had communicated it, managed it and used her intuition that this had to be done, and acted swiftly.

---

[9] Rick Gladstone, *'Liberian Leader Concedes Errors in Response to Ebola'*, New York Times 2015.

Compare and contrast the two cases. In the Soham example, there was multiple system failure, spread over multiple geographical areas. A culture of attitudes may well have contributed to inertia on behalf of the police, a lack of motivation to see Huntley for what he was early on in his sexual offending 'career' – an unstable predator. One young woman's allegation of rape by Ian Huntley was dropped, and it is arguable that this is partly because the police believed she had, in some way, 'asked for it' because she had left a nightclub with him and gone to an alley. Whilst the police made strenuous efforts to find the two little girls in Cambridgeshire, older girls and young women had fared less well in Humberside. A fatal connection developed between both groups of young women. Instead of cutting off Ian Huntley from his prey, the actions of the police enlarged his options to access them.

In Africa, however, entirely different behaviours took place – and the results were different too. Disconnection was actively initiated here, cutting off both geographical areas but also activating quarantine. How different would things be if Ian Huntley had been quarantined? A major finding of the Bichard Report into the events concluded that police data gathering and data sharing was inadequate. He had, after all, moved counties, un-noticed by any new police force. Just like Louise Kamano, known to have been exposed to Ebola but not counted in any system, just walking from one local border to another, only in her case it was from neighbouring country to the next.

A friend of mine who adopted a severely brutalised child told me that the parents would regularly move area, a measure designed entirely to conceal the physical and emotional signs of the abuse they were inflicting on him. It was only an entirely chance meeting with a teacher from a previous school seeing the child turn up hundreds of miles away in a new school that set in train a series of links that eventually freed the child from his enslavement. Serial offenders often move around to avoid detection, it is their mobility which gives them freedom. Geographic profiling now shows just how limited the range of killers can be – they, like Ian Huntley, actually more often than not kill surprisingly close to their homes.[10] But they often take their victims' bodies elsewhere to dispose of them. The quarantine time can be highly valuable and is often overlooked, as the instinct of police forces is often to look at the widest, most connected geography, not the narrowest one.

Tim Berners-Lee, founder of the World Wide Web, has commented that connectedness is absent from many organisations, despite the possibilities that he opened up for them back in the European particle physics lab at Cern in 1989. Of the many quotes listed about his sayings on the internet, the one which stands out for me is not about the internet, but about management of organisations: 'Any enterprise CEO really ought to be able to ask a question that involves connecting data across the organization ... Most organizations are missing this ability to connect all the data together.'[11] For a police force, a government department, a school, or a multinational, 'data' does not just mean digits, it means people. Most organisations do not have the ability to connect people, ideas, problems and solutions. They do not call their databases 'peoplebases', but perhaps they should. They think they are fully connected, and they tell themselves that technology makes it so. But they have forgotten the basic systems and structures of human behaviour and with it Social Health: how we connect and/or disconnect in order to do the right thing.

Now it is time to look at fitness and health themselves and see how and where they can instruct us to apply their lessons to Social Health.

---

[10] João Medeiros, 'How Geographic Profiling Helps Find Serial Killers, www.wired.co.uk
[11] See www.brainyquote.com.

2

Fitness as a metaphor

Person of the year

In 1980 a charismatic Californian college dropout called Stuart Karl came calling on a world famous Oscar-winning actress. He had experimented with trade publishing Spa & Sauna *magazine, what* The New York Times *later referred to in his obituary as magazines 'for purveyors of waterbeds and hot tubs',[1] before becoming interested in the burgeoning video cassette market and publishing* Video Store *magazine. He became convinced there was a market for non-entertainment video, featuring documentary interviews and 'how to' guides. He founded 'Karl Home Video' and featured, amongst others, an interview with John Lennon. Then his wife, a fan of Jane Fonda's Workout, had an idea. The rest, as they say, is history.*

As she later said: No one had ever done a fitness video before. I don't remember exactly when I realized that, in spite of myself, this little workout video had given birth to a new industry. Women began to hear about it. Friends were telling each other, "Hey, check this out! This really works!" VCR players became cheaper as the

---

[1] Obituary by Richard R. Stevenson, 7 February 1988, *New York Times*.

demand grew and, before I knew it, 17 million copies of that original video had been sold.[2]

Jane Fonda's workout video became the bestselling VHS of all time.

Fonda embodied all the sassy, experimental, new-found energy, optimism and ambition of American women in the 1970s, leading the world in a new wave of American feminism.

We talk about standing on the shoulders of giants. In Jane Fonda's case, and perhaps unknown to her, she stood on the shoulders of someone considerably smaller. A petite blond telephone operator called Abbye 'Pudgy' Stockton,[3] *who worried about her weight, became the first woman to work out like men with dumb bells on 'Muscle Beach' in Southern California, a generation before mass media made Jane Fonda a moviestar. Her all-female gym, the Salon of Figure Development on Sunset Boulevard, Los Angeles, opened just two years after the World Health Organization defined wellbeing as being a composite of physical, mental and social wellbeing. Sometimes it just takes time for old ideas to catch on again, reignited by luck, timing and something else, too: the tools of communication.* [4]

Jane Fonda connected to such a wide audience because she tapped the zeitgeist. Her connection was fuelled by technology. The video came out in 1982, the same year that Time *magazine named the computer as 'Person of the Year'. Technology brought an ancient fitness, practised communally or in public spaces, right into the home. Fitness was returning to something ancient: an all-encompassing kind of mental, physical and emotional power not seen since someone far older than either Fonda or Stockton – Aristotle.*

---

[2] Jane Fonda, '30th Anniversary of My First Workout Video', 24 April 2012, www.janefonda.com.

[3] Brooke Siem notes in an article on barbend.com entitled '*Abbye "Pudgy" Stockton is the reason why women lift weights*', that 'After World War II, she opened a gym for women on Sunset Boulevard and began writing the column "Barbelles" for *Strength and Health* magazine', 6 April 2016.

[4] Health Fitness Revolution, '*Top 10 Heath Benefits of Zumba*', 10 April 2015, www.healthfitness revolution.com.

Our bodies, ourselves

Toe bone connected to the foot bone

Foot bone connected to the heel bone

Heel bone connected to the ankle bone

Ankle bone connected to the shin bone

Shin bone connected to the knee bone

Knee bone connected to the thigh bone

Thigh bone connected to the hip bone

Hip bone connected to the back bone

Back bone connected to the shoulder bone

Shoulder bone connected to the neck bone

Neck bone connected to the head bone

Now hear the word of the lord.

DEM BONES, JAMES WELDON JOHNSON

At school in London in the 1970s, before we sat at our hard wooden desks at Gospel Oak School on the edge of leafy Hampstead Heath, North London, we sat on our bottoms on hard wooden floors in morning assembly and sang songs. A favourite was the famous negro spiritual, *Dem Bones*. Originally written a year before the Great Depression in 1928, it was recorded countless times during the twentieth century by near-forgotten greats such as Shirley Caesar, the Kingsmen, the Lennon Sisters, and Rosemary Clooney, aunt of the actor George. Everyone, the world over, seemed to relate to this catchy tune.

What does it mean to be healthy? Let's start at the beginning. Everybody has a body. Big, small, fat, slender, brown, black, white, beige. Pear-shaped or apple shaped. Tall and bony. Short and fleshy. We speak of 'able-bodied' or 'disabled'. Language and meaning in health revolve around the body itself, whatever its shape, size or condition. As individual as a snowflake, connected by biology, history, geography and humanity. And by blood and bone.

Dem Bones reminds me of a children's book called *Funnybones* in which skeletons come out to play at night, the bones clanking out of sync with each other.[5] The oddness of this makes it funny. But my children always laughed with a hint of anxiety: bones are supposed to be connected to, not to swing independently from, each other. If they are not connected, they are broken. Even when very young, children understand that to be broken in pieces is wrong, hurts and needs to be mended.

I like the idea of the connected body, with all of its bones and joints joined together, as a metaphor for healthy connectedness in a wider context. The longing to be part of a physical structure that is whole is both ancient and entirely natural. Not just our own individual physical and spiritual or religious self, but our social and collective ones too: a family, a village, a community.

We want to belong and be whole but we also strenuously want to avoid breakage. The language of the body is often used in relation to society: we describe a 'fracture' or 'fissure', which then widens into war. When a system collapses, it is described in much the same way as a collapsed vein. A mechanistic system, a car maybe, has a 'breakdown' – just as we describe a person whose mental health needs mending. An organisation that is broken is described as 'dysfunctional' as in 'not functioning' – i.e., broken. Bodily language abounds: computers become 'infected' with 'malware' and 'viruses'.

The Social Health that I described earlier is about how we treat our physical and emotional connections in a world which is full of connectedness and its many discontents, just as we connect to our physical and mental health and fitness. But attaining this particular state of health is not quite the same as losing weight or toning up; it is much more holistic than that. At the core of it is belonging and completeness – just like the cautionary children's tales tell us. While the whole business of connection, and the word 'social', feels hijacked today by the idea of an electronic connection, it is of course far less to do with whether it is on Snapchat

---

[5] A classic children's book by Janet Ahlbern and Alan Ahlberg, Puffin, new edition 1999.

or Instagram, and more to do with who you connect to, and whether you feel connected, disconnected or, worse, discarded. The writer Johann Hari has a point when he says that 'the opposite of addiction isn't sobriety. It's connection.'[6]

There is a famous scene in another children's story, the Pixar movie *Toy Story 2*. The hero Woody, a kind, skinny ragdoll cowboy rips his arm by accident while his human owner Andy is out. Later, the boy rushes in, grabs his beloved toy and immediately notices the ripped arm. 'Oh,' he says slowly and sadly. 'You're broken.' There is incredible pathos with Woody swirling, discarded by his beloved Andy, deep down in a dustbin. He is, in fact, having a nightmare, waking to remember that he has been discarded: 'shelved' like a bad product on the top shelf of Andy's bedroom, alongside another broken toy, 'Wheezy', a dust-covered penguin They comfort each other. The pain of being once loved and then abandoned is at the core of the movie. The universal appeal of the *Toy Story* trilogy, apart from its child–adult scripts and jokes, and the premise that toys have feelings, is one of community: the toys band together, they create unlikely alliances, and they mend each other's broken feelings.

Aristotle's Gym

Archaeologists show that from the time we began to develop systems for harnessing food and growing stable societies some 70,000 years ago, our bodies showed the wear and tear from those exertions. Ancient skeletons display signs of hernias and arthritis.[7] There is some discussion these days that stress can be good, that it somehow keeps us connected to what energises us. But when it is twinned with anxiety, it definitely is not. As technology, speed, pace and connectededness rise, so too does stress. A major European study of work-related stress found that 'the most obvious risk factors are linked to workload,

[6] Johann Hari, *Chasing the Scream: The First and Last Days of the War on Drugs*.
[7] Yuval Harari, *Sapiens: A Brief History of Humankind*.

quantity and intensity of work and working hours.'[8] The young, especially the Millennial generation, so caught by capitalism's late-stage limitations, feel it deeply, perhaps because they have more stresses than they have jobs. They have to hurry and hurtle around with few obvious rewards.

I always talk to people if I can, at bus stops, in taxis, in a queue or in shops. It is a good way to just read the world, to take a snapshot of how things are (plus, I am naturally friendly). I started chatting to a young woman wrapping up some clothes for me in a shop. Was she a student, I asked? 'No, but this is not my only job', she said. 'I have two. Both are part-time. I wish I had only one.' I saw, beneath her youth and her prettiness, the signs of worry and stress. The signs of overload. The writer Laurie Penny, born in 1986, puts it like this: 'Anxiety has become the defining disorder of our generation. My own anxiety disorder is as much of a millennial accessory as my smartphone and my skinny jeans'.[9]

How do we mend what is broken if we cannot see the breakage? This applies very obviously to mental health. It also applies to systems where breakage is internal, and often endemic. A fracture can happen to a weakened bone – a bone that is weakened from the inside by osteoporosis, for example. What happened to the World Health Organization to weaken its observational and response units to the extent that it admitted that its reaction to the Ebola crisis had been inadequate? 'The most egregious failure was by WHO in the delay in sounding the alarm', wrote Ashish Jha, director of the Harvard Global Health Institute, and Professor of Medicine at Harvard Medical School, in a report assessing all the systemic failures involved in the crisis. 'People at WHO were

---

[8] A major European Commission Study in 2015 entitled 'Scoping Study on Communications to Address and Prevent Chronic Diseases: Final Report', commissioned by 'Directory C – Public Health' of the European Commission behemoth Directorate-General for Health and Food Safety, showed the findings of an opinion poll conducted in 2013 conducted by EU-OSH, which found that 'more than 50% of all workers indicated that work-related stress is common' and which cites up to 60% of working days lost in Europe being attributed to this: www.ec.europa.eu.

[9] Laurie Penny, 'Fighting Words: Yes, Most Moaning Millennials are Middle Class. But That's Exactly What Should Worry This Government', The New Statesman, 18–31 March 2016.

aware that there was an Ebola outbreak that was getting out of control by spring ... it took until August to declare a public health emergency ... Those were precious months.'[10]

Where Social Health failures occur because things happen too slowly, a large part of stress is often due to shortage of time and the disease that always accompanies it: hurry. I wonder whether the growing popularity of running and cycling worldwide – a marathon in every major city, bicycle sales soaring – is a metaphor for the urgency with which we all now live our lives. They mirror society's desperation to make progress, fast. Movement, agility, speed – these have become metaphors for success, as well as for some kind of social survival.

Social Health arises out of the definition of the healthy physical individual body but I use it here as a metaphor for the wider body too, the institutional and organisational one. The word 'corporate' originates from the Latin 'corpus' – of the body – and 'corporare' – to form into a body.[11] Bodies need to be nurtured, shaped, invested in, and treated in certain ways in order to get what we want from them. By looking at health as a metaphor for how we connect, and specifically fitness and our changing attitude to it, we can start to visualise the steps, the synchronisation, pattern and configuration to move forward, both meaningfully and productively.

Using learned techniques and a mixture of tangible behaviour changes, it is mindset and organisation that lie at the heart of physical and mental health and fitness. There is a locus for the investment that goes into this kind of health – it is called a gym. The gym and the fitness class: a feature of everyday life today, which people use to moderate and manage their health. So embedded is it in modern culture that sales of global sportswear, leisure apparel and

---

[10] B. D. Colen, 'An Indictment of Ebola Response', *Harvard Gazette*, 22 November 2015.

[11] An interesting take on the etymology of the word 'body' can be found in a blog called '*Gin a body meet a body*' by Anatoly Liberman, published by OUP on 14th October 2015, see www.blog.oup.com.

'activewear' are estimated to reach over US$160 billion by 2020.[12] That is a lot of tracksuits, trainers, yoga pants and sports bras. We wear our health regimes outwardly, or we signal through clothing that we have them.

Modern, urban society takes a certain kind of health and fitness very seriously. US$3.4 trillion seriously. That is the amount that the new Global Wellness Institute suggests represents the entire economy of everything from workplace wellness to the spa industry, as well as the new kid on the block, 'wellness tourism' (flourishing in the United Arab Emirates). A third of this, US$500 billion each, are the 'healthy eating, nutrition and weight loss' end of the market and 'fitness and mind-body'.[13] In Italy, the man described as 'the Napolean of Gym',[14] Nerio Allessandri, founded one of the gym equipment business behemoths, Technogym, which is expected to make its own modest contribution to this global sum with a predicted turnover of £7.7 billion by 2020. If this blizzard of statistics is impressive, it is in this much: the scale at which the world has embraced health and fitness as a market and what it represents in relation to other industries. Let me put it another way. It dwarfs global military expenditure: Amnesty International has reported the arms market as rising fifty per cent in just over a decade to US$1.7 trillion.[15]

Of course, statistics can be massaged more than a guest undergoing a spa treatment. I can imagine that the Global Wellness Institute caters for purveyors of products and services who have every vested interest in looking big, but such figures cannot be entirely without foundation. What is highly interesting about the wellness/wellbeing market, however, is not just how rich it makes its founders and financiers – how much of a *market* it is – but that it is so active and participatory. Consumers literally do not sit on the couch with these

---

[12] Morgan Stanley reported in 2015 that 'sports apparel and footwear' sales had risen in just seven years to US$270 billion and were predicted to grow thirty per cent over the next five years.'*Athletic Lifestyles Keep Apparel Sales Healthy*', 30 October 2015.

[13] *Global Spa & Wellness Economy Monitor*, Global Wellness Institute, 2014.

[14] Times Magazine,'*Have you been on this man's treadmill? Probably*', David Aaronovitch, 15 August 2015.

[15] '*Killer Facts: The Scale of the Global Arms Trade*', Amnesty International, 24 August 2015.

products, they become active. People *get fit* and *behave* with what they consume (just look at Jane Fonda's workout sales on video, DVD and in books). The leisurewear sector has only enlarged this market and is probably not fully accounted for in the figures; wearing the clothes of fitness is halfway to doing the fitness class – it demonstrates, at least, being in the mindset. The rest is the physical grind of the doing.

Technogym reports a rise in women users from fifteen per cent in the late 1980s to nearer sixty per cent today. Transformation, change, movement: women and their bodies know how to do this. Nevertheless, the original gym movement was decidedly male. In his panoramic history of the gym, *The Temple of Perfection*, historian Eric Chaline takes us back to Ancient Greece and the origins of the homoerotic Olympiad nearly 3,000 years ago, in which 'exercise and male nudity were so closely linked that the greek verb "to exercise", *gymnazien*, translates literally as "to exercise naked"'.[16]

Back in the days when men honoured the Gods and oiled themselves (and each other) to perfection in men-only spaces, something else was stirring: a sensibility that fitness, health and wellbeing were connected. Classical Athens and its gymnasia provided, as Chaline tells us, 'the closest thing to tertiary education in the ancient world, with philosophers and sophists visiting the gymnasia to exercise themselves and lecture to friends and pupils afterwards either in the shelter of buildings or under trees'.[17] By the time Aristotle founded his school in the fourth century, the concept of excellence, of happiness potential attained through rational endeavour linked to both physical fitness and a moral, social and intellectual education had a name: *arête*. What seems to have happened is that today's health-as-narcissism, combined with a distinctly arête-like focus on complete holistic 'wellness', is mirroring the ancient Hellenistic model of health with its almost mystic Hippocratic notions of the *chymoi* 'humours' of

---

[16] Eric Chaline, *The Temple of Perfection: A History of the Gym*.
[17] Ibid.

pre-modern Western medicine. We are returning to a concept of completeness in health, fitness and wellbeing arguably not seen since Aristotle himself.

The gym is in many ways the opposite of a 'gymnasium' for joined-up connection between mind, body and spirit. I was a member of my local gym for nearly ten years before one intrepid member started a salon for discussion, prompted by the UK's 2016 referendum on its membership of the European Union. Culturally there is nothing systematically social or intellectual about the modern gym. It remains a temple to physical perfection, not mind–body–social connection. It is a pity. Social Health clubs inside gyms seem the most natural next step, echoing the rise of the co-working spaces which see community activity as an essential part of the 'sell' to the new generation of entrepreneurs, the 'solopreneurs'. When everyone has become atomised and individuality threatens community, Social Health is a fundamental requirement, along with physical and emotional health.

Diet, fitness and health regimes are good benchmarks from which to approach a holistic idea of health. Not simply for their positive possibilities, but because of their preventative ones too. What will it cost us not to look after our Social Health, that is the health of our networks and relationships, our knowledge flows, and how we assign and spend time tending to them in the spirit of arête?

Flourishing habits

We first make our habits, and then our habits make us.

JOHN DRYDEN

Recovering from pneumonia and sepsis in my early forties was not the first time I addressed a 'lifestyle' change in my habits. Most women who have babies need to readjust at least one clothes size up afterwards (often several). I had never been good at understanding diet – by which I mean, understanding the first thing about nutrition rather than blindingly 'going on a diet' – but part of the process of getting well was to get my head around both my physical and mental health. I turned to some 'assisted self-help', including some highly valuable sessions with a splendid American business coach, Ginger Cockerham. Ginger and I had phone coaching, not because I was short on time but because of distance – she lives 7,000 miles away from my house. This was pre-Skype days, so I would sit on the telephone, twirling the cord for 50 minutes as I talked to her in Texas. Ginger taught me to take myself seriously. She talked to me as if I was not just a lowly entrepreneur but the leader of a great enterprise. She explained how and why I needed process, pattern and technique with which to cope with a hostile landscape of challenges. With her help I was able to stop draining energy by doing things I was less good at and focus on what she calls the 'highest and best' – effectively, do most of what you are really great at and leave the rest to others.

I used this approach nearly a decade later. When I approached 'the big "five-oh"' and entered the physical foothills of perimenopause, a time of inevitable change. Out of neccessity, I finally tackled something I found even harder than work–life balance: regular physical exercise.

At the gym I walked around the gleaming machines, clutching a big white card of exercises carefully marked up by my cheerful personal trainer, and felt nothing but the gloomy doom of inevitable failure. I just knew I had not got the will – or the willpower. Then I recalled Ginger's sage advice. I threw the gym card away. I was not under anyone's rules or orders except my own. Instead, I began to design my own workout, based simply on using the machines I felt energized by, enjoyed using, and where I could feel I was working up a sweat without screaming for the ordeal to end. Willpower is, after all, now regarded as finite a resource as energy.[18] The result? I ended up with a

---

[18] The idea of 'ego depletion' that willpower is essentially finite has been around for some time. See Baumeister et al., '*Ego Depletion: Is the Active Self a Limited Resource?*' See also research findings published by the American Psychological Association in 2016. Although some take issue with this and debate the idea of ego depletion; *The New Science of Willpower: Can Self Control Really Get Used Up?* Stephanie Pappas, 14 October 2016. See www.livescience.com.

system I have used pretty much three times a week ever since: a very rapid 20-minute regime of cardio plus weights.

Aristotle had another word to describe wellness, a complete life satisfaction he called *eudaimonia*, which translates best as 'human flourishing'. The sociologists and statiticians call it something else: wellbeing. The definitions of it are rather imprecise and somewhat catch-all. The OECD helpfully publishes ten different aspects of wellbeing: 'real wages, educational attainment, life expectancy, personal security, political institutions, environmental quality, income inequality and gender inequality as well as economic growth in the form of gross domestic product (GDP) per head'.[19] That is the driest way to describe the concept of flourishing, and makes it very hard to imagine that individual agency or action has much to do with attaining it. My experience showed that it is precisely by personalising and using your instincts that you can develop habits which help you to flourish.

In the seventy years since the World Health Organization was formed (and since the inception of the OECD, which came into being fifteen years later), we have begun to look at ways to adapt our living, lifestyle and environment to one in which we do not just survive but in which we can thrive. In purely health terms, the great questions of the day in 1946 did not focus on how to personalise cancer treatment to extend life in Manhattan, nor the provision of keyhole surgery in Singapore, nor how to grow vegetables with Vitamin A in rural Bangladesh and thus reduce night blindness in children.[20] It is a very short time ago that we lived or died in mass numbers because we had no underlying wellbeing and no medical advances. The 'Spanish flu' epidemic that came immediately after the First World War arrived less than ten years after

---

[19] OECD Insights 2/10/14 Sue Kendall, '*Mapping the History of Wellbeing*'.

[20] Nobel Laureate Dr Mohammad Yunus, founder of pioneering microfinance provider Grameen Bank in Bangladesh, teamed up with food conglomerate Danone Foods to form Grameen Danone, a 'social business' that provides affordable fortified yoghurt containing enough vitamin A in a daily dose to wipe out the blight of night blindness caused by vitamin A deficiencies in the rural poor in Bangladesh, see www.danonecommunities.com.

the first antibiotics were discovered. Even so, it killed many more people between 1918 and 1919 than had died during the Great War itself. This disease was airborne and spread person-to-person, until around 100 million poor souls had perished. It remains the most devastating epidemic on record, but the disease itself was not, and should never have been, so deadly. Previous mortality rates were less than 0.1 per cent. It is not such a lethal bacteria as the truly awful Bubonic Plague, or Black Death, that was carried by rats in the Middle Ages. This killed up to 200 million people between 1347 and 1352, and was transmitted by fleas carrying the *Yersinia pestis* bacterium, jumping between rats in a basic society with little or no sanitation.

We can look back on the flu pandemic of 1918–1919 and see that the underlying conditions, the very lack of wellbeing in society, contributed to the fact that this strain seemed to have a strength of its own: the mortality rate jumped to 2.5 per cent.[21] Many of the people it infected were weak – specifically, weak from war. Many of those drafted to fight were not the fittest in the first place. The rigours of working-class life had already taken a toll on a new emerging European army: nearly thirty per cent of volunteers for the British Army in the 1860s were rejected on fitness grounds.[22]

Health changed by introducing a social component, through arriving at the ancient idea that people need holistic wellness, good education, sanitation and employment, as well as pure medicine. Yet how we view health needs an update: to try and operate efficiently and healthily today requires great adaptation skills in order to thrive as well as survive. The social tools that surround us – constant connection, ever-present technology, the rushing waterfall of information, choice, deadlines and competition – all mean we need new skills. We desperately need to acquire some new habits.

---

[21] Molly Billings, 'The Influenza Pandemic of 1918', www.virus.stanford.edu/uda/.

[22] Of 2.5 million recruits examined in 1917 and 1918, over forty per cent were deemed 'unable to undergo physical exertion'. Only three out of nine recruits were fully fit. Welfare reform was accelerated at the end, not the beginning of the war. See George Robbs, *British Culture and the First World War*.

One of my favourite jokes is the one where the psychoanalyst asks his patient, 'Do you really want to change?' 'Of course I do!', replies the patient indignantly. 'I'm a lightbulb. I'm all about change.' Humans are built to evolve, adapt and to change.

Balancing patterns

Health then, Social Health, is partly about connecting to a system and belonging, and not breaking, but also something to be practised and kept in balance. These are all core ingredients of functional health. The sports and fitness cultural historian Eric Chaline writes in his history of the gym that Ancient China, Greece and India all regarded health as 'a balance and proper flow of different energies and elemental substances, and diseases as imbalances or blockages'.[23] At the time of writing, the favourite word in the corporate language to describe this state is 'resilience', because the pursuit of a holistic and 'well' life is not confined to the individual but extended to the corporation. Wellbeing has become mainstream and mindfulness is firmly on the business map. But life is not always balanced. A freak of nature – from a tsunami to what in business life, or life in general, the trader-turned-philospher Nassim Nicholas Taleb calls 'the Black Swan', an unthinkable but theoretically possible event which with the benefit of hindsight was dismissed as improbable and unlikely to happen when it was all too possible[24] – can throw us off balance. A sub-prime mortgage crisis triggering an economic earthquake, or a long-term obesity crisis due to a combination of the car, the television and the sugar industry are all laws of unintended consequences.

---

[23] Eric Chaline, *The Temple of Perfection*.
[24] Nassim Nicholas Taleb's prophetic study of what happens when those who run society fail to 'think the unthinkable', published at the same time as the 2008 financial crisis: *The Black Swan: The Impact of the Highly Improbable*.

Network science shows clearly the patterns of inbuilt randomness existing cheek-by-jowl with highly predictable systems. A study of the way teenagers spread sexually transmitted diseases showed that there was always someone sleeping with someone outside the normal predicted 'set' who would ensure that the network effect expanded.[25] This is also why police talk about someone 'slipping through the net'. Their meaning: we could not see the pattern clearly enough; there were too many random factors.

Being uncertain and prey to serendipity is not in the script for most people, certainly for many managers. But the principles of Social Health require adaptability and flexibility as central tenets of survival. To maintain your balance when the waters around you are choppy requires skill. A survivor's account of the 2006 South Asian tsunami is instructive. Out at sea in a tiny fishing boat, a man had the luck to be with a captain who 'told the six of us where to sit, based on our weight and height, so we would balance out the boat. He asked us to hold tight . . . suddenly there was a huge noise and jolt. The wave had hit. Astonishingly, no water splashed in and no-one went overboard. He had saved us all.'[26] We all know we are 'captains of our own destiny'.

The shaping of behaviour, the *action*, is what I am interested in, rather than the dry theory alone. We all understand the word 'behaviour' to be about action in response to some kind of stimulus. The origins date far back to late Middle English and the twinning of the concept arising from 'behave' as a mix of 'be' and 'have' in the sense of 'have or bear oneself in a particular way',[27] through to 'behaviour' itself, described as 'the pattern of demeanour'.[28]

---

[25] The sociologist Charles Kadushin, a pioneer of Social Network Analysis, writes up the case study of a syphilis epidemic in a community of teenagers, an early example of the use of sociometric techniques to analyse the link being made between social network analysis and public health, specifically the importance of social influence in 'diffusion' of a disease that can be caught and spread. See Charles Kadushin, *Understanding Social Networks: Theories, Concepts and Findings*.

[26] Ralf Obergfell, '*I was out to sea when the tsunami struck*', The Guardian, 22 January 2016.

[27] Definition: oxforddictionaries.com.

[28] Ibid.

With pattern, the shape itself acts as a metaphor for movement or action. One aspect leads to, interlocks and interacts, flows well into and with another. It is not ideal to start from the position of pillars, or pyramids, or anything vertical because they reflect hierarchy and its bedfellow, the silo. Silo thinking, as the anthropologist and journalist Gillian Tett reminds us, can be a fatal flaw in an organisation: 'The word silo does not just refer to a physical organization or organization (such as a department). It can also be a state of mind. Silos exist in structures. But they exist in our minds and social groups too. Silos breed tribalism. But they can also go hand in hand with tunnel vision.'[29]

When it comes to changing our behaviour, especially by stopping something, surprising numbers of us experience optimism bias, the psychological trait by which we think things are either better than they are, or not as bad, or that we will be the lucky ones (at the gym many suffer from the exact opposite: pessimism bias). We take risks in accordance with this bias: risks in driving, drinking or smoking, for example. These days, food alerts are reaching the point where you could include salami, bread with gluten, or anything with fructose on a list of dangerous substances. Certainly anyone living in a city with air pollution levels rising to historic highs feels as if they are in the middle of risky conditions just by the act of daily life. But optimism bias is something else. It is when you know you can change what you are doing and, addictively, stubbornly, reluctantly, or for any other reason, you do not. Instead, you rationalise things in order to carry on doing what you know is bad for you and possibly causes harm to others too.

I realized just how much optimism bias I had when attending my second 'drive aware' course for poor driving. Over the course of a three-hour morning in a hot hotel suite with an ugly patterned carpet (and even uglier coffee), thirty of us from very different walks in life began to understand that we were, in fact, united by something similar: we all thought optimistically, at the time

---

[29] Gillian Tett, *The Silo Effect: Why Every Organisation Needs To Disrupt Itself to Survive.*

of our driving offences, that we were driving better than we actually were and that 'everyone else' was the bad driver.

Another obstacle to changing behaviours and mitigating risk is social proof. This 'herd behaviour' is a type of conformity, from mass teenage hysteria to really quite bizarre small-scale specifics. The psychology and marketing professor Robert Cialdini, an expert in social proof, noticed how newspaper stories of suicides generated copycat actions to the degree that 'stories of pure suicides, in which only one person dies, generates wrecks in which only one person dies; stories of suicide-murder combinations, in which there are multiple deaths, generate wrecks in which there are multiple deaths'.[30]

Making change of any kind requires habits to develop and a new form to follow. Some people think you can change behaviour in as little as two weeks, but others believe it takes far longer, anything from sixty-six days to two years.[31] In fact, the tenets of Social Health as I am defining them here – namely to maintain a balance of activity, mindset and connections, which enhance well-being and productivity – can only operate in a culture that is receptive to forming new habits for new reasons. Being in other words, like that lightbulb who really wants to change.

Humans need a lot of practice. In terms of adapting physical change and pace, we are very often beaten to the punch by many of the very species we have overtaken in social terms. Take one example: the humble lizard. Lizards belong to a superclass of reptile called Tetrapoda, of which there are over 6,000 species – roughly the same amount of tweets posted per second in the world.[32] But it turns out that they have an adaptive evolutionary trick up their sleeve that we

---

[30] Robert B. Cialdini, *Influence: The Psychology of Persuasion*.

[31] '*Busting the 21 days habit formation myth*' by Ben D. Gardner, Health Chatter, the UCL Health Behaviour Research Centre blog, 29 June 2012. See also 'How Long Does It Take to Form a Habit?', UCL News Report, 4 August 2009, following the work of Philippa Lally and colleagues from Cancer Research UK Health Behaviour Research Centre.

[32] Twitter's astonishing growth is best understood in the statistic that 6,000 tweets are posted a second, making 200 billion tweets a year, or 500 million tweets a day in 2013, up from a mere 25 million tweets per day in 2010. Source: internetlivestats.com.

do not, and which might put our struggle to adapt to technological change into better perspective. In just fifteen years – a period too miniscule to normally register on any grand-era measuring scale – scientists working at the University of Austin, Texas, noticed that the green Carolina anole lizard, native to Texas, managed to evolve over only twenty generations to develop different toe pads that would give them a better grip on trees than their competitors, the brown anoles. The researchers described this speed as both 'astonishing' and also 'character displacement': these lizards had adapted at, no pun intended, superhuman pace to ensure their survival and superiority in their environment.[33]

In human terms, memory could be seen as our equivalent of the toe pad. We need it to survive. We want it to adapt and to increase in capacity. But in our society the only advance memory we can really generate is outside our bodies, electronically. RAM, or Random Access Memory, on a laptop can hold approximately 32GB. The human equivalent, located in the hippocampus part of our brains, cannot operate at the same speed or scale. Our brains can only go as fast as 40Hz, which explains the speed limit at which computer screens refresh. We can do minimal tricks to teach our brains to store memory more effectively, and to retrieve it efficiently, but we cannot fundamentally increase the size or scope of our brains any more than we can substantially stretch our lives. We may live longer, and that brings a whole set of social challenges, but we certainly are not about to start living forever.

So, we are no lizard. For all our technological acceleration, which is ravishing, thrilling and astonishing, we have to outsource it from our actual bodies – bodies that have remained startlingly unchanged and unevolved for over 200,000 years. This binds and connects us ever more tightly to things we literally do not control: computers and technology. And not necessarily in a healthy way; too much dependence is rarely a good thing.

---

[33] 'Florida Lizards Evolve Rapidly, Within 15 Years and 20 Generations', *UT News*, 23 October 2014, www.news.utexas.edu

Let me put it another way. By 2016, the average time people spent connected to Facebook was fifty minutes, or a sixteenth of their waking hours, while in the UK the amount of time people spend online per day across all their devices, social media and the internet has leapt to 2 hours 51 minutes a day, easily a third of working hours.[34] That is at least the equivalent of some serious toe pad evolution – except we only use our fingers to type on someone else's toe pad. Practice, after all, makes perfect.

Pattern management, as I call it, is hugely helpful when trying to change habits. Having a pattern helps us refer with as little willpower as possible and just get on with the *doing*. The pattern for Social Health is one particular shape above all others: the humble hexagon.

Hexagon thinking

Bees . . . never begin one cell at time, always several; they can judge distance to certain extent, and those that make their spheres or cylinders so that if completed, would intersect, make an intermediate flat wall. Then assume perfect judge of distance . . . in hexagonal prism

CHARLES DARWIN[35]

'Birds do it, bees do it . . . Let's fall in love!', goes the song. It turns out that *Apis mellifera*, or the humble bee, is one of the most efficient, organised and social of species, which operates in a system of pattern management that would make

---

[34] Globally, Facebook users spend just under a sixteenth of their waking time per day, fifty minutes, on the social network. See James B. Stewart, '*Facebook has 50 Minutes of Your Time Each Day. It Wants More*', New York Times, 5 May 2016. Meanwhile, in the UK the Internet Advertising Bureau UK (IAB) and the UK Online Measurement Company (UKKOM) found that Britons spend two hours and fifty-one minutes a day online across their devices, www.thedrum.com/.

[35] Charles Darwin, Memorandum to W. H. Miller, 15 April 1858, *Darwin Correspondence Project*, University of Cambridge.

every architect and structural engineer on the planet weep with envy. Bees have a way of going about their daily life and business that is highly productive and relies strongly on both leadership (the queen) and community (the hive). The honeybee has, according to research on the wisdom of bees, 'mastered a great society and it would be hubris to think we have nothing to learn from them'.[36]

We would not need to think about bees if everything was hunky dory in the garden of humankind. We ought, by reasoning and right (two very human values), to have reached a point in social evolution when our systems, patterns of community and leadership deliver prosperous peace. But we have already established that modern life does not feel too healthy, and that it does not appear to function in an organised, collaborative or joined-up way as much as it could and should. The hardware of modern life is designed in shapes all around us, principally in the form and structure of architecture. It was great twentieth-century architects such as Frank Lloyd Wright who connected in the public mind the idea that buildings needed to be spaces designed to serve and reflect human values. The great design engineer Cecil Balmond talks of pattern in the following terms:

> *The idea starts with finding a unit of pattern and using it over and over again in different interlocking adjacencies. What appears to be random will grow to cover the plane. To keep the feeling of sameness and have the capacity to be different, I wanted to seed a self-similarity of pattern, necessary to realise these ideas, replicating 'network', and not fixed pattern.*[37]

So in order to offer a pattern of thinking for Social Health, I want to use not just words, but shapes too. The most obvious shape is the circle. We talk of a 'social circle', we hold 'roundtables' and we 'circulate' in a room or a group. But

---

[36] Michael O'Malley, *The Wisdom of Bees*.
[37] See Cecil Balmond with Jannuzzi Smith, writing about patterns in architecture in *Informal*.

I prefer the six-sided hexagon as the model for Social Health and its patterns. I take my inspiration from nature. This six-sided, two-dimensional geometric figure is abundant in the natural world, from snowflakes to the interlocking columns of volcanic rock forming the Giant's Causeway in Ireland and then the hexagonal poster species of Social Health: the honeybee. When it comes to snowflakes, snow crystals first grow in simple hexagonal prisms before literally branching out. Their beauty lies in their symmetry but also, in respect of Social Health, their individuality: no two snowflakes, despite all beginning in the same way from the same ice crystal lattice, are ever the same.[38] The behaviour of the collaborative and intelligent social industry of bees make them most worthy for the hexagon of Social Health. Charles Darwin spent exceptional amounts of time observing bees, and their value to the ecosystem is now seen as fundamental to the survival of our own species. Honeybees organise their hives – the place in which they live, work and store their goods – in hexagon-shaped honeycombs. The clincher for me in deciding to use the hexagon as my main model for Social Health, replacing any pyramid shape or indeed circles, is the fact that scientists now know that the original design of honeycomb actually begins as circular shapes, which are then squashed and moulded by the heat of the honey before hardening into hexagons as their final fixed shape.[39]

The traditional sociogram, which visually maps relationships between people, was the prototype for modern social network analysis, which uses edge, not circularity, to measure the strength, length and thickness of 'ties'.[40] The way we look at modern connection, in everything from culture to epidemiology,

---

[38] Kenneth G. Libbrecht, *Snowflake Science*, www.snowcrystals.com.

[39] An article in *Nature*, the international journal of science in 2013 *How honeycombs can build themselves* by Philip Ball explained how the honeycomb begins as a circle, which hardens over time into a hexagon shape.

[40] See *Sociometry and Social Network Analysis: Applications and Implications*, Diana Jones, ANZPA Journal, 15 December 2006.

has to be mapped and made visual so that we can understand the patterns and see with our own eyes just how connected things are. It was the Austrian-American psychiatrist and psychosociologist Jacob L. Moreno who pioneered both the study of what he called 'the science of society' and with it the sociogram in the 1930s.[41] The sociogram helps us map the terrain. Networks are all about mapping, distance and the journey. The writer A. A. Gill put it well: 'When you're a visitor to a city, you like to hurry up the habits, lay down a pattern, gain predictability in place of roots'.[42] I find a tool developed by Professor Herminia Ibarra of INSEAD to visually chart your own influential connections a good example of how looking at pattern can show you how to act – in this case who your networks really focus on and flow from (see Figure 2.1).

II. How Connective is Your Network?

Connectivity refers to your capacity to reach out far and wide outside your immediate network and to connect people and groups who wouldn't otherwise be able to reach each other. Connectivity increases your external perspective and allows you to add unique value.

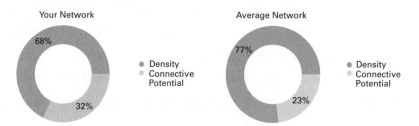

Depending on your line of work, if the percentage of your current contacts who also know each other is above 50–60% you are at risk of having a network that is closed to outside influence. A highly dense network means less time for relationships outside your tight circle. After a while, no new information circulates. To improve the connectivity of your network consider:

- Are there people in your current network who might benefit from knowing each other? List the pairs that you will introduce to each other.
- Are there people in your current network who might introduce you to others you don't yet know? List the person you already know and the person you will ask them to introduce you to.

FIGURE 2.1 *How connective is your network?*

© Herminia Ibarra 2016

---

[41] In April 1933 the *New York Times* published a graphic of '*Emotions Mapped by New Geography*', featuring Jacob Moreno's measurement of social encounters. The following year Moreno published a book entitled *Who Shall Survive? A New Approach to the Problem of Human Interrelations*, which contained some of the earliest graphic depictions of social networks, later known as sociograms.
[42] A. A. Gill, *To America With Love*.

Back to the hexagon and its role as the model for looking at Social Health. Ancient Islamic art depicts hexagons prominently in geometrical lockstep alongside its traditional calligraphy and arabesque, reflecting the ancient idea of logic interrelation. Art and design's depiction of the hexagon is never far from nature and its patterns. In arts and craft patchwork, and its counterpart quilting, the hexagon is used extensively, dating back as early as the twelfth century. Today some of the twenty-first century's most impenetrable coding tech has its own application: hexagonal architecture. Recently a coalition of designers called Architects for Society, from Spain, the US, the Netherlands, Canada and Jordan, have designed 'The Hex', a hexagonal flat-packed portable home for refugees. The forty-square-metre units 'can simply be arranged next to one another in appropriate patterns or they can be joined and share walls for enhanced thermal performance'.[43]

The number six also features in the study of epidemics and pandemics: the first 'wave' tends to last six weeks. It often takes six weeks for confirmation that the 'viral load' of diseases such as HIV has taken root in the body. In the 1918 flu pandemic, the peak wave of mortality occurred in New York City in the six weeks between February and April. Jeremy Farrar, director of the Wellcome Trust, one of the world's largest medical charities, cites a six-week window for getting on top of emerging epidemics.[44]

Six is a number which matters both as a symbol to remember within the cognitive limit and because it is a significant number in both science and nature (including, of course, the brain's six-layered cerebral cortex). Hexagon Thinking can therefore give structure and pattern to allow us to change behaviour around our connectedness and its discontents. (see Figure 2.2).

---

[43] Jenna McKnight, 'Architects for Society Designs Low-Cost Hexagonal Shelters for Refugees', Dezeen, 2016.
[44] Jeremy Farrar speech The Future of Global Health Hay Festival, May 2016.

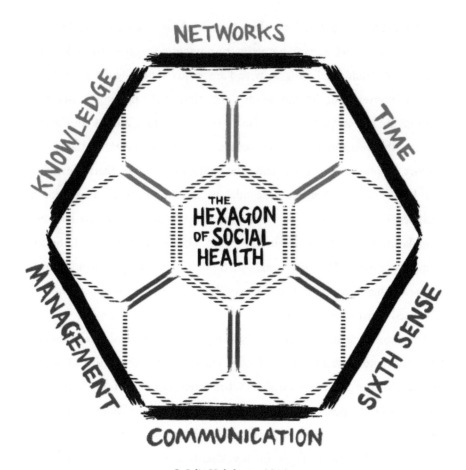

C Julia Hobsbawm 2016

FIGURE 2.2 *The Hexagon of Social Health.*

Earlier in the book, I identified the six disorders of Social Health, or its absence, as Six Degrees of Overload: (i) information obesity; (ii) time starvation; (iii) network tangle; (iv) techno spread; (v) organizational bloat and (vi) life gridlock. The Hexagon of Social Health comprises six healthy interconnected elements, which, taken together, act as correctives to the 'disorder' of connectedness, that is, dysfunction. Remember the stories of Anoushka and Ellen, and of Holly and Jessica? Or of the spread of Ebola? Or your own experiences of overload? Where most of us know exactly how to structure actions around taking greater control of our diet, nutrition, physical exercise and mental wellbeing, no such obvious pattern exists around health concerning who and what we connect with, how often, and how we combat overload in general.

Top knots and coping mechanisms

The top of the hexagon contains three core factors that are often knotted up and confused, and which we need to untie, simplify and clarify if we are to gain control of our Social Health: *knowledge, networks* and *time*: The KNOT. If we are to overcome information obesity, network overload and time starvation, we need to unpick and unpack their components. These form the essential DNA of the Hexagon of Social Health.

Each element of the hexagon of Social Health's top KNOT is inherent in the way I look at the challenges and creative solutions to the Age of Overload. Knowledge, Networks and Time are literally threaded throughout our lives. The challenge is to cope with them adequately. You cannot function without *knowledge*, but navigating your way to find it without a guide or curator is increasingly hard, and not unlike trying to retrieve your camera if you drop it in Niagara Falls: the onward rush sweeps everything away in a blur. Shortage of *time* and the pressure to multitask is a stalker for every modern worker, and society is increasingly geared to the idea that time can be 'saved', as if to emphasise the reality that most of us are neither surviving nor thriving in an Age of Overload. Then there are *networks*. Of course, all of modern life depends entirely on travel, communication and infrastructure, which we take so entirely for granted that they only warrant our attention when they malfunction or seize up. As to our human networks, well, the people side of our networks grow in a tangle around our lives, as neglected as arteries that gradually fur up with cholesterol. Instead of being created, nurtured or managed in any kind of systematic way, a personal or professional network is often insufficient, inadequate or simply out of date. Databases become graveyards of data, not 'peoplebases' or living records of relationships.

The ability to navigate and negotiate through the oceans and rivers of information, to know what is dross and mindless noise rather than useful, believable comment or news, and to create and build networks that can act as bridges across these rivers as much as deep dives into them, and having the time to do this without accidentally triggering the tripwire of overload, these are the cornerstones of good Social Health. The KNOT of *knowledge, networks* and *time* is our scaffolding. We can begin to meet our needs if we have a system that focuses on these three elements.

However, the cornerstones need underpinning. The foundations have to be laid, foundations that are a hybrid of values, attitude and behaviour. We need a trio of coping mechanisms to help to untie the KNOT. These are *management, communication* and *sixth sense.*

Management

The management guru Peter Drucker wrote a seminal paper in 1946, the same year that the UN first mooted the idea of a World Health Organization. In *The Concept of the Corporation*, Drucker argued that changing social values and the growth of the knowledge worker called for a fundamental focus on the organisation not just as an economic system but a social one. *Management* is dominated by the idea of productivity. My definition to put to the WHO is that Social Health itself is achieved by *the ability of individuals and organisations to have access to sufficient knowledge and networks – and to manage time to use these in a balanced way – so that they flourish. Those with Social Health can combine face-to-face relationships with technology to be productive without being overwhelmed.*

To have Social Health is to be productive. We all strive for productivity. Call it creativity if you like, or the driest of economic jargon, 'output', but it is what it is: generating results of your liking (or of someone else's). Productivity has been somewhat in the doldrums for many years – as I pointed out in the Introduction. Even if you contest how we measure productivity, we know that overload slows rather than increases it. There is clearly a correlation between sluggish growth, productivity and the willingness for corporate leaders to look at wellbeing and other 'answers'. The data about the impact on productivity as a result of happy, motivated workforces is compelling.[45]

Applying the M-word to the Hexagon of Social Health provides an umbrella for three systematic behaviour checks: *pace*, *process* and *performance*. The speed and pace at which we all expect to operate is critical, but often out of sync with a true, intuitive understanding of what can actually be accomplished and by when. Not that this stops the political or corporate cycles being relatively short-term, sucking their people into agendas that reflect this. One of the big breakthroughs in the thinking around diet was the shift, somewhere around the mid 1990s, from flash crash to sustained change.

The idea of *performance* must be in the management mix because some kind of measurement is needed to help track progress. While I detest some of the more crass human resource management systems around 'appraisals', the rise of performance fitness and app productivity software demonstrates the strength of the human appetite for competitive comparison. Process is, for me, the most undervalued of nouns. Many basic bodily behaviours are a series of mechanistic processes, albeit unconscious ones. We put one foot in front of another; we have rituals we take for granted but which are, in fact, processes we have picked out and follow. Just taking something for granted should not negate its validity: out in the world you might want to eat food which is not itself processed, but a clean, thorough and safe process for preparing that food is one you value highly. We often overlook process in our personal lives; people

---

[45] See OECD, *The Future of Productivity*, OECD 2015.

often rightly decry too much process and call it bureaucracy, but the right kind of process is actually essential.

Communication

Calling for *communication* in relation to Social Health is becoming more central, as the 'electronic mob' gains force, bringing with it the good, the bad and the downright ugly. But in the general swirl of overload, the risk of 'miscom' remains high. The first half of my career was in communications. I would probably be described as a 'good communicator', but I regularly fall into the trap of poor communication myself – we all do, because communication is complex and needs careful consideration. Do I mean to say this in *that* way? Have we missed something out in our emphasis? Who are we communicating with? Is the time right or wrong to be asking this? Are we inviting a two-way communication or is such siloed information just a form of top-down control? These are just some of the issues to contend with on a daily basis. Reading reaction to something is part of how you gauge whether your communication has 'landed' or is merely a glancing blow. Effective strategies and tactics are fundamental to the coping mechanism mindset. We have to survive the fully connected world, and thrive in it.

Sixth sense

Everyone knows the five senses in the same way that they know the alphabet, and can count them on the fingers of one hand: sight, hearing, touch, taste and smell. The impairment of our senses hinders some of our social functions as well as our sensory ones; we cannot read someone's face, and thus their emotions, if we cannot see all of their features, for example.

Social Health really concerns a sixth sense: *intuition*. Others might call it emotional intelligence. What we feel intuitively about a thing, a situation or a person is critical to how we experience it with our other senses: 'It doesn't smell right', or 'It feels OK', or 'I can't see this happening', or 'I am so close I can taste it'. Described as 'a process that gives us the ability to know something directly without analytical reasoning, bridging the gap between the conscious and nonconscious parts of our mind, and also between instinct and reason',[46] intuition is a critical sixth sense. When the acclaimed human rights lawyer Philippe Sands spoke about his quest to uncover hidden family history and how it connected to uncovering the origins of the legal framework for the terms 'genocide' and 'crimes against humanity' in the Nuremberg Trials of 1945–1946, he spoke candidly of following his intuition and a 'lawyer's sense' that he could uncover more, adding that there were a series of coincidences and happenings associated with his work that 'no novel could possibly match'.[47]

Reasoned instinct amounts to a set of observations, judgements which lead to actions based on the facts, plus a smattering of something *additional* and based on intuition. Using your senses, your common sense, and thus your sixth sense, makes up the sixth branch or side of Hexagon Thinking and the Hexagon of Social Health. These three coping mechanisms of *management, communication* and using a *sixth sense* can smooth the way to successful application of the KNOT of *knowledge, networks* and *time*. The Hexagon of Social Health is designed as as pattern, which, in turn, is a guide and a navigator. When all at sea in a tsunami of overload, factors such as calm process, balance and a guide to follow may be just the cure we need.

---

[46] Francis P. Cholle, '*What is Intuition and How Do We Use It?*', Psychology Today 31 August 2011.
[47] Professor Philippe Sands QC, *Eric Hobsbawm Lecture*, Hay Festival, 29 May 2016.

3

New hierarchies of need

The boy on the Paris Metro

The train doors closed at Place de L'Opéra on the Paris Metro, just as the little boy started to scream. A warm rubber smell permeated the carriage. It was crowded, and the hard bright plastic orange seats, rimmed in grey, were full, with the added squash of luggage. At first the passengers looked around to see if he had caught his fingers. All carriage doors carry a picture of a child-friendly small animal and the message 'Do not put your hands near the doors, as you could get them badly squeezed!' But the boy's fingers were entwined with his mother's, who was looking down, away. She looked stressed, but she did not seem surprised. She looked like she simply had to get through this, that it was familiar to her, and neither sudden nor surprising. He could be neither communicated with nor comforted.

This little boy was in an anguished autistic world of his own, far along 'the spectrum'. He had no language. I have seldom seen such isolation.

The screaming was not rhythmic, but it was relentless. It raised and roiled in a howl of wordless protest not of deprivation – a tantrum over something denied – but of excess, even of pain. The anguish of sensory overload.

Studies on neuroplasticity show the particular brain areas that respond acutely to stress. In technical terms the synapses in his amygdala and orbitoprefontal cortex in his brain would have been firing furiously. Even without autism that environment could trigger a stress response to overload. Imagine having no defences against sound and sensation in an everyday environment. Then imagine having no ability to communicate these feelings, or to have language to describe them. I felt a squeeze of helpless pity. I turned to my own children who were oblivious to the idea that something might be wrong. 'Hey Mum,' whispered one blithely, with the insousiance of the well. 'I bet you're glad that isn't me having a meltdown'.

The ability to form social bonds and to communicate feelings is the first form of connection. Babies track their mother's voice with their blurred eyes from birth. Instinct comes before sentience. Extensive studies, including evolutionary psychologist Robin Dunbar's famous experiments showing that the prefrontal cortex size of a species predicts the size of its social group,[1] point to the human's ability to connect as being the primary definition of it as a social being – and one with the biggest brain as a result. The first hominids with brains as large as ours, the ancient Homo heidelbergernsis, *preceded our own* Homo sapiens.[2] *The social brain of the boy on the Paris Metro may have been interrupted by autism, but its evolution can be traced directly back 700,000 years after his ancestors first developed brains resembling our own, and his unafflicted mother was able to keep him safe and tucked in her arms to shield him from a world against which he had no protection. The neuropsychologist Matthew Lieberman has not only shown that the default position of the human brain is to concern itself with its relationships but that, to the brain, any kind of social pain is experienced in a similar way to physical pain.[3] Pain of any kind is a sign that something is wrong.*

---

[1] Robin Dunbar is the evolutionary psychologist who has done more than perhaps any other scientist to popularise our understanding of the primate brain and its impact on social behaviour and social network behaviour in particular. Before his popular science book, *How Many Friends Does One Person Need? Dunbar's Number and Other Evolutionary Quirks*, was published in 2010 he had written two papers in particular which focused on the primate brain and organisation of its social settings: '*Primate Social Systems*' in 1988 and '*Social Dynamics of Gelada Baboons*' in 1975.

[2] Emily Esfahani Smith, '*Social Connections Make a Better Brain*', The Atlantic, October 2013.

[3] Matthew Lieberman, *Social: Why Our Brains are Wired to Connect*.

The boy needed, above all, connection to someone who could protect him. He might have needed food and shelter too, but his first line of defence was, in fact, love. What he needed above all was connection. Just because he had a condition which made it hard to ask for such a connection did not mean he could do without it.

Menlo Park millennials

In 1948, the same year that the WHO officially came into being and developed its definitions of 'health', an American psychologist, Abraham Maslow, invented a model to look at human needs. For over sixty years, it has endured as a framework for people trying to understand human complexity and behaviour. Maslow's hierarchy of needs has five simple organising principles, based around a hierarchy that ascends from basic to premium: by the time you reach the top of the pyramid, and all your needs are met, you are somehow complete, whole and, by implication, healthy (see Figure 3.1).

Maslow's hierarchy placed physical needs for food and shelter at the wide base point of the pyramid, followed by safety. Love and belonging, esteem and self-actualisation follow, up to the sharpest point. There is, however, a glaring gap. There is no mention of the word 'connection'. It is implied, perhaps, but not actually there, nor the word most obvious to the condition of belonging – 'social'.

In some sense you could argue that Maslow's hierarchy has stood the test of time well enough. It is a pithy way of visualising different human states and behaviours. But some, myself included, are challenging the idea that this hierarchy of needs is right for today's world. Maslow's version is out of date because connection is given secondary status, and also because the dimensions of it are wrong: it is missing a crucial piece. Connection, either our access to the hardware of connections such as energy or communication systems, or the

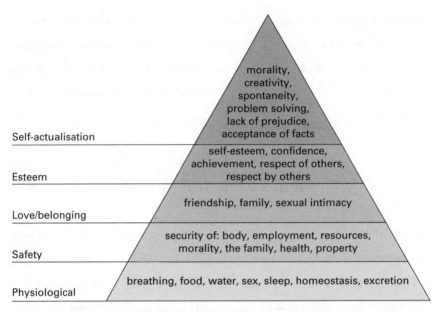

FIGURE 3.1 Diagram based on Maslow's paper, *A Theory of Human Motivation*.

ability to psychologically understand the way in which we connect to others rather than our 'self-actualisation' selves, is simply not present. A significant challenge was published in *Psychology Today* in 2011, noting that 'None of these needs – starting with basic survival on up – are possible without social connection and collaboration'.[4]

Our sense of the growing importance of connection reflects its pervasiveness. We want the 1.3 billion people on the planet who are currently without electrical power[5] to be connected to fresh sources, preferably clean energy ones, for instance. Argument is fierce over how to harness solar energy to new battery power, which can then store energy locally rather than require it to travel hundreds of kilometres

[4] See Pamela Rutledge, '*Social Networks: What Maslow Misses*', Psychology Today.

[5] Sixteen per cent of the global population – 1.3 billion people – have no access to electrical power. Seventy-nine per cent of them are in the fifty poorest nations of the world, mainly sub-Saharan Africa and across parts of Asia (300 million in India for instance). See International Energy Agency data, www. worldenergyoutlook.org.

into remote lands, by which time much of it has dissipated. Emotional connection does not suffer from degrading over distance or even time, and it is embedded in not just one pillar of Maslow's hierarchy but all of them.

How we frame our needs is social and psychological. What one human needs at any time differs. Yet the principle of a list of needs which unite us still feels right. In itself, it connects us. And the present giants of connectivity coincidentally link directly to Abraham Maslow himself. He died in Menlo Park in California, where a century earlier Thomas Alva Edison had invented the phonograph and ushered in the beginnings of the age of connection. Menlo Park is also where Google's founders originally set up shop in a friend's garage and renamed the site the 'Invention Factory'. Today's millennials do not just need connection but take it completely for granted. However, I suspect we underestimate their sophistication about their connection needs and overlook my own more binary, twentieth-century approach. It is true that when I tried to explain to my kids, that I grew up with a four-channel television, a cassette radio player, and only got a computer when I was in my twenties, they looked incredulous. And it is true that our children sleep with their mobile phones as the closest thing to their pillow, after their heads. But they have friends who they see, talk to, play with, hang out with, touch, hug and love. They know full well that they need to be connected to others and to the wider world – for this reason, perhaps, graduates are consistently demanding more of blue-chip employers than just a desk, good money and career prospects. Their generation is often mistakenly branded as the digital native one, where everyone has lost the power of intimacy. But where our teenagers are socially ambidextrous, it is us, the older generation of baby boomers and Gen X, who are the ones who shut ourselves away behind desks and desktops, operating in silos, severing social links at the expense of LinkedIn and a transactional approach to our networks. One thing is clear: the modern connected social person needs – not wants but *needs* – to have friends on Facebook that they actually see face-to-face.

Face-to-face in a Facebook world

Then he told me he had 60 million friends – that is, none.[6]

TANYA GOLD

Taking Maslow's hierarchy as a reference point, I have been illustrating different forms of connection using the model of a 'hierarchy of communication' in corporate classes, when teaching executives or executive MBA students. I want a generation that is starved of time, or too junior to have grown up with 'the long lunch', to understand how the time-intensive, face-to-face meeting is actually at a premium compared to a broadcast model of, say, blasting out 140-word posts to all and sundry.

Despite the infinite variety of messages that communication gives us, the ways we use words, pictures and other media are actually finite, and far less than than there are types of sport, colour, pop music or even species of butterfly.

There are six principal ways to communicate:

1   **Face-to-face:** meetings.

2   **Voice:** phone calls (or Skype, a permissible hybrid of 1 and 2).

3   **Physical word:** writing and using the postal system.

4   **Virtual word:** email with enclosures or links.

5   **Broadcast message:** spreading messages to individuals or large groups.

6   **Social network conversation:** interacting digitally and directly.

These six forms can be condensed into a communication hierarchy mirroring Maslow's pyramid:

---

[6] Tanya Gold in *Sunday Times Magazine* Writing about the celebrity paedophile, Jimmy Savile, December 2015.

1   Physical face/voice.

2   Written word.

3   Broadcast.

The pyramid does not reflect the interconnectivity of communication, which is not actually so much a hierarchy as a cycle. You do not tend to use just one form of communication with one person, but possibly several: you email to fix a meeting and then follow up, possibly by broadcasting to social media or by reporting that meeting somewhere.

It would be simplistic to say that writing an email or a passage in a novel, or sending out a tweet is inherently less effective or forceful than speaking directly to someone's face. What is incontrovertible is the power of intimacy and the trust that accrues from using our physical selves, and not proxies. The ways in

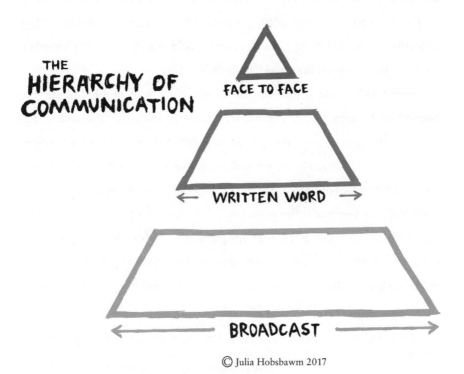

© Julia Hobsbawm 2017

FIGURE 3.2 *The Hierarchy of Communication.*

which we distribute our thoughts, words and feelings can and should be used to achieve scale: book printing and publishing, television networks and distributed forms of connection are all excellent ways to communicate. The rise of the 'spoken book' and distributed services such as Audible show this clearly. Audible has built a library of over 200,000 audiobooks in less than a decade. Don Katz, Audible's founder, told *The Wall Street Journal* that 'the consumer doesn't think of the difference between textual and visual and auditory experience'.[7]

One form of reading and listening and reading aloud trumps all: the book festival. The Hay Festival for Literature started in the small Welsh 'book capital' of Hay-on-Wye in 1998. The town itself has 1,500 residents. In that first year, the festival attracted 1,000 people to some 25 events. By 2012, an estimated 100,000 visitors attended over 800 events spread across 11 days.[8] Hay had to relocate to a bigger site, taking up several nearby fields. Nowadays, most events are sold out. Some of the best conversations happen in the queue to get into its no-fuss tents to hear some of the greatest living thinkers and writers. Many Hay afficionados follow its festivals further afield than Wales – to Colombia, Ireland, Mexico, Spain, Peru and Bangladesh.

Woodstock's music conference in upstate New York in 1969 began the connection between people and music, and coincided with the arrival of the extreme fan. But it was the power of Live Aid in 1985 which began the connection between audience and artist, live in some kind of experience together, connected not just by the physical moment, but by technology as well. Specifically, by television. The musician Phil Collins was famously whisked by Concorde, the now-defunct supersonic passenger jet, from Wembley Stadium in the middle of the concert in one time zone and arrived to perform live again in Philadelphia in the same concert, but in another country, a matter of hours

---

[7] Alexandra Alter, '*The New Explosion in Audio Books: How They Re-emerged as a Rare Bright Spot in the Publishing Business*', Wall St Journal, 1 August 2013.

[8] Andrea Collins, Dimitris Potoglou and Andy Fryers, '*Reducing the Impact of Visitor Travel: Reflections on Hay Festival, Hay-on-wye, Wales*', study undertaken by Cardiff University 2016.

later. The effect was to connect a global audience of 1.9 billion across 150 nations in a single live satellite TV broadcast. In the UK alone (where Live Aid was masterminded by Bob Geldof and Harvey Goldsmith), more than 25 million combined visits were made to see live music in a single year.[9]

I watched Live Aid live on my television screen, and I can remember it as if it was yesterday. It was just before my twenty-first birthday. I watched it alone in a room in my parents' house with the window open, high above the Hampstead Hills in a summery north London, and wished I was there at the stadium itself. I was aware, perhaps for the first time in my life, of other people in the rest of the world who were watching and who were *just like me*. Other young women called Julia, or Giulia or Yulia in Italy or the Soviet Union, somehow connected and united by this extraordinary day. I still watch YouTube videos of Freddie Mercury striding about the stage in his flared white trousers and think there has never been a performer like him who connected via television with pretty much the whole world – with the possible exception of The Beatles, Elvis Presley and Mohammed Ali. YouTube's videos of that Freddie Mercury have generated millions of views – but they are still, at 12 million, a fraction of the numbers who watched Freddie Mercury's rendition of Bohemian Rhapsody live on TV that day, with his phrophetic lyric 'too late: my time has come'. Today, the new kid on the social media block, the 'synchronous social network' The Houseparty videochat platform, allows teenagers and twentysomethings the opportunity to be live with each other on video, on the move, on their smartphones. But it is a fragmented togetherness, by comparision with the Live Aid experience, in that faraway galaxy of 1985.[10]

Yet it is always our desire to see each other's faces, to use touch, smell, sight, hearing in direct proximity to another person – that is the top of the hierarchy of

[9] Market Value data on UK music industry, www.thecreativeindustries.co.uk.

[10] The Houseparty app is a 'synchronous social network', which launched in October 2016, developed by *Apptopia*. At the time of writing it is expected to be the new kid on the social media block to dominate, after Twitter, Snapchat and Instagram.

connection and communication. Generations Y and Z may think mass socialising began with Facebook, but they couldn't be more wrong. The YMCA began in 1844 and still has fifty-eight million 'beneficiaries' in over 11,000 branches worldwide and is 'the world's biggest youth movement';[11] working men's clubs started in 1862; the Women's Institute in 1897; and, in 1907, the Scouts (still active today in 216 countries around the world, with over thirty million members). Some of the biggest social and political changes have been brought about by mass connections, live, of large groups of people: Tahrir Square and Tiannamen Square, a Rolling Stones or Taylor Swift concert, or Live Aid. These are moments in which connection is augmented and amplified by technology but where it is us, real people, who are firmly in the driving seat.

In 1985 there was no mass medium other than cinema in my life, and at the time any hierarchy of communication would definitely have placed broadcast media at the top. It was another twenty-one years before Twitter arrived and ushered in a whole new era of live-TV connectedness. The instant message effect of reporting and commenting on shared culture happening live: that felt thrilling, too.

Already, however, the blush is falling from the rose. There is so much opportunity to connect with everyone, all the time, that the numbers are falling at worse or fragmenting at best. Twitter in the summer of 2016 was struggling against the new kid on the block, Snapchat. Mass connection and mass communication feel excessive and cloying. People are beginning to go private and niche, or at least try to. They cannot connect via servers and the internet completely securely, no matter what anyone tells them, especially after Edward Snowden's revelations, but also, because, as anyone sensible knows, in today's connected age 'you have zero privacy, get over it'.[12] There is always time to take a screengrab or record someone, and then spread it around.

---

[11] YMCA Annual Report 2015.

[12] Scott McNealy of Sun Microsystems told a group of analysts and reporters in 1999 'you have zero privacy anyway. Get over it'. Reported in *Wired*, 26 January 1999.

I do more face-to-face connecting than ever before. No matter how busy I am, I make a point of seeing people in person, both professionally and personally. I meet for coffee or a walk, I hold small suppers or attend conferences and festivals. I am careful which ones I go to, because time is so valuable (and because I value my time) but I do not stint on getting in the room with people rather than communicating and connecting virtually, or not at all. If I want to thrive in the age of overload, more face-to-face connection is not just nice to have – it is a must-have.

Not so long ago I attended a conference in New York. The co-founder of *Wired* magazine, which celebrated all things digital and arguably virtual, had come full circle in his thinking. Speaking about the growing trend in co-working spaces, which spell the end of atomised units within skyscrapers or in siloed offices, he said,

> *If you are not in the same room, you're using up a lot of the (digital) bandwidth to express yourself with other human beings. It's going to be more valuable to spend time physically. If I were an investor, this is where I'd put my money – by being counter-instinctive'.*[13]

What was remarkable was that a technology titan was giving a shoutout for face-to-face connection in a Facebook age, but also that he was framing it as 'counter-instinctive'. As the writer Will Self drily remarked, no-one is suggesting that people start to 'parent their children by Skype'.[14] Skype has its uses as a proxy form of face-to-face when needs must. The evolutionary psychologist Professor Robin Dunbar commented to me in an interview I did with him for one of my BBC radio programmes on connectedness: 'social media certainly help slow down the natural rate of decay in relationship quality that would set in once we cannot readily meet friends face to face. But there is something

---

[13] John Battelle, the co-founder of *Wired* magazine at the DLD conference in New York City, 3 May 2016, making the point that face-to-face connections matter increasingly in a digital age.

[14] The British novelist, writer, teacher and broadcaster Will Self, writing in the *New Statesman* in 2014, made the point that proxy and proximity are not the same when it comes to face-to-face connection.

paramount about face-to-face interactions. Seeing the white of their eyes from time to time seems to be crucial to the way we maintain friendships'.[15]

How we maintain 'friendships' is social, but is not confined to social settings. It is not just that work culture and networked technology allows us to wear less of a metaphorical (and actual) uniform to work, and be both a worker and someone with an obvious domestic life, reflecting the increase in part-time and flexitime arrangements to the degree that 'dress down Friday' whirled through work culture and blew itself out, as these days people can increasingly wear what they like to work.[16] Research consistently shows that blending social factors associated with friendship, family and kinship, such as trust, can make a significant difference to business and professional settings.

Two academic papers, one studying garment producers and the other studying legislative collaboration in the Senate in the United States, both concluded that, whilst not perfect, the relationships in settings which had more of the connective tissue and intimacy of friendship with high face-to-face quotas were stronger and more productive than those without.[17] One American CEO said, 'It is hard to see for an outsider that you become friends with these people – business friends. You trust them and their work. You have an interest in what they're doing outside business'.[18] In the case of politics, 'a conversation on a trip to Europe activated relational benefits that ultimately proved instrumental in the passage of important legislation six years later'.[19]

So here's a question: how else could that have been achieved?

---

[15] In 2014 I interviewed the evolutionary psychologist Professor Robin Dunbar about face-to-face contact for my BBC Radio 4 series 'Networking Nations: The Science of Networks'.
[16] The British employer/employee help service ACAS reported homeworking rising from 16 to 28 per cent, flexitime rising from 19 to 26 per cent and switching from full time to part time rising from 46 to 64 per cent in the UK in the 2005 Survey, right at the start of the fully connected era.
[17] Brian Uzzi, 'Social Structure and Competition in Interfirm Networks: The Paradox of Embeddedness'.
[18] Ibid.
[19] Bruce A. Desmarais, Vincent G. Moscradelli, Brian F. Schaffner and Michael S. Kowai, 'Measuring Legislative Collaboration: The Senate Press Events Network'.

Futureshock

*One of the effects of living with electric information is that we live habitually in
a state of information overload. There's always more than you can cope with.*

MARSHALL MCLUHAN

It was in the late 1960s and early 1970s that we began to live with the concept
of 'information overload'. In 1969, the Canadian social theorist Marshall
McLuhan, who introduced the idea of the 'global village', was advocating that
'faced with information overload, we have no alternative but pattern
recognition'.[20] Within a single generation, between 1975 and 2017, 'Futureshock'[21]
had arrived, bringing us mass consumer electronics, the desktop computer, the
fax, 24/7 TV, the internet, web browsers, search engines, the mobile, the laptop,
the smart mobile, web streaming, social media and now occulus rift, AI and
robotics. The internet critic and social observer Andrew Keen points out that
today we all live in 'a networked world in which the volume of data produced
between 2012 and 2013 made up ninety per cent of all the data produced in
human history'.[22]

The effect of this is billed as entirely liberating. Choice and excess are the
consumer society's baseline offering. The difficulty quickly becomes one only
of overload, Futureshock's main byproduct. Not tuneout, but burnout. When
I ask students what they read and what they listen to, they often look blank.
Their frame of knowledge reference is reduced to the physical size of a piece of
supermarket cheese on their mobile screens, reflected back in a small scrolling
circle of restricted information sources, the same 'feeds' of news. Yet the amount
of times a day they are connected is only rising.[23] Since 2015 major news

---

[20] Marshall McLuhan, *Counterblast*.
[21] Alvin Toffler, *Future Shock*.
[22] Andrew Keen, *The Internet is Not the Answer*.
[23] See '*There's No Place Like Phone: Global Mobile Consumer Survey 2016*' from Deloitte and their
Deloitte Insights blog, 'How Do Today's Students Use Mobiles?'.

providers have begun to programme specifically for these devices, which on the face of it is good. Except that you cannot give depth on this dimension, only shrinkage and speed.

This creates two problems. One is a wealth of partial, myopic and undiverse information. Like tourists going to a sunkissed holiday destination and honing in on the one restaurant that offers them the same food as they eat at home. (I am thinking of a restaurant that I once visited in Greece, where the waiters were incredulous that I wanted kleftiko. 'Are you sure, Madam?' they asked. 'Everyone else wants steak and chips.')

The second problem is knowledge. You need to know stuff these days. The interconnected world of finance and politics, of sport and media, of culture and education, and of everything threaded in between, requires people to thrive and survive if they have little snippets of diverse information rather than siloed blocks of only one or two kinds. Why? Because this is the generation that has to make its own luck. It is now the post-corporate world, where jobs and workplaces are mobile, and where we all face invisible competitors with better information systems and communications than our own. Forget the CV, we now tell our children: fill yourself with knowledge, ideas and experiences. In other words, be interesting. The Futureshock world is inhibiting because it is just so vast. The Royal Navy, one of the oldest and most choreographed of all the armed forces, knows the power of snippets of information narrowing down vast oceans. Andrew St George chronicles the way in which stories, or 'dits', are exchanged on a regular basis:

> The Royal Navy has a highly efficient informal internal network. Leadership information and stories known as dits are exchanged across it – between tiers of management, generations, practices (branches), and social groups. With the help of dits, the Royal Navy's collective consciousness assimilates new knowledge and insights while reinforcing established ones. Visitors to naval

establishments or ships are often invited for a few dits; crews are encouraged to share theirs.[24]

We need to know a lot, or a little about a lot, but what do we trust, where do we go to find it? The term 'truthiness' was coined by the American comedian Stephen Colbert in 2005, and by 2016 during the Trump/Clinton American Presidential campaign this had become 'post-truth' and then, 'Fake News'. But the enemy stalking the information corridors is less truth than nonsense: how can we have de-cluttered, clean minds when they are filled with such media noise? It was interesting when Buzzfeed began to separate out its news from entertainment video feeds in 2016,[25] because at least there was an acknowledgement that information has variations and difference: it is not all one thick and indistinguishable flow.

So you have to be enterprising and entrepreneurial just to swim through the vast oceans of information. Like Dory, the charming forgetful fish in the 2003 Pixar movie *Finding Nemo*, which captured the zeitgeist of the Futureshock and the Age of Overload very well, featuring a vast, limitless ocean. Dory's forgetfulness is a useful metaphor for overcoming overload and tuning things out.

Information has also become something we do not entirely trust. In plenty of countries in the world, internet regulation still misdirects or denies us all the knowledge that exists, but recognising what is true is just as hard as finding it in the first place. We paddle insecurely in a rowing boat on choppy media waters, hoping to spot dry land when we can. Hoping to get lucky. What is our 'family' of information, of knowledge? The truth is that we often forget to even ask, as we place blind faith in the idea that it is 'out there' somewhere, at the click of a button. Of all the practical tools I developed for our clients at Editorial

---

[24] Andrew St George, '*Leadership Lessons from the Royal Navy*'. See also, Andrew St George, *Royal Navy Way of Leadership*.
[25] Benjamin Mullin, '*Buzzfeed Undergoes Company-wide Reorganisation, Separating Entertainment from News*', www.poynter.org.

Intelligence (a company that we bylined 'Knowledge Networking'), the most popular is the 'Knowledge Dashboard', which helps people curate their own flow of information across a range of sources (you can see more in the Appendix).

The other problem with Futureshock knowledge and information is that we can be pulled way off course by the internet's currents of algorithms. This famously happened with Facebook being accused of bias in its feeds and reintroducing humans after the 'disaster' of leaving it all to algorithms.[26] But I have also experienced this firsthand with Google. I created my own website in order to manage and archive a growing list of articles, interviews, a blog and some news (this for promotional reasons), so that I would have a 'shop window'. But I quickly realised I was doing something else. I was organising the chronology of my life and work in a way that was no longer possible just to search for. The 'ranking' of what people found when they looked me up altered the sequence in which I was appearing. This meant that perhaps a piece of writing which was fairly central to my work and of interest, I hoped, to people asking me to speak or consult, was being dragged down into the undertow by a completely different search, often related to someone or something else to which I was linked. A case in point was when my father died in 2012. My search rankings leapt, but they did so around his name, pushing others searches out. When you have large bodies of information or news coming in to the algorithm's reach, you risk it giving off what is effectively a false reading; it is not that the facts are wrong, but the location of those facts in relation to others, which is a distortion in itself.

The antidote to Futureshock is understanding that our needs are changing. To be overwhelmed by uncurated information in fast currents of feeds is not sufficient. In order to navigate we need to curate, we need proper guidance and

---

[26] Sam Thielman, 'Facebook Fires Trending Team, and Algorithm without Humans Goes Crazy', The Guardian, August 2016.

effective signage, as if we were travelling through a transport hub. Imagine arriving at an international airport and not seeing the departures or arrivals board clicking away? Or having the boards adjusted by naughty school kids who were having fun with Hamburg instead of Hanover as a destination, and assigning random gate numbers? We need to recognise that there are times when we need less information, not more. That we need it presented by sources we can trust, in the same way that the best journalists cultivate their 'sources'. The next challenge, of course, is the big one: how on earth do we find the time?

Timescalebending

We have lost patience with our body's capacity to heal itself; because time is of the essence and we have to keep going.

REVD LUCY WINKETT[27]

In his contemporary history, *The Pleasures and Sorrows of Work*, the contemporary philosopher Alain de Botton spent several days with an electrical engineer tracing the 175 kilometres of power line between Dungeness and Canning Town, bringing electricity to a large part of London. He noted the transference 'from a prodigious 400 kilovolts to a more moderate 275 and thence to a placid 132, until it emerged from sockets, shorn of all impetuousness, at a mere 240 volts'.[28] Scale and speed: these are the twin determinants of modern connected life. We mark the speed at which we can do things partly by their scale. Only a 'mere' small number? And how fast?

We all know that feeling of pressure. Growth is a word embedded in the core psyche of capitalism. The philosopher Martha Nussbaum notes how we

---

[27] 'Thought for the Day', BBC Radio 4, August 2015.
[28] Alain de Botton, *The Pleasures and Sorrows of Work*.

wish to 'transcend finitude'.[29] Venture capitalists talk about how fast you can get 'to scale'. It was refreshing to hear the media theorist Douglas Rushkoff scorn this 'digitally steroidal economy' comprehensively at a New York conference full of tech geeks and digital entrepreneurs. The pursuit of scale and growth is 'why Google has grown from being a tech company to a holding company'.[30] The culture of veneration around awesome scale and speed, which may be just that and little else, was beautifully captured by Michael Lewis in his book 'Flash Boys', about the lengths financial traders would go to in order to gain a fraction of a second's advantage over a competitor:

> Brad's desk to the BATS exchange in Weehawken, was about 2 milliseconds, and the slowest, from Brad's desk to Carteret, was around 4 milliseconds. It took 100 milliseconds to blink your eyes; hard to believe that a fraction of a blink of an eye could have such vast market consequences.[31]

This 'death of distance', as the Oxford Don Frances Cairncross put it in 1997[32] – around the time that the electronic everyday landscape changed forever with the internet and computing capacity becoming supercharged, ushering in the Age of Overload – brings with it the idea that not only do we have to deal with very large numbers of things all the time, but that we must do so very quickly indeed.

Then there is not just speed but relentless 'not stopping'. In 2015, *The New York Times* ran an exposé of working practices inside Amazon, describing the rise of a particular kind of worker, the 'Amabot', essentially trained and treated like a human robot. They quoted an anonymous worker as saying 'One time I didn't sleep for four days straight – these businesses were my babies and I did

---

[29] Martha C. Nussbaum, *Upheavals of Thought: The Intelligence of Emotion*.
[30] Douglas Rushkoff spoke at DLD, 16 May 2016, New York. www.dld-conference.com.
[31] Michael Lewis, *Flash Boys*.
[32] Frances Cairncross, *The Death of Distance: How the Communications Revolution Will Change Our Lives*.

whatever I could to make them successful'.[33] Back in the twentieth century, when we were just beginning to realise that we were all being forced to go faster on the 'information superhighway', I was a young book publicist at Penguin Books. In 1985 images were not digital but stored in vast filing cabinets; books were not downloaded but stuffed into jiffy bags and sent, often by expensive courier, to literary editors in between their long lunches and their offices. I was set the task of calling a 'big author' – the novelist Edna O'Brien. She did not answer, but her high-tech new answerphone did. The disembodied voice on the other end of the line explained what the machine was and what it did, and how there would be pause after the bleep in which to record a message. 'It will', she said, in her dulcet Irish lilt, 'give you time to think'.

The knock-on effect of being obsessed not only by scale but also by speed is that it confuses our human system, which remains stubbornly slow to change much in terms of physiology. When I present statistics to illustrate the scale and pace of modern life to students and corporate audiences, they can all relate to the big numbers: no-one is surprised that 50 million Americans belong to a gym, or that LinkedIn has 433 million members. It is the small numbers they have the problem with. Some have heard of the 'Dunbar Number' (of 150; discussed later in this book) but the number 168 always draws blanks. It is a relatively small number. Not as small as the optimal heartbeats per minute, and not as small as the number of seconds in a minute, but smaller by some margin, as we have seen, than much else: smaller than the number of times the number 5 appears in 24 hours, for instance. The number 168 is less than the number of countries in the world. It is less than the number of types of music, art, named sexual practices or types of cuisine. It is less than the number of recorded languages or polyphonic sounds. But to humans it is in fact a large number because it represents a total. As, I have pointed out earlier in this book, it is the complete number of hours in the week.

---

[33] Jodi Kantor and David Streitfeld, 'Inside Amazon: Wrestling Big Ideas in a Bruising Workplace', New York Times, 16 August 2016.

For all the vast inequality in the world, end-to-end, from the billionaire banker to the slum dweller, all have an equality of time to play with. A third of our precious time is used to sleep. The body can stimulate itself into staying up later and longer, but biologically we need six to eight hours of sleep a night (actually broken up into different segments but the norm is now a single unbroken period). That means there are only 112 hours left (can you feel the clocking ticking?) in which to live, to work, to multitask, to connect and to have everything done. This small number is incredibly shocking and disappointing to people. We are living in a world of such scale, where excess is sold as desirable, that the term 'living within our means' is supposed to apply to prudent financial management but not, somehow, time itself. Small wonder then that impatience is on the rise. I found myself grinding my teeth in irritation one day when I opened a locker at the gym and found someone had left clothes in it without putting a padlock on outside. They had wasted my time. I fumed. Whatever the time – seconds, nanoseconds – it felt too long. It felt like a *waste*.

Wherever we look, speed is celebrated. The entire news media, upended first by 24/7 'rolling news' pioneered by CNN in the 1990s, and now happening on every TV, tablet and mobile in an online, on-air continuous sequence, has become enthralled to speed first and everything else second. The Pulitzer Prize winners Howard Rosenberg and Charles Feldman noted, in their aptly-named book *No Time to Think*, that news programming has been designed to satisfy this appetite for consumers 'so that they can receive it without breaking stride the way a marathon runner grabs a cup of water on the run'.[34]

Our bodies and our psyches seem to be beginning to rebel against the swift and the speedy as the only way to be. The 'Slow Movement'[35] started in 1986 and was the first sign that we need to balance out the frenetic pace of life with

---

[34] Howard Rosenberg and Charles Feldman, *No Time to Think: The Menace of Media Speed and the 24-hour News Cycle*.

[35] The Slow Movement originated in 1986 with Slow Food, started by Carlo Petrini in Italy. See www.create-the-good-life.com.

something else, something less instant and temporary. Nearly twenty years later, the big cultural box office lies in boxed set TV mini-series, with phrases such as 'binge watching' and 'marathon viewing' entering the lexicon. Netflix's *House of Cards* was a good example, as were the BBC's 'Scandi Dramas', *The Bridge* and *Borgen* – series which were consumed, on average, between two and six episodes in one sitting. It seems to me that people want to reclaim time, to stretch and elongate it and that sitting in one place watching one thing compulsively is a rather good way of slowing down.

Techno Shabbat

After speed and scale (the size of US President Donald Trump's twenty million-plus Twitter following @realdonaldtrump gives him an additional power to the @POTUS status itself), comes time. We want literally to bend it to our will, to control it. We control our time, the symbol of which for many is the diary or the schedule, rather poorly, if we control it at all. We outsource the management of it to others in ways that would be unthinkable if it were our own bodies. There is no cloud-based group i-cal or Outlook calendar equivalent of your diet, in which others can design and manipulate what goes into your body. But the diary, the metaphorical body for the way we spend our time, is always up for (someone else's) grabs.

The Age of Overload is full of contradictions. A sense of disconnection stalks many at home and at work. My own working life – spanning Telex to Twitter, Ink to Instagram, Analogue to Digital – has been one in which I stay connected to childhood friends living on different continents but struggle to make time that is not pre-determined by a schedule or diary and to connect directly with those around me whom I love. Blocks of time to help us meet and connect our ideas, projects and gatherings. The less time we have, the more we crave to control it, but only because it is a system for measuring a certain kind of meaning – and what has more meaning than who we connect with, and who we are connected to?

We use the 24-hour clock, and the 60-minute hour in almost everything to do with organising our lives. When the Sumerians of ancient Mesopotamia first divided time into sixths some 5,000 years ago, they could not have predicted that they would bequeath modern life two of its most important tools: the wheel and time. In fact, time itself would not be measured anything like as acutely as it is today were it not for the wheel itself, or rather the railroad wheel. The Scottish engineer Sir Stamford Fleming, dubbed 'the father of standard time', first introduced time zones in 1883 (after allegedly missing a train due to haphazard organization of schedules).[36]

So wedded are we today to time and its measurement that Apple launched its latest 'wearable' tech not as a handheld computer with a little clock on the top but a wristwatch with an embedded computer.[37] The message was clear: in the teenage twenty-first century we wear time (and how we spend it) as a statement of who we are. Being busy is seen as better than not being busy. Apps that attempt to help you control time are in a section of their own called 'productivity' on the digital shelf. Not only are watches one of the few objects that dominate the luxury product market (Rolex alone was estimated to have a brand value of seven billion Swiss Francs in 2014),[38] but those who control their time are generally more wealthy and have higher status than those who do not. Yet the behavioural zeitgeist-watcher Rory Sutherland frequently points out in his Wikiman column in *The Spectator* magazine the foolishness of a society which

---

[36] Standard time in time zones was instituted in the US and Canada by the railroads on 18 November 1883. Before then, time of day was a local matter, using community clocks based on solar time. Standardisation in tome zones was established in the Standard Time Act of 19 March 1918, with the nine time zones of Coordinated Universal Time or UTC still in place today.

[37] Apple launched the Apple watch in April 2015, which in its first year outperformed the iPhone in sales, according to the *Wall St Journal*, although subsequent quarters saw significant dips in revenues as consumers did not adapt wholesale to this new addition to personal computing, www.wsj.com reference in bibliography.

[38] See https://www.statista.com.

thinks only in terms of time, and specifically time-saving, rather than other ways of measuring success. Writing about the new British high speed rail link HS2 he puts it thus: 'The prospect of saving 30 minutes twice a month is not a gamechanger'.[39] People tend to believe, however, that it is. The MIT sociologist and psychologist Sherry Turkle, who has pioneered much thinking about the connectedness of humans in a technological age, notes in her latest book, *Reclaiming Conversation: The Power of Talk in a Digital Age*, that the cost of apparent time-saving in corporate meetings ('it is common practice for lawyers, even at the most senior level, to keep phones and tablets out during meetings') is a disconnection of attention: a kind of opportunity to tuneout is presented culturally as some kind of great time-saving device. Thus the conference call – which I regard as about as socially unhealthy as a big bag of fast-food fries, to be consumed as a one-off at great intervals – becomes an opportunity 'if they are alone, to listen to the call and continue to work at their screens. They will miss the face-to-face conversations but they'll be able to multitask'.[40]

Time, they say, is the great healer. But increasingly, our approach to time, the anxieties it provokes in us, is anything but healing or healthy. When we think about connection, we often think how fast we can connect. And inevitably, when we think about how fast we connect, we think about how much time it takes us. Social Health puts paying attention to time at the heart of the idea of contemporary rounded health precisely because we are generally so badly out of sync with it. My own antidote to the time crunch is to bend or stretch it. In my mind, of course. I often do less in order to try and do more. One day a week I slow things down, going on *techno shabbat* away from social media and the internet, in order to bring my mind's eye on time down to the real-time pace, not the frenetic, machine-led one. I do not so much practise 'mindfulness' techniques, which require some focus and concentration as well as time, as I do

---

[39] Rory Sutherland, '*The Most Important Test That HS2 Doesn't Pass*', The Spectator, November 2015.
[40] Sherry Turkle, *Reclaiming Conversation: The Power of Talk in A Digital Age.*

mind*lessness:* ways in which I switch off rather than tune mind*fully* in. I think back to my childhood, when my father, an academic, would write constantly for days and then slump in front of the TV watching the American cop show *Kojak* with me. Dad would stretch out his long legs and we would transport ourselves to someone else's time pressure – cop shows are always about deadlines and rushing, as well as about character – while he forgot, momentarily, his own.

My friends in business look forward to 'wheels up' on their trips, when time is suspended. They cannot be scheduled to do anything like a conference call or a meeting in the air and they disappear, momentarily, into their own time, bending it to their will, not anyone else's. We crave control in our lives, but Social Health requires us to take it – and to craft it. There is a word for this, of course: 'downtime'. It is just important to remember to have it. Remember: the power of being connected is also know the opposite – when to disconnect and unplug.

PART TWO

THE BLENDED SELF

4

The social soul

Naomi and Gladys

'Can you let me in a little bit, just a little?' The person asking the question has neat features in a strong face which has lived eight decades. She is Naomi Feil, a German-born American-raised social worker. She has a steady gaze and voice and bright eyes, and is leaning towards another woman in her eighties whose eyes are closed, her face slack and silent. 'When people are old and deteriorated and no-one speaks to them they will withdraw more and more', says Feil of her work. 'Then the desperate need for connection is all now inside.'

Naomi Feil is talking to Gladys Wilson, who lives in a facility for elderly people with dementia who are labelled 'non-verbal'. She is using a method she has devised, called 'validation', to bring 'communication through empathy' to cognitively impaired individuals. The work is startling in both its intensity and its effect. Gladys is rocking her hands with an unfocused movement. You can see the institutional blue plastic of a chair peeking through a pretty crochet blanket, which itself is full of soft pastels – pinks, greens, yellows. The purple in the blanket picks up the colour of Gladys' jacket, under which is a crisp white shirt, but everything else about her has no colour, and is crumpled and sad. 'Are you crying?' asks Naomi gently. 'I can see a tear.'

Gladys and Naomi are of a similar age and look like they might have had similar strong features when young: clear, clean skin – white for Naomi and caramel for Gladys – and beautiful expressive lips. Naomi talks firmly and softly to Gladys, but it isn't her words that you notice. It is her hands. They are gently touching Gladys just by her ears, stroking the sides of her face. 'Every cell remembers this is how they were touched as an infant by their mother', she says. Her face is level with Gladys' and perhaps fifteen inches away. 'You're very sad', says Naomi. 'Can you open your eyes just a little and see me?' The eyes, which are wilted with inner neglect, open a tiny peep and look out. They meet Naomi's steady gaze and immediately Gladys' hands start to slap the arms of her chair. At the same moment, Naomi starts to sing. 'Jesus loves me, yes I know. For the Bible tells me so.'

Gladys' hands start to thump the chair more strongly, so Naomi raises her voice and sings the Christian hymn louder and faster. She refers to this direct mirroring behaviour as 'exquisite listening'. At this moment, both women are locked in an identical communication with each other. All disparity has disappeared. They are fully connected in this moment.

Naomi now leans right in. Her nose is nearly touching that of Gladys, their strong aquiline features a reflection of each other, a symmetry. Then Naomi changes song. 'He's got the whole world, in his hands, he's got the whole wide world . . .'. She sings and she pauses a tiny beat, knowing instinctively what will happen. Gladys, half-blind, a mute woman incarcerated by isolation, finishes the chorus and softly whispers '. . . in his hands' back at Naomi.

'Do you feel safe?' asks Naomi gently, still holding her face, still looking close as can be into her eyes. Then she states it. 'You feel safe.' Gladys says a word. Her mouth opens wide, her two remaining teeth shine as white as her shirt and she speaks, probably for the first time in many, many years. 'Yeah', she says quietly.

What drives the human being more than anything – and arguably lifted and drove us from the swamp to the skyscraper in 100,000 short years – started with the tools of fire and cooking pots and grew with the ability to communicate through stories and language, through touch and tenderness. We are social souls. We advanced our tools of civilisation with cooking, culture, cities and faith to leapfrog over our evolutionary competitors. Full connection was our chariot of fire. Modern civilisation relies on a set of increasingly sophisticated systems to function in increasingly complex ways, both commercially and politically, but they only need one outcome: to preserve this essential social DNA.

All human behaviour puts connection at its centre, with perhaps the exception of the people we might call 'inhuman' – the handful of psychopaths and sociopaths devoid of sufficient empathy to function like the rest of us, and unable to place connection at the centre of everything. Matthew Lieberman, Director of the Cognitive Neuroscience Laboratory at UCLA puts it like this:

> *Our brain is profoundly social. Our social wiring motivates us to stay connected. It returns our attention again and again to understanding the minds of people around us ... to ensure that we harmonise with those around us.*[1]

The great management thinker and social philospher Charles Handy said that 'part of any psychological contract with any group, family, firm or society is an exchange of some individual freedom in return for the rewards of belonging'.[2] We have a word for the choreographed series of social settings we organise around ourselves as individuals and institutions: society.

Neuroscience shows that the default position of the healthy brain, when not concerned with basic cognitive function, is connection and our social world. Love, life, birth, and funeral rites, death and loss. These are what concern us all, subconsciously, all of the time, regardless of whether we give the impression of being super busy and super achieving or not. In 2001, during '9/11', our minds were seared by the phone calls and texts from people trapped in the buildings and planes. As they faced death, they wanted to communicate the essence of life: love. When politicians talk about terrorists 'spreading fear', they understand that the fear of a loss of connection to someone you love is the most powerful emotion we can have.

---

[1] Matthew D. Lieberman, *Social: Why Our Brains are Wired to Connect.*
[2] Charles Handy, *Understanding Organizations.*

A modern illness, FOMO, or fear of missing out, joins its equal and opposite emotions – increased loneliness, isolation and alienation. Loneliness is becoming entrenched, even endemic.[3] More people divorce, live alone, and have emotional and mental illness (or the absence of wellness) than ever before. We are all connected to our families, and those without such support groups are universally acknowledged to suffer and have our pity: to be truly unconnected or disconnected socially must be the biggest deprivation most of us could possibly imagine.

The distinguished sociologist Zygmunt Bauman said shortly before he died: 'loneliness, abandonment is the great fear of our individualist age'.[4] Individualism does not always have to be lonely, of course. Narcissism is on the rise. I am as guilty as anyone of posting a 'selfie' on Instagram. The endemic isolation and atomisation of society is stimulating not just a craving to connect but also to be visible. As if we might disappear, unnoticed, if we do not declare loudly just how present we are. Instagram has 400 million monthly active accounts and it lends itself to individual look-at-me-ism perfectly: my life, my clothes, my impressions of the world around me. And yet Instagram, and other micro-social media (many people who have public Twitter accounts use Instagram privately), are also utterly social, sharing with others information on places to go, architecture, gardens, art. These all thrive and are themselves the product of intense individuality. There is a curious symmetry in this connection, both an isolated voice and a shared one.

One of my favourite Instagram accounts is in fact called '@symmetrybreakfast' (500,000 followers) which posts images of double-portioned, perfectly aligned and arranged breakfasts. This is ostensibly about food, but it is not purely about that. It is about the very individuality of food. It

---

[3] Research by Professor Julianne Hol-Lunstad and colleagues in 2010 made empirical links between loneliness and mortality. See Holt-Lunstad et al., 'Social Relationships and Mortality Risk: A Meta-Analytic Review'.

[4] Zygmunt Bauman (2016) interview by Ricardo de Querol, El Pais, www.elpais.com.

asks us to connect to the idea of how it is prepared, and how it makes us feel. The rise of the food fad itself, with cookery programmes and book sales soaring, and restaurants booming, is a reflection of our social DNA: we *want* to break bread with each other. The late British food critic and travel writer A. A. Gill wrote about the civic value of food, from street food to the top tables. He believed that food is a metaphor for society. Breakfast, he wrote 'is everything. The beginning, the first thing. It is the mouthful that is the commitment to a new day, a continuing life.'[5]

The family clan

Blessed is the influence of one true, loving human soul on another.

GEORGE ELIOT

When we break bread or post selfies, we do so for ourselves but we also do it for others. Offline, how many people do we actually socialise with? The answer, famously, is 150: a very small number when you consider the metrics with which most of us live on social media, where to aspire to have 150 'likes' can be regarded as puny.

This 150 is called 'Dunbar's Number', after Professor Robin Dunbar, the evolutionary psychologist at the University of Oxford, whose famous experiments on the neocortex size of primates uncovered a whole series of observations about how humans are hardwired to behave. Specifically, Dunbar found that by looking at the shape of group size in monkeys relative to their brain size, it would be possibly to do the same for humans. Dunbar dug into the anthropological fabric of human societies to observe that within the layers of large cities and organisations something like this number does

---

[5] A. A. Gill, *Breakfast at the Wolseley.*

exist as a pattern. 'Once you start to look for them, groups of about this size turn up everywhere', he says, in, *How Many Friends Does One Person Need: Dunbar's Number and Other Evolutionary Quirks*.[6]

It is said that Neolithic farming villages numbered 150 and the fourth-century Sacred Band of Thebes consisted of 150 pairs of male lovers forming an elite force to fight the Battle of Leuctra. Modern big businesses are often arranged into manageable divisions of around 150 employees. One global company leader I know deliberately keeps his 1,000-strong workforce in different locations, 'so that they will all feel they still work in small little companies with individuality rather than one giant one'. The whole point about this number, naturally arrived at by humans, is that it represents closeness and proximity, mimicking the clan size of a large family. It also, says Dunbar, represents the cognitive limit we can manage: in short, how many Christmas cards can you send? Or how many people actually get your 'out of office' holiday bounce-back email?

When Dunbar's Number was first bubbling up into popular consciousness in 2010, I was conducting an experiment in my networking business. Up until that point we had organised one-off events to bring together professionals in our network who wanted to hear ideas and meet stimulating people. These were usually held over breakfast in interesting venues. This was not as pervasive a format then as it is today, where there is an excess of events with RSVPs directed to virtual stationery such as Eventbrite and Paperless Post. But its novelty could not hide its drawbacks: people came, they saw, they spoke and they left. They would instantly forget their experience as the rest of the day's busyness swallowed them up. I wanted something deeper.

Noticing that the World Economic Forum's flagship event took place in splendid isolation, on the top of a Swiss mountain near Davos, I wondered

---

[6] Robin Dunbar, *How Many Friends Does one Person Need? Dunbar's Number and Other Evolutionary Quirks*.

whether the fact that people raved about it was something to do with its location as well as the power it conveyed. If eighty per cent of the appeal of Davos was the people, surely twenty per cent was the surroundings and ambiance? I had a hunch that it was not just world leaders who wanted this kind of experience but ordinary professionals too. Acting on the hunch that people wanted to connect to ideas and people in small, intense groups, I booked the entire holiday village of Portmeirion, high in the mountains of Snowdonia in North Wales. Designed by the architect Sir Clough Williams-Ellis in the 1930s, and made famous by the 1970s TV show 'The Prisoner', whose refrain was 'I am a name! Not a number!', Portmeirion remains one of the best celebrations of individuality in a mass age. I called the conference 'Names Not Numbers'.[7]

Walk and Talk

Portmeirion stands on a rocky peninsula surrounded by sea, rhodedendron bushes, and a series of intensely quirky and beautiful Italiante cottages and houses, whose wooden frames are all painted in a traditional greeny turquoise, my favourite colour in the world. I used to visit Portmeirion as a child when 'Clough', who always wore plus-fours with knee-high yellow socks and whose shock of silver grey hair swept back from his craggy face like the relentless cliff winds, rented holiday cottages in the nearby mountains to my parents and a series of other quirky Cambridge academics. We holidayed for many blissful years at 'Parc Farm' at the foot of a village under the tiny mountain of Cnicht. The houses and cottages all featured wooden frames, painted in this same signature colour that stood out so vividly against the slate, bracken and moss. My father used to take me and my brother Andy walking to the lakes

---

[7] www.namesnotnumbers.com.

overlooking Bethgelert, where the only movement for miles would be the odd divebombing gull, a sheep dragging some grass into its mouth, and the tinkle of a clear mountain stream. We would stop on some rocks and look for our usual gap, 'The Robber's Cave'. Inside, our Dad would bring out chocolate bars: *Ice Breakers* for us kids and *Bourneville* for him. We would sit together, cramped in the musty quiet dark with our torches and chocolate, and be happier than anyone could be.

On special occasions the whole family would come down to Portmeirion. Clough gave us a pass to go beyond the main tourist areas and thus have hotel access as guests. The pass was actually a letter, sort of a cross between 'To Whom It May Concern' and some kind of financial bond. It was my first taste of upgrade treatment and I was greatly impressed as we swung into the grounds with nothing to pay and headed down to the hotel where real paying guests rather than day trippers were allowed to park. There we would swim in the tiny pool overlooking the estuary, which was as blue as a Hockney painting and always, no matter how warm the weather, as cold as a bucket of ice. But, oh, the glamour of it. Sometimes the Williams-Ellis clan, including the grand Lady Amabel, a member of the old English aristocratic Strachey family, who erected a thirty-foot Christmas tree at Brondanw farm and invited all the scrappy local kids to take home a tiny wrapped present, just like in the best Victorian novels, would throw lavish buffets served on the hotel's terrace. Guests would look up at the *trompe l'oeil* features Clough had installed high on the cliff ledges overlooking the hotel and appartements: statues of people leaning over the railings, surveying the ribbed tidal sand of the Llyn peninsula below.

So there could only be one place in my mind when I had the idea for an 'experiential residential' conference, emulating the splendid isolation and theatre of Davos, for a cultural conference of ideas for professionals. Conferences at that time were all about scale and volume: you made money by packing as many people as possible into a large featureless 'venue' or 'complex', sticking a badge on someone and hoping to induce them to wander down to a bland exhibition hall to buy some merchandise. I wanted to do something different. I wanted Names Not Numbers (NNN) to allow people time to develop relationships over a period of days, not hours, and to do so in a physical setting that was arresting and sublime, so that their senses would be satisfied and they could really connect with each other. I had one golden rule: no name badges. It would not kill anyone to just make conversation and ask.

NNN worked. In our first year it snowed and we nearly did not make it up the M1 motorway from London. But as the coach curved around the road off the drab A470 from Lake Bala and into the lush landscape created in a unique partnership between Clough Williams-Ellis and nature, a hush descended. There was no 'green room' for the artists, no matter how famous they were: the historian Simon Schama and the singer Annie Lennox. There were people who were not names, but they were not numbers either: how could they be? They ran on the same body clock as everyone else, they walked and talked along the beach just the same. We all belonged in one place, together. Perhaps most of all, there was no phone signal. People had to disconnect, whether they liked it or not. NNN became a success, and is still running today, but I was determined to preserve the intimacy at the expense of lucrative expansion. So instead of growing the scale of it to more than 150, I expanded the number of conferences and locations, but kept the core grouping the same. I found that at the end of NNN, people behaved as if they had experienced something rich and comfortable at the same time. They sent thank you cards, some sent candles and flowers. They had experienced a closeness at NNN that I hope had something to do with the setting, the programming and the event organisation, but which I think also had something critical to do with the scale.

The social soul likes to belong to a family. And a family, even a clan, is not vast but a series of small interconnected groups (if you are lucky, you have siblings and cousins – or even better, a 'blended' family of step-children and their families). Even if we do not, we like to behave as families, with people we trust, even when we are at work. Here is the biggest discovery of all: no matter where people work, they want what they want as a blended self, a person who has a life in and out of 'the office'. They want their senses stimulated, they want their sensibility addressed. If you are not helping them do that, will they stay motivated or will they look for the fastest opportunity to professionally disconnect?

Coffee cup conversation

The coffee house must not be dismissed with a cursory mention . . . coffee houses were the chief organs through which the public opinion of the metropolis vented itself.

T. B. MACAULAY, *THE HISTORY OF ENGLAND*

It seems that our hunger for connection is matched only by our thirst. Whether at work or play, we social souls often talk about things over a cup of coffee. Today, one hundred million bags of coffee are exported each year (the world buys almost twice as much Arabica as Robusta).[8] The modern coffee house is four centuries old. The journalist Tom Standage, who specialises in analysing the evolution of media and technology culture, described the face-to-face culture of coffee houses in the age of Enlightenment:

> *Whatever the topic, the main business of coffeehouses was the sharing and discussion of news and opinion in spoken, written, and printed form . . . conversation between strangers was encouraged, and distinctions of class and status were to be left at the door.*[9]

---

[8] Coffee Market Report, International Coffee Organization, www.ico.org.
[9] Tom Standage, *Writing on the Wall: Social Media – the First 2,000 Years.*

In the heady early days of eighteenth-century bohemia, you might not just drink coffee, either. Hogarth famously painted a louche scene featuring a well-used punch bowl in 'Midnight Modern Conversation', painted in 1732 at St John's Coffee House in London's Temple Bar.[10] Soho and Covent Garden establishments, like Old Slaughter's and Tom and Moll King's, put conversation so much at the centre of the community that Hogarth painted an entire set of conversation pieces, which were commissioned throughout his career. The coffee houses were a giant petri dish of art and poltics, gossip, culture and literature. Out of them grew separate clubs and associations: the poet Dryden may have frequented Will's Coffee House but soon it was clubs such as The Kit Kat Club, followed by the Society for the Encouragement of Arts, Manufactures and Commerce (now RSA), which began a more academy-focused aspect to social gatherings. You learned, and exchanged knowledge as much as you engaged in the more bawdy side of life.

There is no trace, bawdy or otherwise, of this exciting, dynamic exchange in today's modern coffee house – and more's the pity. Yes, you can get specialist coffee, you can have a double machiato or a drip-coffee, and the word 'barista' has a cachet for now, but something is missing: where is the actual conversation? Lee Siegel's account of the internet age, *Against the Machine: Being Human in the Age of the Electronic Mob*, is scathing: 'It's not the community that the laptop-ization of the coffeehouse has dispelled. It's the concrete, undeniable mutable fact of our being in the world'.[11] Of course social groups do go to coffee houses today but they are not called houses anymore. They are called shops. This needs to change if the social soul of coffee houses is to come back at all. The spontaneity and instinctive acceptance that meeting strangers to just *see what happens* is almost entirely absent. It may only be a matter of time before they do. The coffee house chain that introduces strangers to each other

---

[10] See Vic Gatrell's *The First Bohemians: Life and Art in London's Golden Age.*
[11] Lee Siegel, 'The World Is All That Is the Case', in *Against The Machine: Being Human in the Age of the Electronic Mob.*

and encourages connection may be on to something. If the social neuroscientist Matthew Lieberman is right, that 'we are hard wired to connect', and the sociologist Mark Granovetter's seminal findings from over 40 years ago, in *The Strength of Weak Ties*,[12] show that people can make all sorts of valuable and rewarding connections from unlikely sources, then it tells us two things. Firstly, we need to connect face-to-face more often, rather than less; and secondly, we need to do so in ways that put technology on the back burner. As Lee Siegal puts it:

> *The people you encounter on the internet are half people and half building blocks for your fantasies. You yourself fill in their pixelated or digitized blanks . . . They are at the mercy of your mouse, of your disconnecting finger.*[13]

Or put another way: for the social soul, you have to be in the room with each other for something good to happen.

This comes right back to Dunbar's Number and the trust that builds up and crystallises with closeness. It is hard to do this if you are not actually in front of someone. In 'Free Radicals', a short story by Alice Munro, one of the characters acknowledges that it's the physical act of holding a warm cup of coffee that is important – 'that was the aid to thought or whatever it was she practiced'.[14] But the act of meeting someone for coffee, or a meal . . . well, that is a kind of commitment. I think of the business relationships I have developed over the years and they almost always began over a cup of coffee. I think of the friendships I have nurtured over a meal, a glass of wine, a place from which to look into their eyes and – yes, that cliché itself – connect.

Connection is the very essence of life. Although this book looks at its perils and excesses, and explores the possibilities of disconnection as something

---

[12] Mark Granovetter, '*The Strength of Weak Ties*' American Journal of Society, 1973.
[13] Lee Siegal, *Against The Machine: Being Human in the Age of the Electronic Mob*.
[14] 'Free Radicals', from the *New Yorker* magazine, February 2008.

positive, it is connection itself, in its pure, raw human form, which, if it takes place with trust, is rarely a bad thing. Trust gets much more complicated when you exchange more than just voice, eye, face contact. When you start to touch, let alone introduce sex, then connection, of course, becomes a whole lot more complicated.

Tinderbox sex

Spread thy close curtain, love-performing night,
That runaway's eyes may wink and Romeo
Leap to these arms, untalk'd of and unseen.

ROMEO AND JULIET 3.2.1

Is there a more anonymous name than John or Jane Doe? Originally borne out of an obscure British legal process called the *Action of ejectment*, they are names used in popular culture to define the nameless, those victims of crime who are never identified. These are also the names of those people involved in the US$500 million lawsuit against the internet dating site Ashley Madison (motto: 'Life is Short. Have an Affair'), whose anonymity, along with thirty-nine million others, was hacked in 2015.

The Ashley Madison incident could, no pun intended, have signalled the beginning of the end of the affair that people have been having with internet dating. The statistics, however, suggest otherwise. Social souls happen to like dating. And sex. Badoo is one of the largest internet dating sites in the world, with 300 million users in 190 countries worldwide – that's definitely bigger than 'Dunbar's Number'.[15] Tinder, which introduced the active 'swipe' mechanism to allow users not to just connect immediately but to communicate

---

[15] BBC Online article, *'The Dating Game: Which Dating Apps are Winning the Hearts of the World?'*, 12 February 2016.

their amorous interest, has more than fifty million monthly users and one billion swipes a day.[16]

The casualisation of sex has become a cultural norm in Western and westernised democracies, as the Millennials who watched their divorcing Baby Boomer parents eschew traditional monogomy have decided that they want something entirely different. Technology is aiding and abetting what they want, rather than creating a market out of nowhere. It is aiding adultery, as Ashley Madison has shown, and it is creating a buffet of sexual grazing for everyone else. *Rolling Stone* magazine featured the new sexual mores in a candid feature. The writer was surprised that monogomy seemed to have become quaint.[17]

It is often women, not men, leading the trend. 'I want to be meaningfully connected and involved with a lot of people, whether or not that means in a sexual way', a young woman tells the reporter.[18] There is a new term for Tinder-encounters: 'hookup sex'. This means, in old language, 'no strings attached'. The American comedienne Amy Schumer, who has honed a glorious line of post-feminist sassy standup by focusing on telling it how it really is for women of her generation, put it like this:

I will speak and share and fuck and love and I will never apologise to the frightened millions who resent that they never had it in them to do it. In every group of girlfriends, there's that one who is the sluttiest. If you don't have that friend, you're that friend.

I admit that a part of me, quite a large part actually, recoils from this sentiment, despite being a fan of Schumer and having laughed myself silly at seeing her perform live at the GQ Men of the Year Awards (at which she said 'That's so great, because men need more awards.') because I do not recognise

---

[16] Craig Smith, '*By the Numbers: 41 Impressive Tinder Statistics*', 29 May 2016, www.expandedramblings.com.

[17] Alex Morris, '*Tales from the Millennials' Sexual Revolution*', Rolling Stone, 2014.

[18] Ibid.

the idea that sex and intimacy can become so disconnected – for either men or women.

It makes me wonder whether casual sex, or swift encounters which lead with little or no preamble to bed, represent a longing to use physical connection as a release and a connection which is denied as our lives are increasingly locked away behind screens. We want, in short, to let our hair down. Cast your mind back a few hundred years, to coffee house days. The historian of bohemian London, Vic Gatrell, records the sheer scale and exuberance with which the Enlightenment years were conducted in London, blending a new-found flourishing in art, ideas, coffee houses and clubs with another kind of face-to-face connection, sex:

> *If sexual freedom is a condition of bohemian life, Covent Garden was especially blessed with it. Apart from vegetables, flowers and fruit, the most intense of its miasmas was the sex that well-attuned nostrils might breathe in its very air.*[19]

There are downsides and dark sides to internet sex, making it a different kind of tinderbox. Courting anonymity often appeals to people with something to hide. In the UK, on Christmas Eve 2015, a 23-year-old woman, Katie Locke, was strangled by Carl Langdell on a first date, after having met on an internet dating site. The 'beautiful and vibrant' history and politics teacher did not, the prosecuting counsel told the court, know of the mental health history of her 'date' when she agreed to meet him, even though he had confided in a mental health care worker, only a matter of months previously, exactly what he wished to do to someone while they were alive and after he had killed them. He re-enacted this fantasy with someone alive and then he killed her. That someone was Katie Locke.[20]

---

[19] Vic Gatrell, *The First Bohemians: Life and Art in London's Golden Age.*
[20] ' *"Depraved" killer Carl Langdell jailed for first date murder*', BBC News, 3 June 2016.

There is another way of looking at internet dating, where you have to pay to play. The moral philospher Michael Sandel notes the devaluation that comes when you put transactions into everything. He paints a comically awful picture of American lobbying companies paying homeless people to queue for them outside Congress, for instance. And of the oldest social connection there is, he said, 'Consider friendships. Suppose you want more friends than you have. Would you try to buy some? Not likely. A moment's reflection would lead you to realise that it wouldn't work. A hired friend is not the same as a real one.'[21]

Back in my late twenties, when I feared I would be on the shelf forever and never find a husband, I joined a dating agency. It operated on email rather than internet. You had to submit a picture of yourself (mine was of me looking homely, leaning against a five-bar gate in Wales; it was a one-time-only selfie that you had to submit, no range of poses allowed), and answer all the usual questions that algorithms now calculate in superfast time. But this was really a sort of 'lonely hearts' ad mixed with putting my entry in front of some other people who had signed up and looked vaguely compatible. It was not, in other words, very scientific. A friend told me something very prescient. 'You won't meet the man of your dreams, Julia,' he said. 'You will, however, discover exactly who you *don't* want to meet, and it will help you choose the right one when you do find him.' This gloomy prediction haunted me as I traipsed around on 'dates' with people I had never laid eyes on before. I met a handful over a period of weeks, but I only remember two. The first was a meeting in a pub in Leicester Square. It was packed with people in the mid-evening, after-work rush, and I remember feeling panicky because London was at the time in the middle of a vicious IRA bombing campaign. I now think my panic about being trapped in a very full 'target' place – I almost had a full-blown panic attack – was as much to do with acute anxiety at the situation I had put myself in than anything else. Plus, I loathe pubs, being far more at home in, well, a

---

[21] Michael Sandel, *What Money Can't Buy. The Moral Limits of Markets.*

coffee house. I fought my way through the throng as fast as possible. I remember nothing whatsoever about the man I met, only my feelings about the whole encounter.

The second thing I remember is a date I had in London's Camden Town in Café Delancey, near the famous tourist spot of Camden Lock. Now a wholly unprepossessing venue with a high turnover of owners, Café Delancey was a 1980s style icon of an eaterie, at a time when there were not many around. A glorious faux-French café serving great café au lait and odd but delicious Mittel-Europa food like frankfurters and rösti, it was no-fuss yet glamorous. You sat at small round marble-topped tables with iron feet, under the watchful gaze of a series of paintings of legs and feet playing 'footsie' with each other. The café is long-gone and so is the date. I remember knowing instantly that there was no chemistry. As a recent divorcée remarked to the BBC when, in 2016, they did a survey of internet dating habits to mark Valentine's Day,

> *You create this perfect profile, using your best photographs and most creative lines of text, to create this persona, and you start to believe this persona that you've created. You spend a few weeks sending lines of text to each other, and you eventually arrange to meet. At the meeting, it's instantly recognisable that neither of you can live up to the expectations and you part company. If there's no chemistry, there's no chemistry. The fallout is the trip home, where you feel crushed and defeated and you know you're going back to square one to start the whole process again.*[22]

At the end of the appointed hour, with a mutual sinking feeling, we wrapped up the meeting. This is what it was: an assessment meeting, not a romantic date at all. I assumed we would split the bill – it was only a daytime coffee and these were the dungaree-wearing, Greenham-common-protesting, fat-is-a-feminist-issue years for young twentysomethings like me in London: women did not

---

[22] *'The Dating Game. Which Dating Apps are Winning the Hearts of the World?'*, 12 February 2016.

expect men to pay for them. However, I was taken aback when he asked me to pay for him too. He had just come back from an overseas trip, he explained, and had no English sterling – 'Unless you think they will accept payment in pesetas?' I confess that, at this point, I knew that there was something worse than not having chemistry: I simply did not *know* this man, nor any of the others. They were total strangers. The whole point, I realised, of my wanting to meet someone to spend the rest of my life with was to find someone I felt to be familiar, with whom there was recognition. The randomness of being match-made so imprecisely was, I realised, not for me. As it happened, several years later, I did meet the man I was to marry. Not through a dating agency; I already knew him. We reconnected and the rest is my marital history.

For me, marrying was a way of connecting to social ties and connections I already had; in fact, to reconnect to them. This is not to say that dating complete strangers cannot work perfectly, or that using algorithms to increase the statistical possibility of finding the right person is not perfectly viable. For me, what endures about romantic connection is something you can build together. When you take sex out of the equation, in a wider group for instance, that shared purpose, knowledge and mission is called something else: social capital.

Clearing the beach

When the historian and commentator Niall Ferguson bought a beachside house in South Wales he was troubled by the amount of litter that was left strewn around. It was a beautiful landscape that was supposed to be 'unspoilt', but in fact was the opposite. Each weekend he set about clearing it up, bit by bit. To his surprise – he had fully expected this to be a solo exercise – he found himself joined by neighbours. 'I want to cast doubt on the idea that the new social networks of the internet are in any sense a substitute for real networks of the sort that helped me clear my local beach', he wrote.[23] But he went further, drawing a wider connection between the absence of such community participation in civic society and calling it a contributory factor to the so-called 'Great Degeneration' of societies, which have become atomised, atagonistic and unstable. There are echoes of this back in Yuval Noah Harari's claim that the rapid ascent of man has left the human immature, fractious and actually unsocial.

In many senses we are encouraged and exhorted to attend only to our own needs, rather than those of the people around us. The idea that the generation of shy, withdrawn but talented designers who have built some degree of isolation into everyday technology (headphones attached to personal sound systems, screens that you have to look down at and tap, avoiding eye contact), often described as 'geeks', may in fact be products of high functioning autism and other social communication conditions is beginning to be voiced.[24]

Social capital is now a measured currency, an economic form of output which began to be taken seriously at the turn of this century when the American political scientist Robert Putnam famously introduced the concept in his book *Bowling Alone*. He warned of a society becoming isolated and disconnected from itself, in which 'financial capital – the wherewithal for mass marketing – has steadily replaced social capital – that is, grassroots citizen networks – as the coin of the realm'.[25] This analysis has been echoed and imitated widely, with the idea of group social connectedness at street and community level being accepted as healthy, compared to isolated, atomised and lonely groups who are only in it for themselves.

How we pull together, to clear a beach or improve a community (or stop it from becoming atomised and hostile to anyone but itself), is a function of

---

[23] Niall Ferguson, *The Great Degeneration: How Institutions Decay and Economies Die.*
[24] Lauren Silverman, '*Young Adults with Autism Can Thrive in High-Tech Jobs*', NPR Morning Edition 2013.
[25] Robert D. Putnam, *Bowling Alone: The Collapse and Revival of American Community.*

social capital. The World Bank describes this social capital as 'the connectedness of citizens to their community'.[26] Not least of which is how to get local people to clear a beach – either by leading by example and having some kind of social standing, or because the community itself is motivated and engaged. People want to pull together rather than go bowling alone.

Social capital obviously features in my definition of Social Health. You cannot join things up, or get things done, without it. To be fully connected as an individual or community of some kind, a business community or a civic one, requires the three main components of Social Health – good *knowledge* management, *networks* and networking capability, and sufficient *time* and space in which to achieve everything. These are partly created by the right social capital: who do you turn to for knowledge about x or y? How can we get such-and-such done? Oh, x or y will know. We need to get this done quickly. That requires us to reach x + y + z. A certain kind of generosity is required to build and maintain social capital; you have to have give and take. The management academic Adam Grant wrote extensively about this, placing reciprocity and generosity at the centre of people's ability to help themselves – by helping others.[27] He cites the example of Enron, whose spectacular collapse marked the beginning of the end of trust in 'Big Business', and notes that the founder, Kenneth Lay, used a large photograph of himself in every corporate report and only ever referred to the achievements of the company when prefaced by 'I' and not 'We'. Selfishness and social capital are at opposite ends of the spectrum.

The social soul can be anti-social – i.e. selfish, for them*selves* – or, literally, egocentric and concerned only with one (ego). The networks that lie at the heart of social capital resist this solo effort. I like the way that sociologists have begun to look not just at the individual in relation to the group, but what they

[26] Partha Dasgupta and Ismail Sergaledin (eds), *Social Capital – A Multi-Faceted Perspective.*
[27] Adam Grant, *Give and Take: A Revolutionary Approach to Success.*

can achieve together – what beaches they can clear. The Said Business School economic analyst Marc Ventresca, a man I first met under the blazing Abu Dhabi sun at a World Economic Forum summit, calls for more of what he dubs 'The System Builder' in society: entrepreneurs who 'have a vision but also implement it in complex ways that involve pulling apart what exists, reusing that, re-purposing what is already in place'.[28]

The point about social capital and Social Health is not just that it gets things done, that it activates rather than sits back in an inert way, but that it is to some extent spontaneous and reacts to what needs to be done at the time it needs doing. This seems to me very healthy: how do you know if you need to clear a beach until it begins to fill with litter? To return to my point about productivity as a key measurement of Social Health (slowing global levels of productivity tend to match rising obesity levels), the neuroscientist Matthew Lieberman, who has measured how brains are hardwired to concern themselves first and foremost with matters of connection and love, says:

> *If you take a moment to think it through, the benefits of social connection in terms of productivity are self-evident . . . social connection is a resource in the same way that intelligence or the internet are resources. They facilitate getting done what needs doing.*[29]

Who has social capital and who builds it, other than the entrepreneurial? Social enterprises are often associated with it, but what about individuals? Enter the broker. People who can network, bridge and build and connect between communities have social capital. They are the mavens and connectors that Malcolm Gladwell first brought to our attention in *The Tipping Point*, published the same year as Putnam's *Bowling Alone*. It is ironic that the biggest

---

[28] See Marc Ventresca's '*Is "System Builder" the new founder? An Oxford Lecturer's Myth-Busting Guide to the Word Entrepreneur*',12 June 2013, www.theheureka.com.
[29] Matthew Lieberman, *Social: Why Our Brains are Wired to Connect*.

cultural event of 2000 was to become associated with a kind of isolated selfishness that has reputationally dogged the computer business ever since: Sony released its Playstation 2, selling over 155 million units worldwide. That same year, one of the most popular films was an exploratory celebration of isolation, *Cast Away*, based on the writer Lucy Irvine's spell alone on a desert island. The world was becoming connected and yet isolated, yet longing to connect. These were – and remain – the contradictions of the Social Soul.

5

Worker beings

By day the skyscraper looms in the smoke and sun and has a soul.
Prairie and valley, streets of the city, pour people into it
and they mingle among its twenty floors and are
poured out again back to the streets, prairies and valleys.
It is the men and women, boys and girls so poured in and
out all day that give the building a soul of dreams
and thoughts and memories.

CARL SANDBERG, *SKYSCRAPER*, 1916

The bad job interview

The impeccably dressed woman asked the slightly dowdy interviewee sitting in front of her an impossible question. 'So,' she said. 'Who are your contacts?' In an instant, and with crushing humiliation, the younger woman knew that despite having been picked for this interview, despite having been given an 'in', despite all of that, she simply wasn't ready. Why would she be? This job was one of the most prestigious in publishing and she had worked in mainstream publishing for a mere five months. She has kidded herself that, having worked her way up up from in-tray filing in a small medical publishing house in North London, having dropped out of college with no degree and landed a marketing job at the publishing giant Penguin largely on the strength of her connections, she would carry on sauntering effortlessly up the ranks. She had, after all, been talent-spotted by a founding director of the fresh new kid on this publishing block, who popped up from behind a filing cabinet one day when the girl had only been there five minutes and said 'I'm putting you up for a job'. How foolish she'd been! At around the time that this bright young know-nothing was thinking she'd won the lottery, a penniless writer was scribbling away in a café and would end up being published by this new publishing kid. The writer was J. K. Rowling, then undiscovered, writing in an Edinburgh café. The publisher who lit a literary touchpaper with Harry Potter and the Philosopher's Stone *was called Bloomsbury. The young woman who did not make the grade to work at Bloomsbury (coincidentally, the publisher of the book that you are now holding in your hands) that day was me.*

At the time, the defining mass-connecting technology of the day – other than paperback books – was not the Internet but still the telephone and television. CNN was the key new brand, broadcasting continuously a new phase: 'rolling news'. For my part I was a regular user of the telex – a great lumbering dinosaur of a machine which looked like an obese typewriter – which I had used to send publishing copy to my first boss when he was away at the Frankfurt Book Fair.

What I did not have, physically or metaphorically, wasn't down to technology at all. It was something my interviewer instinctively understood that I needed to acquire and practise using before I could come back and play in the big league of her company. This technology was smaller than a telex, and had no wires or plastic or plugs of any kind, except for a wheel on which several pieces of paper flipped up. What I needed was a Rolodex. This was the ultimate organiser of contacts. I had only seen one on sale in New York. You can't know people you don't yet know! You have to fill the Rolodex (or it's British counterpart of the day, the Filofax, which I bought the minute the interview ended) with actual names. At the time I was asked for my media contacts I was only able to name one: my dear Uncle Wal, the distinguished Guardian journalist Walter Schwarz, who at the time was Religious Affairs Correspondent. By name-dropping, I felt foolish and somehow disloyal: as if I was sacrificing a small mouse to a very hungry, elegant python. 'Yes,' my impeccably polite interviewer asked kindly, sensing my dismay but doing what she needed to do. 'Who else?'

The interview took place in the Groucho Club in London's Soho, the newly opened drinking and socialising den started by a handful of smart publishing and media people. The Groucho Club was a vision of the future and I wanted to be part of it so much that, when I did get my next job, I negotiated membership there with one of the founders in lieu of a pay rise. In those days I was so nervous and overawed that I used to practise my facial expressions in a shop window in nearby Wardour Street before I dared to walk through the revolving door and into its slatted-blind, womb-like interior, dark in the daytime and full of writers not waiting for cocktail hour to begin before they started drinking. Louche, it was. I adored and feared it with a passion.

When it opened in 1984, 'The Groucho' – named, of course, after the Marx brother who famously said he wouldn't join a club which would accept him as a member – foresaw today's time of continuous overlap in networks across media, news, entertainment and the arts. Technology and digital in those days meant video and DVD, and nothing else: we are talking a lifetime ago, really. It foresaw the connection of new worlds and the disconnection of old ones: members' clubs like The Groucho heralded the demise of two old institutions: the 'old boy network' epitomised by gentlemen's clubs of the day, and the staid office itself. Today, parts of the Groucho Club are mobile places of work. The coffee houses of today are like cheap-seat versions of Soho House, which quickly followed the velvet-sofa chic of the Groucho. The new kids on the club block are now co-working spaces, blends of not just types of professionals, but how and where they work. Without realising it, with my lack of any formal introduction to the world of work, I was given a ringside seat at precisely the time it all began to change.

I learned more about the world of work in those short disastrous minutes of my interview in the Groucho Club that day, and more about the world of networks, than possibly anything before or since. I learned that being parachuted into a job or an interview counted for nothing if you could not do the job itself.

I learned that not being able to turn to the people in your field to get things done – in this case, media contacts – rendered all other skills useless. I learned the value of the searing effect of failure in galvanising, in being a prerequisite of future success. Finally, I learned that the world changes fast: Only a few months earlier I had landed the Penguin job and felt on top of the world. Suddenly I had a whole new skillset I had to learn; both what I knew and who I knew needed to change. The wheel of work does one thing constantly: like the world it mirrors, it constantly moves and revolves. The question is this: is the fully connected world of work generally too fixed and too unmoving to connect its workers as fully as required?

Paperweight

Working life is long. 10,000 days long, more or less[1] – about the time it takes a person to start their descent into old age after nearly half a century of living. Of course, we live our non-working lives in these forty-five or so years too – I'm just counting the 225 or so working days per annum. This factors in weekends and public holidays, as well as between one and four weeks a year off for your own rest and relaxation.[2] Still, that is a ratio of five days worked for every two off. By any metric that is a majority of your time, excluding sleeping, that you are working. That is if you are one of the lucky ones who has work at all. Work is wealth. Work is identity. Work is, for many of us, community. Work is where we belong. Work keeps us healthy. Or at least that is what it should do.

---

[1] There is no global standard, but the OECD lists an average of 1766 annual hours worked, which, if we assume at least forty-five years of work between the ages of twenty and sixty-five (although it varies greatly and in many countries is extending significantly) gives a picture of most full-time paid workers spending close to 80,000 hours, or 10,000 days, working.

[2] The OECD's 2009 Special Focus study, '*Measuring Leisure in OECD Countries*', in their 'Society at a Glance' Social Indicators report cited an average of forty-one total weeks a year worked when weekends, national holidays and annual vacation time is factored in but, again, there are considerable variations.

Work is also a journey – through the years and across lands of different skills. A journey discovering what you are good at and what you enjoy; who and how you can make a difference. That is the aspiration for the professional working classes anyway. That is often the aspiration of people who would like to become 'professional'. That is not everybody, nor is it a valuation of professionals as somehow better at their careers than anyone else. But the professional worker is more likely to be aware of the desire to feel satisfied at work and to aspire to be somehow compensated by more than just money. Eighty-seven per cent of Millennials believe that 'the success of a business should be measured in terms of more than just its financial performance'.[3]

The definition of 'career' means a course or journey through life.[4] It originates from the sixteenth-century French word 'carriére', meaning road or racecourse, and that from the original Latin 'careria', a track for wheeled vehicles. The association of the noun with the course of a working life is as recent as the start of the nineteenth century. Travel at work is venerated and retains glamour. The domestic journey to and from work affects wellbeing: some people have jammed, sweaty, long commutes, while others catch up on reading in peace and quiet. Some sit in traffic on flyovers, humming along to the local radio or shouting at it during the morning political shows. In cities around the world, the walking and cycling commuter revolution is well under way. We go 'to' work. We go home 'from' work. It is, literally, a journey. More and more of us work, even as artificial intelligence and the doom-mongers of 'the second machine age'[5] predict human obsolescence in the workplace; 3.5 billion people will require jobs by 2030.

---

[3] The 2016 Deloitte Millennial Survey, *'Winning Over the Next Generation of Leaders'*.

[4] For an etymological definition of 'career', see Robert Barnhart (Ed.), *Barnhart Dictionary of Etymology*, H.W. Wilson Co., 1988.

[5] The phrase 'Second Machine Age' was first coined in 2014 by MIT's Erik Brynjolfsson and Andrew McAfee in their influential book *The Second Machine Age: Work, Progress, and Prosperity in a Time of Brilliant Technologies*.

Which is about half the planet.[6] Half the planet, working for half their lives. Over a third of Americans already work on a freelance basis, and by about 2030 probably the rest of the world's workforce will mirror this ratio – that is, many millions of people on all five continents of the world who are making their own luck, will be freelance, self-employed and not going anywhere near a static place of work, either a factory, an office or a shop-floor.[7] But they will still work. We will all still want satisfaction, community, identity and clarity from what we do, won't we?

Work is also a weight. Even for those like me who have enjoyed the vast majority of their work, feeling energised, creative, productive and stimulated, it is still often a dominant, domineering, heavy creature. It can sometimes feel like a burden. I notice that I often see the pattern of how I find my work in the shape of the paper on my desk. Although I often work on the move, on my iPad with its little keyboard clicking magnetically onto it, I still have a desk. Not having one would feel wrong; it would feel disconnected from work. Even though I use that desk less and less, the decision to have *no* desk still belongs to others. So I have a desk and it is covered with paper. Some people are paperless. Some people trust that they can retrieve what they want and need on a just-in-time basis, like a factory floor. I need the physical evidence. I need to read and underline and hold my work. I like to physically organise it in piles and groups. I like to watch it grow and then diminish. I like to see progress and process twinned together. So, paper. Sometimes it litters my desk, literally. Great messy tracts lie in a tangled sprawl as on a teenager's bedroom floor. At other times I impose order. I tidy. I get on top of the filing, the sorting, the different *piles*, and

---

[6] Richard Dobbs et al., *The World at Work: Jobs, Pay and Skills for 3.5 Billion People*, www.McKinsey.com 2012.

[7] Forbes Magazine reported in 2015 that in the UK and US research shows that 'half the working population could be their own boss'. See David Presser, '*How Freelancers Are Taking Over the World*', The Pew Research Centre also posted a range of findings to support this trend. See Aaron Smith, '*Gig Work Online Selling & Home Sharing*', see also the 2014 Forbes article by Dan Schawbel, '*Top 10 Workplace Trends for 2015*'.

I zig-zag neatly between them and their electronic counterparts lying inert across various email inboxes or outsourced to Dropbox or Slack. It is actually all the same; evidence of a life doing *work*, that journey to make *A* happen and to move to *B*.

At my physical desk I punctuate and control the workload visually through a simple, old system: the paperweight. The paperweight was born during the early nineteenth-century flourishing of art and antiques, criss-crossing networks of seaways to the finest houses in the land. It was for that new status symbol, the working desk, that the craftsmen of Baccarat and Clichy in France made objects of intricate glass and crystal. Sole artisans working away in the 1840s and 1850s became the custodians of objects of beauty designed both to control paper and somehow act as a beautifying metaphor for the very job it represented; paperweights reflected the weight of responsibility we had ushered in. There was no going back from working life.

The past 7,000 days of my own working life have been narrated by diaries, organising systems, the telex, the typewriter, the desktop computer, the PDA, the laptop, the mobile phone and the iPad. But I never gave up on paper. We may have email instead these days – over a third of the world's population will use email by 2020[8] – but the piece of paper remains the most hallowed in an act of work, as signing legal documents or receiving anything handwritten will attest. It is the piece of paper that we carry with us in our heads and in our briefcases, even when we hide them away on memory sticks. The words and meaning we convey are moving with us, just as they did in Carl Sandberg's 'Skyscraper' published in 1916. As well as being an almost perfect piece of poetry it used a wonderful metaphor to foresee the sheer scale of transit involved in business and office life through one bit of paper: the letter: *'ten-dollar-a-week stenographers take letters from corporation officers, lawyers, efficiency engineers, and tons of letters go bundled from the building to all ends*

---

[8] 'Email Statistics Report 2015–2019', The Radicati Group, www.radicati.com.

of the earth'.[9] Work at its best is transit, movement and journey. Why, then, does so much of work feel the opposite? Why, in a fully connected world, does work feel so deluged and overwhelmed? Perhaps the answer lies partly around the desk itself, in the office.

The lonely skyscraper

It's a long old road, but I know I'm gonna find the end.

BESSIE SMITH, JAZZ SINGER, 1894–1937

1994 was the year in which the web browser Netscape first appeared, opening up the world at your desk. It was a year of global social progress. South Africa held its first multiracial elections, with Nelson Mandela inaugurated as President; the first passengers travelled through the Channel Tunnel; and same-sex unions were legalised in Denmark, Israel and Sweden. That same year, a Dutch report grandly heralded the end of the office itself. The report title 'Het Nieuwe Werken' predicted that the virtual office was the new kid in town and that it had arrived thanks to the opportunities of remote-working coupled with big changes in 'the behavioural environment around attitudes to work and flexibility'.[10] The physical space, so it predicted, the place where you worked, would no longer take priority. For many office workers this was a scent of freedom, even if they still had to trudge to their cubicle just like before. The 1990s were to the world of work what the 1950s were to feminism: a sign of 'no going back', a certain kind of freedom from certain constraints, and the shackles around work coming off.

---

[9] Reproduced with permission The Barbara Hogenson Agency.
[10] See '*Human Development Report 1997*', Oxford University Press, published for UNDP United Nations Development Programme.

With the benefit of hindsight, I see that I always hated being confined at work or at school. My feet itched early. At our secondary school, the main assembly hall looked out, through a vast plate glass window, several hundred yards to the Camden Road, a trunk road in North London, one and a half miles from Oxford Street's shopping mecca, and along which, in the mid-1970s, cars and lorries thundered all day going somewhere North. I longed daily to be out and about amongst them, to be free and going somewhere. *Out there.* To this day I drive between meetings in London, and spend more time out of an office than in it. Maybe the act of transit, of motion, is a metaphor for connection. I wanted to be *in transit*, picking things up and learning as I went. Largely through academic failure and choosing an unorthodox career path (all my friends went to university, none to polytechnic; all except me graduated), I happened upon a model on which the world of work today relies: mobility, agility, open-mindedness and humility about doing the granular as well as the grandiose. The world of work today is like those Carl Sandburg letters: fully mobile, fully connected. Perhaps the question now is: Where do we locate our working lives?

The idea of office work as a chore, as a burden, as something to be endured, is nothing new. The eighteenth-century essayist and writer Charles Lamb, a London clerk, complained, 'You don't know how wearisome it is to breathe the air of four pent walls without relief day after day'.[11] In the mid-1960s, it was an enterprising American who made a highly successful restaurant chain, still around today, with the name 'T. G. I. Friday', standing for 'Thank God It's Friday'. The burden of work was as much to do with the place of it as the fact of it. The office has struggled for many years to become an enjoyable place in which to work. Today, as much effort is made to make the workplace physically attractive as the pay package itself. The internet giants such as Facebook and Google famously create campuses, with the equivalent of adult play centres

---

[11] Charles Lamb, 1775–1834, essayist and writer, quoted in *'How the Office Was Invented'*, BBC Magazine, 13 July 2013, based on a transcript from Lucy Kellaway's *'History of Office Life'*, BBC Radio Four.

and overflowing kitchens to entice workers to stay, to play and to work – and not to leave the premises. But the office remains as a solo building in which a silo of work is completed. The workplace is not really a healthy, joined-up, connected human space so much as a physical place where the hope is that, if it looks good, it is good. The two are not the same.

Workplace bullying is, the statistics tell us, on the rise. At exactly the time that the age of connection began in the mid-1990s, social science researchers began predicting problems.[12] Even Google, one of the most desirable companies in the world to work for if you are a Millennial, runs internal programmes on 'unconscious bias'.[13] Most if not all of the great global brand name businesses, behind the scenes, face a plethora of well-known signs of poor social health: isolation, bullying, lack of progress ... a 'stuckness'. This is because the actual business of work, of putting people together to achieve linear growth whilst telling them they work in a lateral touchy-feely world, is a disconnect – and people know it. So people in grey-walled offices, or working in those spaces with ping pong tables and primary coloured sofas, will not behave fundamentally differently unless they actually *have* Social Health in their workplace: good flows of knowledge, networks and the right timeframe and pace in which to work; great management, communication and an ability to operate on commonsense and with all their human senses. Jobs do not get done by systems alone, or working for a company with a reputation for being glamorous, rich or groovy; the reality creeps in before long. The office is just a place where the human problems bubble up. It is the human behaviours, attitudes, practices and mindsets that need to change.

How you view these problems is open to interpretation. We need ways of coping with the Age of Overload in which there is a tsunami of tasks,

---

[12] I. Rivers and N. Noret, '"I h8 u": Findings from a Five-Year Study of Text and Email Bullying'; C. Weare, W. E. Loges and N. Oztas, 'Email Effects on the Structure of Local Associations: A Social Network Analysis'.

[13] Revealed in remarks on International Women's Day 2016 at the BBC in a panel on diversity for women.

technology and complexity. Yes, you could be working from the top of a mountain with a beautiful view but it would be marred unless you had the right coping mechanisms to get your job done. Coping mechanisms mean that you have good management and communications, and are able to use commonsense in what work you do, for whom, and in how you are expected to deliver it. But the fact that you need these at all underscores their very absence.

Commonsense is often spectacularly absent in office life, so much so that one of the biggest TV hits of the past fifteen years has been a spoof 'mockumentary' about an incoherent, self-centred, ludicrous manager in a series called 'The Office'. The show has been bought by over eighty different countries, so universally resonant are its themes of the tragi-comic fraught pointlessness of much of modern office life.[14] Even if you do not have an idiot manager or do not have to work in an office but are connected to it by smartphone or laptop, the number of times you send out email blizzards with 'reply all', only to find that the content of those emails, the action points, have become lost somewhere along the way, is well recognised and all part of the cynical malaise which rightly infects our approach to what is supposed to be productivity's finest hours – forty of them a week. I can almost see you nodding. Inside offices themselves, you know that moment when you email someone, only to walk past their desk about five minutes later. The office has become a stilted silo where we forget that the human worker can use their senses rather than outsource their actions to machines and yet homeworking or remote working has its perils and problems, the most obvious being disconnection from other humans.

So clever businesses are mixing and matching techniques to address what really does work – and what really does not. They are not turning their existing

---

[14] 'The Office', was first created and shown in Britain by Ricky Gervais and Stephen Merchant in 2001, its themes expanded on in novels such as 'Then We Came to the End' by Joshua Ferris, in 2008.

offices into funky furniture palaces great for the interior design office workers, or holding endless team meetings, or indeed letting everyone work virtually and losing what little sense of community there is. They are creating and designing their workspaces to reflect people's real behaviour, the real way people move, congregate and communicate. And they are not just looking at the bottom line or the top line, but the space in the middle: the space to connect what is happening with what needs to happen, and how it can best be made to happen.

Hydroponic hives

'Worker bees'. We know what that means. That we work en masse, unremarkable and unrewarded. We associate work with that other expression, 'a hive of activity'. Actual bees are in many ways the poster species for Social Health. Why? Because they organise themselves socially and industrially in one of the most efficient manners to be found on earth: the construction of hives, the organisation of pollination and the storage of honey. Bees are deeply hierarchal in one sense – everything revolves around the Queen – and yet they have to collaborate and choreograph or else they do not survive. And if they do not, neither do we. The bee is a central figure in the insect kingdom, connecting the plants with the rest of us. Small wonder that Charles Darwin devoted such significant amounts of his time and energy to studying them. The many metaphors that integrate the idea of bee behaviour and humans – *hive mind, swarm intelligence, groupthink* – all contain a dystopian underbelly, and yet the central appealing aspect for me is that bees get things done. Bees organise on a collective basis; they create, store and manage what they do incredibly well. Whether they are also kind to each other is not something my research covered, but I shall stick to the image that the very nature of bees, being of and from nature, is something from which we can learn in our human world of work.

Some are already learning. As freelance workers start to match the numbers of statutory workers, as the Age of Overload disconnects us from the need to work only in fixed settings, new office systems are being developed. These are consciously designed like ecosystems. Take Second Home in London and Lisbon.[15] A hydroponic working space that boasts 'thousands of plants and trees, and natural light to provide the perfect environment to grow your business', Second Home is built on a new set of principles about productivity and collective endeavour – that people can work away in isolated unnatural conditions or they can buzz around each other and draw energy and creativity from their working environment. Or The Office Group, set up by a London-based entrepreneur, Olly Olsen.[16] He said in an interview 'workspaces must be designed for purpose as well as aesthetic'. The expansion of freelance office spaces might be a marker of the move towards Social Health at work: people want to be connected, they want to be *productive* but they want a good environment. If we enjoy nice gyms, nice juicers, of course we now want nice offices. No-more skyscrapers. WeWork has hot desks in the United States, Israel, Canada, South Korea, China, France, Australia, UK, Hong Kong, Germany, Netherlands and Mexico. They offer not just space but events in which to 'learn, network and get inspired'.[17] Having hydroponic plants in an office space designed for collaborative, creative co-working is not to be confused with just making the work environment 'groovy': if it aids productivity, then it is, by definition, working.

Calling virtual office space 'home' is smart, too. The companies that nurture family-type settings and small, scaled-down environments and teams do better. Google moved over US$65 billion dollars of stock in a single day in 2015[18] and employs a relatively small workforce of 50,000 people around the

---

15 www.secondhome.io.
16 www.theofficegroup.co.uk.
17 www.wework.com.
18 Matt Krantz, 'Google's 16% Leap Lifts Nasdaq to New High', on www.usatoday.com.

world. It is consistently ranked as the number one desirable place to work in the world, not just because it is glamorous and on-trend but because its layout mimics a kind of home campus.[19] This trend was started by the billionaire media tech philanthropist Michael Bloomberg, who pioneered in-house canteens, gyms and social activities that were designed to both connect workers but also, cleverly, to give them neither the motive nor any real need to leave the building during the working day.

A very different kind of business model, but one worth comparing to the tech giants, is the UK's National Health Service. Beset by problems in adapting to modern financial and managerial pressures, it is the fifth biggest employer in the world. It suffers levels of morale that are so low that, in 2015, junior doctors went on strike over pay. The NHS cannot make its employees feel loved, even though most of them are incredibly loyal. The complexity of structure reflects its scale. Its sheer size prevents any meaningful change or for those changes to be registered or noticed when they do happen. The scale of the problem is linked to the size of the beast. Any government department knows this. Being fully connected means achieving some kind of intimacy. So we need to redesign how we live, who we live and work amongst, to achieve a state in which trust, connection, communication, process, performance, all knit together smoothly and in a way which feels right.

The future of smart, connected work is going to lie in disconnecting 'the office' from a culture of isolation and atrophy. I had a coffee not so long ago with a corporate man who has worked for his firm, a global consultancy, almost all of his working life. He is keenly interested in innovation, and the buzzword for him is 'disruption', the holy grail of commerce and industry. Disruption is what killed Blackberry in a matter of months. It is what has ushered in co-working spaces for the new 'solopreneur', so that ordinary skyscraper office

---

[19] Fortune 100 'Best Companies to Work For' annual rankings, www.fortune.com

space is plummeting in value, while anything with a hydroponic plant in it cannot rent out its desk spaces fast enough.

Disruption on purpose

Disruption is incredibly hard for the old, lumbering dinosaurs of the office jungle. Disruption is better done by the smaller, more agile bees. This man noted that 'people only stay for two years and despite everything we give them, they say it is not enough. They want to leave.' I am not surprised. Part of the new agile, mobile world, the world in which movement is built in to everything, the movement of information and knowledge but also of *knowledge workers*, is the very idea to which corporations and large organisations cling, even as it sinks from view: *retention*. People do not want to be retained in one place or in one job. They can see they will not build networks, satisfy their curiosity or gain satisfaction from one company, one community or one system any longer. This is the biggest curiosity for the corporation. Social Health is all about keeping it real. It often actually is all about something else too: letting go.

Once upon a time, 'globalisation' was hailed as a land of freedom and opportunity. Now it has much more of a mixed report card. The world of working life, as I argued in Chapter 1, is hostile, tense and full of threats. Even for the 'lucky' ones. For a start, the working world of the corporation is struggling to find its way. The word used to describe this hunt for validity for reputation, on top of whatever else corporations may do (which is to produce goods and services that people then buy) is currently 'purpose'. I say 'currently' because over the last ten years alone it has also included 'reputation' and 'corporate social responsibility'. Reputation management has become a massive spend, almost approaching parity with the biggest marketing budget of all: advertising.

Before the last great economic wobble of 2008, the buzzword for corporates was CSR or Corporate Social Responsibility. This was the idea that corporations did not just make giant profits, but gave back to the community to which they belonged. Post-2008, the atmosphere changed and CSR began to be seen as a giant figleaf for giant profits. Millennials began to want more than money and perks from the companies they joined. Consumers wanted more than just cheap products. Activists began to besmirch corporations being donors to causes if they felt their hands were dirty from their profits (oil companies, such as Shell and BP, became targets of corporate activism, even when they gave to globally acknowledged good causes such as art, all as a result of their corporate failings elsewhere). Purpose, the new buzzword, is proving as elusive as productivity.

Productivity levels that are globally low have a well-known link to wellbeing: the World Bank, the International Labour Organization, the OECD and the World Economic Forum have all addressed wellbeing. But none of them have yet addressed Social Health. They look at isolated aspects of social capital or stress, rather than something fundamental, interconnected and joined up, and which clearly affects output. Workers are just not happy, and not clear about what they are supposed to be doing or how they are supposed to be doing it. The communications revolution of the late 1990s should have brought some kind of alignment, some kind of clarity: everyone was connected to every great idea, practice and process on the planet. Something has gone badly wrong. A key reason for this is not purpose at all. It is connection and its polar opposite – *disconnection*. Companies and organisations need to shift their focus to connecting *inwards* as well as *outwards*, and to its workers as well as its consumers. This is something bigger than what is currently called 'internal communications' and it is bigger too than 'L&D' or 'learning and development'. This ends up being a kind of outsourcing. It is a disconnection of purpose, and disconnection of feeling between the top and the bottom, a disaffection which causes much of the wear and tear, the stress, fractures and breakage in morale, and in the physical and mental health of employees. A Social Health strategy would be both prevention and quite possibly a cure.

People who work need to know that they can find what they need. That they can connect to the right information and the right people at the right time. They need to know when they can switch off as well as on. They need to feel connected to what they do, and where and how they do it. They need to feel value and worth. These are intrinsic drivers of output and productivity. Millennials now vote with their feet at work. In Deloitte's global survey of over 4,000 people, spanning China, Columbia, Turkey, Canada, Italy, the US and the UK, twenty per cent expect to stay until 2020 in one job due to financial performance, whilst the figure triples to sixty-one per cent where there is 'value alignment'.[20] In other words, Social Health is there in the data already, waiting to be seen and understood.

The reasons why worker websites such as Glassdoor and ebosswatch have ballooned is for exactly the same reasons that social media uses the viral spread of epidemics: under the right conditions, word catches on. Word of bad businesses, bad bosses and badly run organisations can spread swiftly on social media, just as consumer complaints do. The washing machine manufacturer Maytag experienced the full wrath of Heather Armstrong, a new mother, who blogged about her broken machine. This resulted in her Twitter following rising to more than a million and Maytag having to replace her machine while its sales slumped.[21] What was Maytag thinking? What was happening in the management of the business that meant they were so slow to react? The problem appeared to be reputational: the PR people were ultimately the ones who will have told senior management how critical this moment was. The problem, of course, was not anything to do with public relations. It was behaviour. A customer with a newborn baby could not get her washing done

---

[20] *The 2016 Doloitte Millennial Survey*: winning over the next generation of leader.
[21] See www.theweek.com/*dooce-vs-maytag*.

because of a faulty new machine. The company tried (no pun intended) to wash its hands of its responsibility because, for a brief moment, and forgetting social media's powerful new surging force (this was back in 2009), it imagined that it could. But had Maytag wanted to be joined up, to match products with customer experience while also solving the problem, it could have avoided the crisis in the first place.

The management guru Tom Peters has aways had a refreshinghly practical approach to management, which is just the organisational behaviour needed to get things done – or not. In the early 1990s, when we already had computers in every office and enjoyed 24/7 broadcasting, when email and the internet were still restricted, he saw, like many management thinkers, the future. He began to write about curiosity and its value. The value and worth of wanting to know what you do not know, what you might have missed. The business world and the organisational world cling to notions of certainty, even though that is like trying to hold on to moving tree trunks in a fast-flowing river: you cannot stay in the same place. We are back to motion, movement and transit; the workplace that embraces those things does better than the one which does not. For the populist marketing writer Seth Godin, 'curious has nothing to do with income, nothing to do with education ... it has to do with a desire to push whatever envelope is interesting'.[22]

This is why Social Health is not just its core components – *knowledge*, *networks* and *time*, all of which need to be harnessed well – but coping, corrective mechanisms: *management, communication* and (common) *sixth sense*. They all go together, just like in health and fitness, except there it is blood pressure *and* weight *and* BMI, or diet *and* exercise *and* rest/relaxation. Social Health in the workplace is about movement and choreography. If the moving parts are too stuck or too sluggish, or if they are too siloed, it can be disastrous.

---

[22] Blog by Seth Godin, '*The Secret to Creativity Is Curiosity*', 7 January 2010, www.sethgodin.typepad.com.

The World Health Organization itself was set up to connect and choreograph a global view of health and fitness and, to be fair, it has largely contributed to improvement rather than decline. But its key failing is one of scale, of size, of mobility and of agility. Of achieving balance. It has become bloated and, well, corporate. It risks over-reacting, as it was accused of doing with SARS, and of under-reacting, as it did with the Zika virus. Above all else with Ebola, it did not behave in a balanced, reactive and agile way at all. The central nervous system in Geneva had certain disconnects from the operations out in the field in Africa. They had to wait for certain approvals before acting on what the smaller and more nimble Médecins Sans Frontières wanted to do. Recently the WHO has had to contend with critical think tank reports, with titles such as 'What's the World Health Organization For?', and in 2016, a Reuters' article entitled 'The World Health Organization's Critical Challenge: Healing Itself', which noted the 'flaws in the structure evident in the Ebola crisis'.[23]

The network structure of most organisations is centralised and often what can be called hub and spoke – a nerve or control centre, often referred to in business as the Corporate Centre, and then other divisions that radiate outwards. Management is typically grouped by country, product or region, all of which operate on the same basis. Such structures of big organisations are themselves a hindrance to progress. It may be uncomfortable, and even distasteful, but the successful large-scale organisations that have leadership at the centre and rely on a highly devolved structure, at which informal, self-determined lattice structures replace tightly controlled, top-down ones, can more often be found in criminal and terrorist networks than in legal, legitimate workplaces.

Compare and contrast the ineffectiveness and inefficiency of the six different police forces in Brussels with the agility and devolved, mobile

---

[23] Kate Kelland, 'Doctoring WHO. The World Health Organization's Critical Challenge: Healing Itself', www.reuters.com.

cell structure of the 2015 Paris Bataclan killers? It does not bear thinking about.

We need to go back to some basics, to re-read the great management thinkers such as Peter Drucker and Tom Peters, or contemporary organisational behaviour experts such as Herminia Ibarra and Lynda Gratton, to understand that it is people-centred, versatile, commonsense-aware and highly networked configurations that make people operate well. The answers do not lie in the word 'Leadership'. They lie in the actions, mainly, of people called managers. What motivates the business world? Growth and profit? Tick. What motivates people? Something else. Value and worth. The absences of these cause a simple vital disconnect at the heart of the malaise that we are seeing again and again. The answer lies partly in something as simple as keeping it real, maintaining perspective on common sense, not system sense. Certainly, successful organisations need a highly attuned blend of management, communication and sense-based coping mechanisms, as I call them, drawing on keeping healthy flows of information and knowledge, networks and networking, and allowing time and pace over which things happen. All too often, however, this process stalls. All too often, this system gets stuck. The culprit is often the victim: the Marzipan Manager.

Marzipan Managers

There they are, the managers, stuck below the leadership icing, stuck behind a wall of email, a mountain of paper, jammed somewhere in the middle as if between floors in a skyscraper. No-one is helping them navigate, curating what and who they need to know, devising systems that focus them on the most productive things they could be: engaged and interested. In other words, stimulated.

This group might begin to feel not just stuck but cheated. They have worked hard to get their first and maybe second degrees. They have certainly been questioned in detail in umpteen interviews before they even landed their job. So now, and sooner rather than later, they face a peculiar isolation. They know a lot about their company but not in relation to anyone or anywhere else. The bigger the company or the larger the network, the more technically connected we are, and the higher the risk of being personally more alone. To be even more brutal, their worth does not increase in value as they rise through the skyscraper ranks. It risks doing the opposite: unless they constantly upgrade their skills, managers become like shiny new cars whose value drops the minute they leave the forecourt of the garage.

As if the basic disconnect which seems inbuilt into the system of big business and corporate life is not bad enough, the Age of Overload has hindered, not helped it. Sherry Turkle, the American academic, put it right at the beginning of her book, *Alone Together*: 'Our networked life allows us to hide from each other, even as we are tethered to each other. We'd rather text than talk'. So the Marzipan Manager is a creature of the times. They are encouraged to stay in their offices and indeed, to some extent, have begun to feel safer there. Despite the job title and leadership training, their confidence often seeps away.

Networking could and should be a major liberation for the Marzipan Manager. Networking allows you to create diverse groups of connections and diverse insights and thoughts. But the Marzipan Manager suffers, more often, from acute shyness. They hate networking, using the pressures of work as an excuse. In reality they often feel they have nothing to contribute or say, or that they will be asked to justify the time. So they stay indoors and stay stuck. I am doing a disservice to those who are able to manage both 'presenteeism' and being out and about, and I appreciate that there is some investment in a kind of networking already. The problem is that it is generally the wrong kind.

Firstly, there is the siloed conference, in which everyone is likely to be like everyone else, and where the hidden agenda is business development. (I would go so far as to say please avoid any kind of event with 'networking drinks' tagged at the end: it shows that very little care or thought has gone into understanding even the basics of social network theory and how and why networked behaviour needs to happen at all.) Perhaps this is why MIT *Sloan Management Review*, one of the founts of management thinking noted that:

> *Many companies send their employees off to make connections with a slap on the back and nothing else, and then managers wonder why employees often fall into familiar traps, such as relying on a narrow spectrum of people who are at their same level, from the same department or country, or whom they happen to like. High-performing employees, by contrast, routinely avoid such traps. Instead of allowing their networks to lean in one direction, high performers intentionally build connections with the goal of boosting their performance.[24]*

The second type of corporate networking, which is as dubious as the catch-all 'networking reception', are those events held under the rubric of 'Leadership'. This has become a byword for everything hierarchical, structural and aspirational in the corporate world, but often bears scant relation to the new lateral, connected approach now required. So managers are sent on courses. Or team-building exercises, kayaking down some rapids for old-style bonding. While this can be great, it is not nearly as productive as showing them how to reconnect to ideas and make links between their personal interests and their corporate ones. The Marzipan Manager, just like the rest of us, has a blended self: they are both a professional and a personal person. The more work can marry up who they really are, and what they think and feel, the better.

Deny the Marzipan Manager the oxygen of outside connections and the power of ideas and they do what anyone does in a silo or a bunker: they react as if they are threatened. They do not so much burnout as tuneout. I have

---

[24] Sloan Management Review. *'Building a well-Networked organisation'* Margaret Schweer, Dimitris Assimakopoulos, Rob Cross and Robert J. Thomas, 21 December 2011.

often stared through the plate-glass windows of the world of corporate life, slack-jawed in amazement at the ever-complex ways in which departments charged with the development of people put their 'people' through their paces just to give them jobs and help them to 'retention'. Variously called 'Personnel', and then updated to 'Human Resources' (or what one long-suffering corporate friend tartly refers to as 'human remains'), these departments are often run by some of the most interesting people, who are forced by corporate culture and corporate herd instinct to inflict the least interesting and productive working practices on their 'people'. By far the worst example of this has to be the Appraisal.

My idea of hell on earth is the so-called '360-degree appraisal': large corporations invited – and some still do – co-workers to evaluate and grade each other's performance, in much the same way that quality controllers assess items for display in supermarkets: less about how good the product is, and more how they conform in how they look. It is probably why I have avoided corporate life myself for anything other than the shortest of periods, and why I feel that I can see its failings without any vested interest – I am not the one climbing the 'greasy pole'. The best news I have read in a long time was that major corporations are beginning to drop these unproductive, socially poisonous activities. The management and office life writer Lucy Kellaway of the *Financial Times* nailed it perfectly: 'Wasting £200 million a year on a system that rewards the wrong people, demotivates almost everyone, and spreads boredom and cynicism all round'.[25]

When we began to take people in corporations out of their traditional comfort zone to the Names Not Numbers conferences that I described in 'Social Souls', it was often like overcoming a kind of intellectual starvation. It turned out that many people with big grand 'manager' job titles are actually forced into a sticky-sweet fix of a job, able only to do a handful of repetitive tasks which bear no relation to what actually interests them. When at Names

---

[25] Lucy Kellaway, '*A Blast of Common Sense Frees Staff from Appraisals*', ww.ft.com, 26 July 2015.

Not Numbers we started to place them into an environment where they could talk – and do so freely – about their views, some gasped the air with relief but also guilt. It became common to see them anxiously gobbling up ideas in a discussion as if it were somehow taboo. I found this depressing (even as it opened up a rich business seam). Could this be the key to productivity? Could this be the reason why 'leaders' like entrepreneurs, people with autonomy and independence, rather than shackled managers, could be more productive by pursing *what they actually like to do?* I believe so.

Let us go back to the idea of Social Health and its six core components: the trio of having *knowledge, networks* and *time* under your control and having the right *management, communication* and *sixth sense* to know what is wrong and how to self-correct. How healthy is it, I wonder, to have to spend your time evaluating colleagues or being evaluated by them, and how vauable is it to be unable to really say when something is wrong, because communication is actually quite closed outside of the formal appraisal structure?

I am haunted by the case of the social workers in the London Borough of Haringey, where a tiny child of two, named 'Baby P', was murdered by his stepfather. This child managed to fall off the radar of the social care system, despite being in it and being monitored by people who themselves were victims of a disastrous spiral of social conditions and a work culture almost as ruinous as the conditions experienced by the child. When it was reviewed after his death, a work culture emerged in which there was no Social Health amongst the social workers. There were intense time and workload pressures, so there was no opportunity to look in detail at complex cases, which began to blur into each other. There were no support networks, so they had no intermediary, only managers above them who were concerned with targets and who were themselves jammed in layers underneath others. Social workers changing jobs or changing shifts resulted – a pattern seen in other cases – in knowledge about 'at risk' children such as Baby P literally being stopped in its tracks (an echo of what happened in the Soham Murders mentioned in Chapter 1). There was little or no opportunity to tune into their intuition about the boy, to the extent that at one point this infant – little more than a baby, his blond mop of hair imprinted on my mind for years afterwards from the photo used in the press, innocently and trustingly looking upwards into the eyes of his photographing abuser – had injuries on his face that his mother covered up by smearing them with chocolate. Now I feel I can say with certainty that if I came across an injured child of two with his face covered in chocolate to disguise bruising, then an alarm bell would go off, especially if my job was to look for such signs. I can only imagine that if I could not, I would have disconnected so fully and comprehensively from my job – out of exhaustion, being overwhelmed or as a result of anxiety – that I could no longer do that job. Yet this is what happened. And it happens nearly 100 times a year in the UK alone. Of course, you cannot prevent every murder or every devious abuse. But I notice a pattern here in certain work cultures in public service – when there is no Social Health system, the system breaks down and fails.

Then there is the case of the FBI who, in 2016, admitted that it had briefly monitored an American citizen who was a suspected Islamist extremist – a man called Omar Mateen. This man, who was probably homosexual, with untreated mental health issues presenting as homophobia, went on to commit the largest mass shooting in American history at an LGBT nightclub in Orlando, Florida, in June of that year. Not only did the FBI come out of its surveillance abruptly and fail to do any more of any kind – such as track him in the event of him buying large amounts of armoury and ammunition – but the public agencies in general completely failed to join up something else: this man had been a very violent wife abuser. Had the agencies who had come into contact with him shared knowledge that Mateen had a record of very violent spousal abuse? But they also allocated 'resource' over a short, not long, spread of time: this allowed him to lie fallow and then buy a gun and ammunition with no alerts being triggered whatsoever.

What about business culture? Where are the failings here? Corporate failure is littered with the after-effects of poor Social Health: poor communication, hasty decisions, ineffective management, disconnected emotional literacy, restricted networks which reinforce bad behaviour. Enron, BP's Deep Water Horizon and the collapse of the retailer BHS in the UK are just a few examples. *Every company that performs badly usually suffers from at least three of the six markers of Social Health.* The bigger those companies are, the more liable they are to that failure. The bigger the organisation, the greater the risk that they rely on technological connection, are badly insulated for knowledge, and are badly connected in terms of intelligence and inward flow of knowledge as a result.

Ironically, the Marzipan Manager is superficially hyperconnected. Many spend up to eleven hours a day digitally connected,[26] and research has found that 'the office' can involve up to eighty-eight separate ten-minute episodes of work involving email and other short, interruptive interactions.[27] Small wonder then that business travel is on the up, despite straightened global economic times. It is pretty much the only licensed time for stressed and harried executives to kick back on the flat bed and switch off. Yes, I see some of them urgently tapping away during a ten-hour trans-ocean flight, but mostly they do what I do: put on the headphones and catch up on movies and novels for which they have otherwise been too busy, and to be something else besides: *unreachable.*

The Marzipan Manager is the organisational equivalent of the political stereotype – 'the squeezed middle'. They can often be marginalised within their organisation. They have gone through the educational hoops. They have been interviewed and appraised to within an inch of their lives. But it does not make them more productive, or more engaged, or happier, or more connected to the jobs they are supposed to do. They are unseen, unloved and unconnected.

---

[26] See www.statista.com.
[27] See the chapter entitled 'Working with Constant Connectivity', citing 'frequency and duration of work episodes', in *Pressed for Time: The Acceleration of Life in Digital Capitalism* by Judy Wajcman, Anthony Giddens Professor of Sociology at the LSE and a Fellow of the British Academy.

Some people care about job titles. In fact, most do. Our working identity is like our personal identity. Being called a manager used to mean you got a designated parking space or your own office. You enjoyed a kind of upgrade because you managed others to success. But in order not to be stuck, to be a good, productive manager, you need more than luck, more than skill, more than good leadership skills. You need peripheral vision.

Highly peripheral people

In geometry, an edge is a particular kind of line segment joining two vertices. In a polygon, an edge is a line segment on the boundary, and is often called a side.

WIKIPEDIA DEFINITION OF EDGE (GEOMETRY)

The dangers of over-full connection are clear in health and security situations: imagine if Ebola had reached a major city or a nearby airport. The closeness of some of the fishing villages to an airport in Sierra Leone was one of the major accelerants to the alarm signals during the 2014 outbreak in Guinea, making it so different from the more remote, contained incident in the Democratic Republic of Congo (then Zaire) in 1976. Once people like Louise Kamano (whose story I told in the Preface) were able to walk over a land with no border controls, close to a city (Monrovia), which was close to other countries with major global hub cities, the risks began to escalate. Once a problem incapacitates the hub, the problem quickly becomes, in network terms, 'scale-free'. Or to put it a simpler way: out of control.

Louise came from the periphery. She was not someone already dying, obviously contaminating those around her. The authorities did in fact know of her exposure to the virus, but they were so worried about the political effects of shutting down and quarantining the country that they repressed the advice from Médecins Sans Frontières, the principal local charity, that everyone who came into contact of any kind needed to be quarantined. This small charity was itself not regarded as central – if anything, peripheral – to the major centralised knowledge centre that was the World Health Organization. As such, it was overlooked at a critical moment. The dictionary tells us that peripheral means 'not relating to the main or most important part' or of being 'located on the edge'.[28]

The organisational network analyst Rob Cross has carried out extensive research, clearly showing the value of what he calls 'highly peripheral people'.[29] They may be in the margins or they may be marginalised – in corporate terms, think of people with less important job titles who appear at first glance to be peripheral to power or how things get done. On closer inspection, however, it is often exactly these people who have a key role to play. This can alter health for ill – literally, in the case of a contagious disease, it can be the peripheral player like Louise Kamano or, in the case of sexually transmitted diseases, it is often an outrider who comes into contact with a group.[30] It can also contribute the opposite way – to Social Health. Organisations that bring together diverse groups in order to share knowledge often find that peripheral figures may hold highly valuable information that unlocks many answers.

I owe my career to being a peripheral outsider. I was accidentally at the edge, rather than the centre, mainly because I floundered at school and did not complete a degree. While my social network went off on gap years and to university, I stayed at home and got a job. It was nothing fancy: a receptionist

---

[28] Meriam Webster definition of 'peripheral'.

[29] Rob Cross et al., *'Knowing What We Know: Supporting Knowledge Creation and Sharing in Social Networks'*.

[30] The American sociologist Charles Kadushin, a pioneer of Social Network Analysis, writes up the case study explaining the importance of both predictable and random patterns in terms of infection. He analyses the way HIV-AIDS often spread through the occurrence of 'concurrence' or where 'instability' means that more than one sexual partnership takes place within a community that has not yet realised its epidemiological exposure or judged it accurately. See Charles Kadushin, *Understanding Social Networks: Theories, Concepts and Findings*.

in a small medical publishing house, where I had to open post, file papers, answer the phone, and be bossed around by a rather impressive French woman named Sylvie, who both inspired and terrified me. I would stand for hours photocopying 800-page manuscripts on sports injuries, while keeping my eyes and ears open. I noticed that the post for the publicity manager was far more interesting to me than that of the production co-ordinator. I noticed something else in those early publishing days, when the only expectation anyone had of me was to be back from my lunch break on time and not make spelling errors in correspondence. I noticed that in every company, no matter how atomised or how small, there is a kind of family, waiting to be united. I knew this when I would walk in and out of the editors' rooms, probably the most hallowed place, and feel like the youngest child going in to their big siblings' space, waiting to be shooed out. I found out because one such big sibling, an editor called Sally, went on a skiing holiday and did not come back, killed in a freak accident. I remember the dull shock, the silence, the grief. She had probably not said more than a few words to me – I remember her flat shoes with their interesting bows more than I do her voice – but in the moment of her death the company became just another family.

Carl Sandburg's poem Skyscraper so beautifully captures the way that work and the place of work dominated the landscape for the modern connected age – literally and metaphorically it is never in the end far from the personality and soul of each person associated with it. How the very building itself is embedded with our social DNA inside its walls. Sandburg noticed how everyone connected to the building is not just a name on their door plate but united by 'hundreds of names and each name standing for a face written across with a dead child, a passionate lover, a driving ambition for a million dollar business or a lobster's ease of life'.[31] What he meant was that back then our

---

[31] Carl Sandburg, 'Skyscraper'. With thanks to the Barbara Hogenson Agency. For further information on Carl Sandburg's poetry, see www.nps.gov.

blended selves and souls were locked away in a single uniform of 'work' and that we traipsed in and out of the office as if it were a belching factory itself until they 'pour back out to the streets, prairies and valleys'.

So work connects, even when we feel disconnected. We cannot help it. Like the social souls we are, worker bees have a common aim: to return to the group, to the hive, with honey. It is where we belong. With others.

6

Networks and networkers

The ghetto and the garden

Picture the scene. It is 1770. Sailing in The Endeavour, *a young British cartographer and mathematician, Captain James Cook, lands at Botany Bay, Australia. This is an important leg of his three-year 'voyage of discovery'. He and his crew have become the first Europeans to reach 'that vast unknown tract, above latitude 40'.[1] That same year and in fact that same month, April, a long poem written by the struggling poet Thomas Chatterton is published. 'Kew Gardens' clearly puts the royal botanical gardens at the centre of links to the power and patronage of the times. Flora and fauna is prime bounty from the new endeavours to map and discover the treasures of the world, the unknown tracts. In fact, one of the people on board* The Endeavour *with Captain Cook is no less a figure than Joseph Banks, President of the Royal Society. It is he who later turns Kew into the international centre for botany and horticulture when he returns from this journey, using, it is noted, the fact that he was 'blessed with good connections'.[2]*

---

[1] London Gazetteer notes on James Cook voyage, 18 August 1768. See www.thegazette.co.uk.
[2] See *Joseph Banks, The Plant Collector who made the Exotic Everyday in British Gardens* www.kew.org, Kew Magazine, 2009.

In August 1770, four months after his paean to Kew was published, Thomas Chatterton committed suicide. Although he became an inspiration to the next generation of Romantic poets, he did not have any patronage or connections, certainly not enough to secure him passage on the social networks of the day. He died penniless and starving. In his Last Will and Testament he declared himself to be 'A Boy of Learning and a Bard of Tropes', leaving the care of his mother and sister 'to the protection of my friends if I have any'.[3] He was just seventeen years old.

There is a third connection in 1770 (a year in which the Spinning Jenny marked another milestone in the industrial revolution) but it concerns a different kind of industry, a different kind of creative energy, a different kind of force of nature. A thousand miles away from Australia's Botany Bay, and from Kew Gardens or Thomas Chatterton's pauper's grave, in Frankfurt, Germany, a young man of twenty-six began an endeavour of his own.

This young man's origins were every bit as tough as Thomas Chatterton's – orphaned at twelve, penniless and living in wretched cramped poverty of his own. But through luck, fate and talent he built his life on networks and never looked back. Young Mayer Amschel Rothschild, who had been sent to rabbinical school but had to leave when his parents died, had been sent out of the Frankfurt Ghetto of Judengasse to Hanover to learn about business. By August 1770 he was working his way up as a court trader, dealing in coins and antiques. Although there were no great riches yet, he had direct entry to the wealth and patronage on which success depended.[4] More besides: location. Frankfurt was a hub network city linking several trade routes. Mayer Amschel may well have been attracted to the possibilities of breaking out of a very narrow network. He lived in the highly regulated, closed network of the Judengasse, a ghetto in which people lived literally cheek by jowl and where permissions were needed to enter and exit. He married that year and had the first of nineteen children, ten of whom survived.

---

[3] Thomas Chatterton, 1752–1770, www.poetryfoundation.org
[4] Niall Ferguson, *The House of Rothschild: Money's Prophets, 1798–1848.*

The story of his five sons is what allowed Mayer Amschel to found and build one of the biggest business successes of the last two centuries and to see him undertake endeavours that netted personal, political and cultural fortunes and influence which remain to this day.

In banking, finance, property, art and academia the Rothschild name is known around the world for wealth, excellence, and networks. Mayer Amschel's sons – Amschel, Salomon, Nathan, Kalman and Jakob – fanned out across five continents and as a result he called them his 'five arrows'. Today the family crest of the Rothschilds features this potent symbol, and 'five arrows' remains the name of the investment banking arm of the family firm.

Public gardens such as Kew, and indeed the magnificent Rothschild gardens seen at Waddesdon Manor in Buckinghamshire, are expressions of the power of connection by the most powerful force of all: nature. Plants themselves are a wonderful metaphor for networks: the proliferation of roots, branches, buds and leaves, the interdependence of pollination, cross-fertilisation, the random turns a living organism takes as it grows – these are all features of the behaviour of networks in science itself. The Rothschilds' Villa Ephrussi on the French Riviera, officially classified as one of France's Great Gardens, is designed like a ship – perhaps inspired by Captain Cook's very own. The house itself is framed by the endless beauty of the sea and the lands – in this case, the gardens – that lie around it. Sea. Land. People. Nature. Networks. They are all connected.

Billions of shy people

If you dislike networking, you are not alone. What we do not fully understand, we often fear. And what we fear, we dislike. Why do people dislike networking? Because they are shy. A common myth about networking – and I mean the active verb here, net*working*, rather than the composition and behaviour which happens on net*works* – is that it is for extroverts. Noisy, loud, confident people.

Introverts, people assume, hate it. How many people are introvert rather than extrovert? Quite a lot. One of the biggest bestselling books in the recent 'smart thinking' genre was Susan Cain's *Quiet*, which popularised the idea that networking is superficial and loud. 'Many have a horror of small talk, but enjoy deep discussions', she wrote.[5] I know that feeling. Yet if you knew me and had to label me, you would be more likely to use the word 'extrovert' than almost anything.

So discussing networking (I will get to networks shortly) is already a disconnect. It is misunderstood and misappropriated. In the popularised and polarised mindset of networking, there are two kinds of networkers: thoughtful good ones (introverts) and the others who are by implication not so good. It is certainly true that to walk into a room full of strangers can feel uncomfortable – often the most common way to begin your introduction to networking, as events are usually cheerfully signposted 'networking reception'. I should know. I have walked into a thousand rooms full of strangers and each time my stomach clenches, each time I dread it and each time wish I was, like a Susan Cain introvert stereotype, 'home in pyjamas'.

I think the enemy of networking, of shyness, is the enormity of distance you feel initially. Of course the minute you do manage to make eye contact with one person, to find your voice, to say something – small talk or big talk, it does not actually matter what comes out of your mouth initially – the distance melts away. Once I realised that the model of networking commonly sold to people was entirely wrong – namely to meet *as many people as possible in one go* – and that in fact the reverse was true, I found my own shyness could be kept to manageable levels. I call this 'coming in to land' when I teach corporate students what networking means – and what it does not. That moment when you walk into a room to connect with strangers is not so different from descending in an aeroplane. Sometimes the landing is lengthy, circling above the runway and

---

[5] Susan Cain, *Quiet: Growing up as an Introvert in a World That Can't Stop Talking*.

landing bumpily through clouds. At other times it is smooth, fast and easy. These are the times I like: walking in to a reception or a conference and being quickly at ease; finding someone I know; or being greeted well and efficiently at the front desk.

In other words, huge numbers can diminish us and make us feel small. That is why my Names Not Numbers conference limits its size, and why I avoid large gatherings in favour of small, curated ones. We should guard against large, loud, one-size-fits-all events. Yet everywhere you look, size and scale is presented as better than its opposite: smallness. Around 6,000 tweets are posted every second,[6] and services scream at you with offers to generate false followers electronically, if you so desire. In London, a twentysomething young man calling himself 'KSI Olajidebt' reached ten million subscribers on YouTube in just five years by simply vlogging from his front room,[7] and his success, his scale, is celebrated. Size equates to celebrity. Eric Schmidt, founder of Google, proudly announced that in the near-future, 'at your fingertips will be an entire world's worth of digital content.'[8] Now global national debt is not measured in millions or even billions, but something else, something bigger: trillions. What does it do to a collective psyche when the numbers just keep getting bigger? I think it encourages us to do the only thing we can safely do without blowing a fuse at the sheer scale: we disconnect from it. We no longer notice the numbers – even when perhaps we should.

Of course there are people who are more shy or quieter than others. But the disconnect with the idea of networking is partly that it is all about being social, or being superficially social. The Rothschild business was built on a very carefully built-up mix of social society and straightforward connections,

---

[6] Data from Internet Live Stats, www.internetlivestats.com

[7] Josh Warwick and Philip Allen, 'Meet the 21-Year Old YouTuber Who Made Millions Playing Video Games', *The Telegraph*, 16 October 2014, www.telegraph.co.uk

[8] Eric Schmidt and Jared Cohen, *The New Digital Age: Reshaping the Future of People, Nations and Business.*

but also something else: networks themselves. Specifically, the intelligence that travels on networks. In fact, the main currency used by the Rothschilds in the nineteenth century was not dollars or sterling, but *knowledge*. The historian Niall Ferguson's biography of the family notes that the investment in fast communication networks to better transport intelligence meant that carrier pigeons were a major source of intelligence gathering: 'It was not until after the mid-1930s that the development of the railway, the telegraph and the steamship opened a new era in communications – one in which it would be a good deal harder for the Rothschilds to steal a march on their competitors.'[9]

The history of modern connection was the product of staggering quantities of imagination, ambition and scale – and networks. The first successful transatlantic cables laid in the 1850s were 2,000 fathoms down, stretching 1,600 miles from the old to the new world. Over 2,500 miles of Atlantic cable were ordered, and for each mile of cable over 130 miles of wire were needed.[10] Today the narrative of modern life, dominated by tech giants from Silicon Valley who think that scale and size is the answer to pretty much everything, is that technology is transforming at as great or greater a rate and impact than in the late nineteenth century. Certainly it is true that there will be fifty billion networked devices by 2020,[11] a number almost impossible to grasp. Also true is that what mobile phones bring in terms of transformation to developing nations in the area of health care alone will be both vast and welcome. All the next steps in what Google calls 'our future selves' were laid in underwater cables and overland lines of connection over 150 years ago: electricity, railroads, ultimate networks. Then, in the cradle of the industrial revolution, cables and

---

[9] Niall Ferguson, *The House of Rothschild: Money's Prophets, 1798–1848*.
[10] http://www.cntr.salford.ac.uk
[11] World Economic Forum, '*Hyperconnected World*', www.weforum.org

cars were the connectors, the roads and railways were the network. Today, human beings, holding their mobile device, connecting via the internet, conference call, craning forward to hologram and AI futures, are transporting themselves. The individual, connected en masse to everyone and everything is not just on networks. By becoming networks in our own right, we are transporting ourselves from the isolation, the collective shyness of limitation, and into a limitless dimension. But this brings discontents. It is intimacy, trust, small-scale and real-time connections, face-to-face, which forge lasting human networks, more than anything else.

Often the most powerful networks are shy ones – shy of publicity and shy of outsiders. An extraordinary amount of global business 'families' are just that – dynasties whose 'private offices' manage vast corporate family interests. There are roughly 1,000 companies in 35 countries around the world with a market capitalisation of at least US$1 billion which are family-owned, including Reliance in India, Walmart in America, Richemont in Switzerland, Foxconn in Taiwan, Softbank in Japan, Volkswagen in Germany and Samsung in South Korea.[12] The currency that runs like electricity through these family businesses, and through their strong networks, is trust. Trust forges connection; the lack of trust creates the polar opposite.

Trust is part of a set of psychological codes that large and small groups of people all understand and trade in. Sandy Pentland of MIT, writing about what he called 'social physics', remarked that in economics 'the central reason exchange networks are better than markets is trust. Relationships in an exchange network quickly become stable (we go back again and again to the person who gives us the best deal), and with stability comes trust, i.e. the expectation of a continued valuable relationship'.[13] Which brings us to different kinds of networks themselves.

---

[12] Corey Stern, 'The 21 biggest family-owned businesses in the world', www.uk.businessinsider.com
[13] Alex Pentland, *Social Physics: How Good Ideas Spread – Lessons from a New Science.*

The rules of Guanxi

I traced lines between moments and events distant from one another, I established convergences and divergences.

ELENA FERRANTE, *MY BRILLIANT FRIEND*

When we say 'connected', it has become shorthand for something else – 'relationships'. Elena Ferrante's trilogy of novels has become one of the biggest publishing sensations, focusing entirely on the anatomy of an evolving friendship between two girls into womanhood and their families. Connected relationships are, of course, networks. The structures and patterns that occur in nature and technology alike have remarkable similarities. Looking at network science can explain this complex spinning world of relationships more than perhaps any other branch of science or social science. I use the word 'branch' deliberately. A tree is a good way to start when visualising a network. From biology to electrical engineering, from neuroscience to economics, cells in hummingbirds and humans, cellphones and computers – the structural DNA of modern life as we know it is one of a network.

My path into the science and social science of networks was a reverse journey. I practised it for years with unconscious ease, before I even realised that its roots lay in sociology, biology and an Aristotlean flourishing of thought in the 1950s, during the first flush of the World Health Organization's quest to create a global health policy for the world. Just as the WHO got going, and the world began to think about thriving again having survived the horrors of the Second World War, academics began to study in earnest what a global health policy meant in terms of human behaviour. In the 1950s we had Jacob Moreno's sociograms, Maslow's hierarchy of needs, Milgram's studies – not just on Small World Theory but also on Obedience. How humans behave with each other and in what configurations was suddenly fascinating. Anthropology was hip.

One of my favourite books of the period is *Life is with People: The Culture of the Shtetl*, with an introduction by Margaret Mead, the great American cultural anthropologist.[14] Here, although it is implicit rather than stated directly, the concept of network and community takes centre stage: 'Everywhere people cluster to talk, at home, in the market place, on the street. Everyone is interested in "what people say". News is never kept for oneself. Whether the event is personal or general, it must be shared.'[15] There was a flourishing of ideas around not just the Hierarchy of Needs and the theory of Small Worlds, but the very underpinning of human behaviour; Solomon Asch's marvellous studies of coercion in African societies should be required reading for anyone trying to understand how terrorism flourishes inside prison cells, for instance.[16] Network structures are mathematically democratic – it is the *behaviour* on them which affects everything, one way or the other.

The disciplines that dip into network science and theory – stretched as they are across management and organisational behaviour and into pure maths and physics themselves (and something frankly terrifying called *Random Graph Theory*) – were not immediately apparent to me. I had a rather friendly, personal manner and a somewhat nosy attitude to what other people were thinking and feeling, certainly no method or planned approach. Other than the sting of rejection from a job interview propelling me to know as wide a circle as possible, I never connected any academic underpinning to what I was doing. In fact, it was was only when the internet and email began, ushering in the first signs of overload, that I sensed that people were becoming overwhelmed by too much information, with too little time to develop relationships, and that there might be a business opportunity in trying somehow to be a broker between certain kinds of people – in the first instance between people in communications, in which I was still working, and in journalism. These were the days when

---

[14] Mark Zborowski and Elizabeth Herzog, *Life is With People: The Culture of the Shtetl*.
[15] Ibid.
[16] Solomon E. Asch, '*Opinions and Social Pressure*', published in Scientific American, November 1955.

journalists felt beseiged by faxes of press notices, which often bore no relation to what they were interested in. I saw this first hand while working on the 'Forward Planning' desk of a satellite TV magazine show. Despite informing the PR community about what was of interest, they continued to bombard the desk with ill-matched information. I realised this could only lead to a lack of trust between the two communities, and a flood of bad information. This was my early interest in networks; I just did not realise it at the time. I was, however, curious. I began to note the shifts from a top-down hierarchical media to a lateral one in which there was a spread of channels. Later, I witnessed the arrival of 'citizen journalism' of voice and choice, which burst the control of the media and of those pouring information directly into its funnels.

I am a member of the Jewish Diaspora, a people who have been scattered far from their original homelands. I realised that I adopted a sort of instinctive behavioural diaspora, in that I picked up all sorts of ideas and influences from a wide range of settings; I worked in publishing, television, politics and public relations, before settling on networking about a decade into the new age of connection. This was somewhat at odds with my peers who had gone through a more siloed career path: university, a vocational job in teaching or academia, or even the media, which for years had very distinct pathways. If you were a producer back then, you did not move sideways into editing. Now everyone does a bit of everything, as globalisation and consumerism reached a fever pitch that coincided with the 'triple revolution' of internet, mobile and media that I mentioned right at the beginning of this book. Where I had worked my way up, with no grand titles or status, I began to flourish in my work. I had agility, I had mobility and, above all, I had connections.

The Chinese have a word for the connected, the relationship, the act of building and making networks: in Mandarin this is *Guanxi*. While the word and its connotations are not without controversy, it speaks volumes about the way we feel about networks, and conduct ourselves on them. The Chinese are themselves a diaspora people, whose business strategy has been to fan out across the world, identify commercial patterns and opportunities and bring them back to China to build them domestically. *The Economist* noted back in 2011 'that more Chinese people live outside of China than French people live in France', and that while 'diasporas have been part of the world for millennia' their power as social networks is without rival.[17]

Some of the great thinking about networks has coincided with the point when the 'networked society', as sociologist Manuell Castells put it, was bursting out. He wrote in 1996 that 'power does not reside in institutions, nor even the state or large corporations. It is located in the networks that structure society.[18] The rise of the network society did not happen in a vacuum. It happened in the very context and cradle of connectedness. The 1990s saw a flourishing of ideas that coincided exactly with mass mobile connectivity in technology: the internet, email and the mobile phone. Suddenly we wanted to understand networks more profoundly. There was a rich literature of thought published between 1995 and the early 2000s on network communication, great books that highlighted the excitement, energy and promise around this new drawing together of ideas and behaviours in a newly joined-together world. Geoff Mulgan was one such observer; in 1991 he rather presciently wrote that 'informal networks of "who's who, what's what and why's why" are as important as formal structures' and that 'social networks predate even the most rudimentary information technologies. Networks of kinship, of influence and gossip, of espionage or credit, cliques and cronies, are apparent in all known societies.'[19]

Then something surprising happened: publishing around connectedness in a sociological and anthropological context changed. Why? There had never been more journals or opportunity to publish. It was because of social networks.

---

[17] *The Economist* published an interesting blog in November 2011. See '*Diasporas: Mapping Migration*'.
[18] Manuel Castells, *The Rise of the Network Society: The Information Age – Economy, Society and Culture, Volume I.*
[19] Geoff Mulgan, *Communication and Control: Networks and the New Economies of Communication.*

The arrival of social networks – Friendster and LinkedIn in 2002, Myspace in 2003, Facebook in 2004 and YouTube in 2005 – gave rise to something else in the networked society – the rise of social network analysis. Interestingly, what also flourished was literature about disconnection; Robert Putnam's famous *Bowling Alone* was published in 2000, for instance. There are some tremendous but neglected books on networking that are long since out of print – Lipnack and Skyrme, for example.[20] You can track them down on Amazon but they are almost invisible behind the tsunami of other, fresher, hipper titles on how to work a room and how to use networking as a selling tool.

Whilst Guanxi in Mandarin literally translates as 'relationships' or 'connections', the act (and art) of networking has become associated with advantage, and often an unfair advantage in particular. Never mind that that advantage can in fact be meritocratic, as I will explain later in this chapter; Guanxi has also become shorthand in some circles for nothing short of favouritism. You must draw your own conclusions about networks and the act and art of networking, but to help you frame your thinking here are some of the core ideas that come up again and again in the studies, with papers scattered like a diaspora themselves over the world of academic thought on the subject.

Brokers and builders

Network science shows that the structure is remarkably similar, regardless of whether what we are looking at it as a tree, a computer system or a human society. What is different is that the pattern of *action* and *behaviour* between 'actors' can lead to either bottleneck or uncontrolled rampage, but it can also

---

[20] See Jessica Lipnack and Jeffrey Stamps, *Age of the Network: Organising Principles for the 21st Century* and David J. Skyrme, *Knowledge Networking: Creating the Collaborative Enterprise*.

lead to something else: smooth, agile and connected networks that ease the flow of trust and ideas.

Understanding networks lies at the heart of understanding social connectedness. Since I began to look at the theories and studies spanning psychology, neuroscience, organisational behaviour, management and sociology and social network analysis, I have been constantly surprised by how little either the science or the social science of networks is understood or applied in society outside the rather closed network of academia. Behavioural economics and 'nudge' theory, fuelled by some exceptional communicators such as Daniel Kahneman and Richard Thaler,[21] are beginning to open up the field, as is neuroscience. Management thinkers such as Herminia Ibarra[22] and Lynda Gratton[23] join the greats, such as Peter Drucker, Tom Peters and Charles Handy,[24] in making organisational behaviour mainstream. The public wants to understand and connect the dots in this increasingly complex and compellingly closeknit world. In contemporary studies of the internet and society, business and media, we have the likes of Andrew Keen,[25] Timothy Garton Ash,[26] Margaret Heffernan[27] and James Gleick.[28] But we are in the early days of popularising the culture and science of connectedness, despite its centrality to everything we do and everything we are.[29] This book is an attempt to begin to draw some threads

---

[21] Thaler's reference in *Misbehaving: The Making of Behaviour Economics* to his work with Daniel Kahneman.

[22] Herminia Ibarra, *Act Like a Leader, Think Like a Leader*. See also www.herminiaibarra.com.

[23] Lynda Gratton, *The Shift: The Future of Work is Already Here*. See also www.lyndagratton.com.

[24] See www.drucker.institute.com, www.tompeters.com and Charles Handy's latest book, *The Second Curve*.

[25] Andrew Keen, *The Internet is not the Answer*. See also www.ajkeen.com.

[26] Timothy Garton Ash, *Free Speech: Ten Principles for a Connected World*. See also www.timothygartonash.com.

[27] Margaret Heffernan, *Wilful Blindness: Why We Ignore the Obvious at Our Peril*; *A Bigger Prize* and *Beyond Measure: The Big Impact of Small Changes*. See also www.mheffernan.com.

[28] James Gleick, *The Information: A History, a Theory, a Flood*. See also www.around.com.

[29] Richard Thaler's 2016 book *Misbehaviours: The Making of Behavioural Economics* gives great insight into the zeitgeist around the subject and how his collaboration with the distinguished behavioural psychologist Daniel Kahneman lit something of a touchpaper for behavioural economics becoming fashionable.

together, many of which have lain fallow in different parts of the academic universe, while also standing on the shoulders of some of the giants who have shaped my thinking and brought networks further into the open than ever before: Barry Wellman, Charles Kadushin, Duncan J. Watts, Nicholas Christakis and Albert-László Barabási in particular and Yaneer Bar-Yam.[30]

It is, however, the sociologist Ronald S. Burt who has done the most to shape my understanding of networks and what I would call Behavioural Networks.[31] He coined the wildly interesting and influential concept of 'brokerage and closure' to identify how human relationships form patterns that are influenced by the closeness of each 'tie' to one another. In particular, he identified something rather glorious-sounding called 'structural holes'. As he puts it, *'structural holes are the empty spaces in social structure. The value-potential of structural holes is that they separate non-redundant sources of information, sources that are more additive than overlapping.'* Let me translate: if you only know people who already know each other, then the information 'brokered' between them is not that original and may even reinforce 'groupthink'. This homophily, in which everyone agrees with everyone else and passes around stagnating information and views, can be seen very clearly in examples such as sub-prime mortgage traders prior to the economic crash of 2008.

Ronald Burt built – and networks are fundamentally built and grown, or else they wither like broken branches – on an earlier theory of the 1970s called 'weak tie theory' by another American sociologist, Mark Granovetter. His paper, 'The Strength of Weak Ties',[32] proved critical in understanding that the ways in which people transact information and build relationships are as

---

[30] A highly potent mix of sociology, physics, and the study of network dynamics make up the work of the academics Charles Kadushin (www.kadushin.com), Nicholas A. Christakis (www.nicholaschristakis. net), Albert-László Barabási (www.barabasi.com), Duncan. J. Watts (www.microsoft.com), Yaneer Bar-Yam (www.nesci.edu) and Barry Wellman (www.groups.chass.utoronto.ca

[31] See Ronald Burt, *'Structural Holes Versus Network Closure as Social Capital'*, in *Social Capital: Theory and Research*.

[32] Mark S. Granovetter, *'The Strength of Weak Ties'* American Journal of Sociology 1973.

lateral as they are linear. In other words, how did you get your job? Was it through an ad, or was it via word of mouth? How did you meet your partner? Was it through a dating agency or was it in fact because you rather randomly sat next to them at a gathering organised by a friend of a friend?

Someone who has hugely affected my understanding of networks in practice, in action, in the boardroom and across the businesses I teach is Herminia Ibarra, Cora Chaired Professor of Leadership and Learning, and Professor of Organizational Behaviour, at INSEAD. She co-wrote a seminar paper in the *Harvard Business Review* in 2007 entitled 'How Leaders Create and Use Networks', in which she defined networking as 'creating a tissue of personal contacts to provide the support, feedback, and resources needed to get things done.' One of the keys, she wrote, is to have the ability to 'plug the aspiring leader into a set of relationships and information sources.' Reading about this linking – networks are all about linkages and connections, what Ibarra calls 'network out and across' of the idea of who you know and what you know – was another key point for me in recognising the potency for change and progress afforded by having networks and being able to undertake networking. Just because the perception of networking remains somewhat shallow is too bad for some – the ones who maintain that mindset are far more likely to suffer than those who do not.

The idea of having a diverse set of connections with 'weak ties' and 'structural holes' that make your network stronger is not only exciting in a counterintuitive way, but it also matters in terms of productivity. I have said it before and it bears repeating: productivity is a key indicator of Social Health. If you have *knowledge, networks* and *time/pace* operating in sync, well managed, communicated and done so using common sense, you are almost certainly going to see an increase in productivity.

Understanding the social science, and indeed the hard science, of networks is not just an ideal exercise in looking at the beauty of the honeycomb or snowflake hexagon, tempting though that may be. It is to understand how to improve productivity in a rewarding way, which connects directly back into the 'social wellbeing' originally envisaged seventy long years ago by the World Health Organization.

Brokering and building networks of people who transact knowledge well is one of the key ways to success. As the authors of a study of the collaborative economy say,

> *Under bureaucracy, knowledge is treated as a scarce resource and is therefore concentrated, along with the corresponding decision rights, in specialized functional units and at higher levels of the organization. However, in organizations that are competing primarily on their ability to respond and innovate, knowledge from all parts of the organization is crucial to success, and often subordinates know more than their superiors.*[33]

Another key thinker in networks is the management specialist Lynda Gratton, London Business School's Professor of Management Practice. She has looked extensively at the future of work and how only the connected and the networked will be able to get things done. She writes of 'the shift from isolated competitor to innovative connector,' noting that 'one of the great paradoxes of the future of work will be to simultaneously be a unique specialist and master, capable of standing out from the crowd, while at the same time being intimately connected to the crowd.'[34]

This brings us back to Ronald Burt's point about brokerage and closure. It is ironic that whilst network science is described and delineated with lines and edges, with 'ties' of all sorts of length and thickness, network science is in essence all about social circles. This is all a far cry from the silo mentality that has dominated working culture and thinking around networking. Networking is social, as in it involves one human reaching another and communicating. But its origins are mathematical, biological and scientific. The social and the cultural come after the structural. Its impact can be understood, measured and

---

[33] Paul S. Adler and Charles Heckscher, '*Towards Collaborative Community*', University of Southern California, 2005.
[34] Lynda Gratton, *The Shift*. The future of work is already here.

replicated. Patterns can be deployed to stop network 'spread' – as we saw in the quarantine strategy around Ebola – but also to mimic 'good' spread. Some of the best communications strategies such as 'town hall meetings' have evolved to create small network communities or to allow face-to-face connection between bosses, managers, workers and other stakeholders. This is pure brokerage and closure as per Burt; pure strategic networking as per Ibarra.

Networking has been seen as the preserve of the senior players who have control over their time and who can be 'trusted' to spend it productively. With the benefits of networking collaboratively being understood so much more, it can only be a matter of time before these practices of investing in relationships and building social capital gain traction far more widely inside organisations. Networking helps at every level, and should be done at every level. The value of being able to network and collaborate with colleagues is now being directly linked to productivity. The neuroscientist Matthew Lieberman quotes a study showing that 'individual intelligence may only be optimised when it is enhanced through social connections to others in a group.'[35]

Networking capability is one of fifteen key 'pillars' listed in the annual Gender Global Entrepreneurship and Development Index of High Potential Women Entrepreneurs, on the grounds that 'Entrepreneurs who have better networks are more successful, can identify more viable opportunities, and access more and better resources'. Networking, which relies so much on making your own luck, ranks alongside 'willingness and risk' as an entrepreneurial quality.

When two Italian academics, Fabio Sabatini and Francesco Sarracino, surveyed 50,000 Italian households and showed that wellbeing and happiness levels were far higher in those people who had face-to-face connection

---

[35] Lieberman, Matthew D. (2013), *Social: Why Our Brains are Wired to Connect*. Oxford: Oxford University Press.

[36] Sabatini, Fabio and Francesco Sarrancino (2013), 'Will Facebook Save or Destroy Social Capital? An Empirical Investigation into the Effect of Online Interactions on Trust and Networks', *University of Rome*.

rather than purely electronic and online connections, I was not surprised.[36] Their findings echoed one brought to public attention in Malcolm Gladwell's book *Outliers*, which looked at the Italian–American Roseto community of Pennsylvania. This consisted of overweight men who were all smokers, which baffled researchers because the men suffered none of the heart disease and death rates that would have been expected from such a demographic. Nor were there instances of suicide, alcoholism, drug addiction or crime associated with virtually every other town in the region, the state and the country at large. In fact, the Rosetans bucked every health and social behaviour trend going. After exhausting all the possible reasons a very simple one emerged: networks. These men had strong family ties and strong family rituals. They all sat down together for meals consisting, it must be said, of healthy olive oil and other forms of a Mediterranean diet. But this was not the clincher. The main reason was the connective tissue between these people emotionally.

Social connectedness is a form of social capital. The very connectedness of people in these communities, of which Roseto happened to be an early adopter or 'outlier', shows the power of networked societies in a social context. A century earlier, as the very roads and cables of connectedness were being laid down indelibly in society, the sociologist Emile Durkheim noted that suicides were connected to profound isolation, alienation and disconnection.[37] It is networks that can reconnect people who are lost to loneliness and despair, as much as to the thrilling discovery of ideas or the wealth of global networked trade.

Why then, with all this evidence, do people cling to the belief that networks are more bad than good, that Guanxi is not about meritocracy but about the 'Old Boy's Network' instead? The answer lies in a room far from reach of the ordinary mortal. The answer lies in the Global Green Room.

---

[37] Emile Durkheim, founding father of modern sociology, whose book, *Suicide: A Study in Sociology*, was first published in 1897.

The Global Green Room

The Green Room – where artists go to relax before a show, or where the red velvet rope of nepotism and unfair advantage is held in place to block some but is pulled back for others to allow them 'full access'. This Green Room is often associated with specific places, Davos in Switzerland being a well-known one. It may have originated in mud-filled music festivals such as Glastonbury, but the idea behind a Green Room is anything but peace and love. It is the cold hard edge of exclusivity. But the Green Room is often invisible. It is a club, and is a place dominated by social class and unfair advantage; it hinges on a network. There is another name for the the Global Green Room: the Old Boy Network.

Society is still full of aspirational tendencies, from schools to gaming culture to corporate life, all offering models of progressing upwards, level by level. For some, the ultimate tip of the pyramid is the corner office. For others, it is an academic degree. The concept of an 'upgrade', commonly seen in global airline marketing strategy, also reflects this hierarchical, aspirational approach to life; we all want a better seat, we all want the red velvet rope at the nightclub to be unhooked especially for us, to turn left on the plane to Upper Class, the very language saying 'you're higher up the social food chain than those below'. Anthony Trollope, the great Victorian novelist and social chronicler memorably describes one of his characters as belonging to the 'Upper Ten Hundred' in society.[38] We still revere sporting and acting stars who win accolades, trophies and awards. Yet the past thirty years of networked society have shown us that hierarchies are not necessarily as resilient, fair or flexible as more lateral models. If you are stuck in your corner office, you may be cut off from the 'shop floor'. Furthermore, being seen as 'elite' today is not a badge of upgrade status so much as a having a target on your back, making you identified as 'them' and

---

[38] Anthony Trollope, *Can you Forgive Her?*

not 'us'. Although society still allows celebrity and overpaid soccer and sports stars, it has fallen out with that elite known as 'leaders' – in politics, in business and in public life. Which makes this a particularly interesting time to look at elitism and its role in networks.

There is no doubt that having strong networks favours you. In some ways it is a numbers game – Metcalfe's Law, coined by Robert Metcalfe, who founded the ethernet, holds that 'a network's value is increased as the size of the network increases'.[39] In the numbers game, having access to a small network can be a disadvantage. One of the best effects of the ease of connection, in an age of mobile payments and apps, has been to transform certain small isolated markets into bigger ones. The success of M-Pesa in South Africa, for instance, or the micro-lending of Grameen Bank in Bangladesh[40] all enlarged networks to allow access for poor and isolated communities to trade – and in doing so broke down some market elitism, namely that only the 'big players' could join in. This kind of visibly enlarged access to a network is all to the good. There should be more of it, and networked technology largely aids and abets this. The harder kind of access is less visible, more behind the red rope, more in the Green Room. Like the breakage and fracture I described in Chaper 1, how do you heal something if you cannot actually see what the broken bit is?

Elite networks in public life, business and politics are the places where decisions are munched over in peace, private and informality – all the hallmarks of a trust-based network behaviour, which in itself is not the biological preseve of one person over another. You do not have to be cleverer, richer or smarter – but social networks mean that if you are, and you have the right connections, you have more statistical chance of being invited. So allure grows by the very fact of exclusivity, therefore boosting power around the exclusive Green Room. For

---

[39] For an explanation of Metcalfe's Law, www.computerhope.com.
[40] M-Pesa started in Kenya in 2007 with backing from British Vodafone, has transformed mobile-phone-based banking and microfinancing in the developing world. See www.safaricom.co.ke. Grameen Bank, founded by Nobel Laureate Professor Mohammad Yunus, reaches ninety-seven per cent of Bangladeshi women with its 'Bank for the Poor', based not on credit but on trust. See www.grameen.com.

world leaders and financial movers and shakers, increasingly from the NGO sector, the centre of gravity remains the World Economic Forum, whose annual retreat each January in the Swiss mountain resort of Davos is just the apex of a year-long global programme of invitation-only gatherings. But there are others. The even more exclusive Bilderberg conference, with only 150 attendees, none of whom are formally confirmed or announced (which started as a select affair for the political elites of Europe and Northern Europe at the same time as Abraham Maslow was excluding 'connection' from his hierarchy of needs),[41] is accused of the kind of elite stitch-up that the people of Britain revolted against so spectacularly with the 2016 'Brexit' referendum to leave the European Union. The EU was perceived as being an elite, which the ordinary person could not get in to and yet on whom they could project a wide range of discontent.

What happens in the Green Room anyway? When David Cameron was Britain's Prime Minister – before his political plug was pulled by the Brexit vote – he once divulged a private telephone conversation with Her Majesty the Queen about a previous referendum, the 2015 vote on whether Scotland should gain independence from the UK. As he strolled along a UN conference corridor in New York, he was overheard (politicians and public figures need to realise one global truth: a microphone and camera is always on, somewhere) bragging to Michael Bloomberg, the billionaire who had made his money by connecting financial data to special screens before becoming Mayor of New York, that he had made Her Majesty 'purr'[42] when he told her that the United Kingdom would remain, at that point, united. In so doing, David Cameron (who had previously invited me to join his entourage for another summit, the Nordic-Baltic Gathering in Stockholm in 2012) confirmed two interesting

---

[41] Bilderberg started in 1954. Maslow's original paper was in 1943 but was fully expressed in his book *Motivation and Personality*, published in 1954.

[42] David Cameron, during his tenure as Britain's Prime Minister, was picked up bragging on camera to billionaire Michael Bloomberg at the United Nations General Assembly Climate Summit in New York in September 2014 that her Majesty the Queen had 'purred down the line' with pleasure that Scotland had voted to remain part of the United Kingdom in the divisive and narrowly-won Scottish Referendum.

social network theories in one fell swoop. The first, discovered in 1954 by Elihu Katz, a researcher at the Bureau of Applied Social Research at Columbia University, is that if you want to spread an idea, pick someone with influential social ties. Bilderberg started this same year: so someone was quick to put that theory into practice. The second is the truism that trust networks rely on what David Cameron exchanged: confidences. Being able to broker knowledge is exactly the currency that people can build on. Especially knowledge that someone else does not have. It is knowledge as well as networks that are the mark of a well-connected person. Someone who knows people and someone who knows something others need to know.

In the end the Global Green Room is less of a place than a virtual reality. If you have been brought up excluded from places in which to practise skills in confidently exchanging ideas, or in a culture that does not value knowledge brokering or social connectedness, it can be a disadvantage. When I look at the problem of social exclusion and elitism, I take the opposite view of the telescope to many; instead of looking at the denied opportunities to the large group outside, I look at the behaviours of those inside. I ask myself, 'Can these behaviours be copied, or can access be widened?' The answer is yes and no. Yes, in that, as I said before, these are not biologically determined features, like super-long athletic legs or very brainy mathematical minds, which cannot be shaped so much as inherited. Networking acumen, skill and opportunity can be created and practised. The blockage, of course, is knowing who to know and what to know. But it is also having the mindset, or the ambition to even go there.

In the UK I give talks to schoolchildren as part of a small but highly effective charity called Speakers for Schools. This organisation aims to instill a meritocratic ambition in ordinary state schools – that is, the opposite of the public school, elitist system of Eton College, for example, which embodies the negative associations of the old boy network. What has always surprised and depressed me is the absolute lack of vision, ambition, confidence or curiosity shown by many of the children – teenagers – with whom I speak. They may be bright and capable, certainly, but the culture in which they live is often (not always, of course) prohibitively limited in outlook. The very underpinning of education needs to bring an enlarged world view of precisely the elitist networks deployed so successfully by the powerful if this ratio of haves and have nots is ever to change. From which end of the telescope do you view the Green Room – outside or in?

When I started my career I had an undeniable advantage: my surname. It may not have counted for much if I had tried to work in medicine or the mines, but in book publishing, especially to a house that published my own father, it did: Penguin Books. My surname, distinctive enough to be associated instantly with him, must have pulled my ordinary application for the job of Publicity Assistant, advertised in *The Bookseller*, to the top of the pile. The rest was down to me, but that was all I needed. A break. Over the years I have had many scornful rows with people who believe that this kind of advantage is entirely wrong. I would say this: it is entirely natural. What would you rather do, rewire the human race or take practical steps to increase the level of opportunity available for others to take advantage of? I also point out that the idea that unfair advantage is either sought or given only to people of a certain class is not the whole story. When the highly gifted and popular British comedian and scriptwriter Victoria Wood died in 2016, her obituary noted that she got her first big break on a TV talent show because she knew someone running the queue outside the studio when she went for the audition. The person who knew her put her name at the front. That is all it took. That and her talent, timing and serendipity. Network science is very good at explaining how, despite the pattern and predictability of certain behaviours, Metcalfe's Law being one, something else is a constant: unpredictability. The person who moves across the border at the wrong time with Ebola. The person who puts the audition tape into the hands of the person who can spread it most widely because they have the appropriate influence. Much of networks, and the creation of them, is less planned and Machiavellian and far more accidental and organic than people may think.

Jazz ensembles and orchestras

When I worked in publishing, I was able to see an interesting process in close-up. I watched an idea in someone's head become commissioned and produced, through a series of short interconnected executions, and so create a finished product, a tangible something that could be held – a book. Even today, the process of publishing a Kindle book or a hardback has similar components and moves. The initial manuscript comes in and is copy-edited; it goes to Production for programming a schedule; print prices and print formats are booked, or ISBNs and Amazon listings determined. At the same time, preliminary marketing copy is written, as is cover copy, copy for the trade booksellers and the sales team – 'blurbs' of all kinds, in fact. Then comes the London Book Fair in April and Frankfurt Book Fair in October, and the secondary, tertiary and world rights markets. More copy and more visuals are needed. Then finally, publicity. When I was with a publishing firm in the 1980s, I heard the publisher's wife on the telephone to the Features and Books editors 'selling in' the story of the book, and something clicked in me; this was my bit in the process, my calling. I felt like I had found the music I liked, as well as my instrument. I began to move from the edge to the centre of something that I could call a career. That process took a year or so and taught me something else: that work happens in a sequence but it is often an improvised one.

The best careers are full of haphazard moments that have ended up leading to a point where we now find ourselves, rather than a dedicated, straight-line journey. If you think about the way you walk up the side of a mountain, meander along a canal path or navigate through traffic, life at work operates in much the same way: you are on the move. You take turnings. You rise up, you level out. You have to negotiate and navigate some tricky passages. And you do so in a continuous state of communication of one kind or another: by talking, writing, meeting, agreeing, disagreeing, instructing, listening, advising, studying, paying attention, zoning out, travelling, worrying and enjoying – all with other people, either face-to-face or electronically.

In music they call this improvisation. In social science a keen interest began to be taken (at precisely the point that the communications revolution of the 1990s started) in the value that different kinds of organisational behavioural movement and choreography could have on success. A flurry of academic papers began to appear, with titles such as 'Improvisation as a Mindset for Organizational Analysis'[42] and 'Exploring the Empty Spaces of Organizing: How Improvisational Jazz Helps Redescribe Organizational Structure.'[43] Published in the years that saw, in networked technology, the founding of Google and, in the jazz world, the posthumous awarding of the Pulitzer Prize to Duke Ellington (1988 and 1989), they echoed a sentiment that someone had expressed even earlier.

Valdis Krebs was born and raised in Ohio. He moved to California in the early 1980s and joined the HR systems project team at Toyota in Los Angeles. It was the first major corporate computerised HR system and he was interested in what technology could do in terms of people management. Valdis describes himself as a 'curious guy', which probably explains why he began to take night classes in AI and systems analysis at UCLA. His challenge? To see what the combination of AI and management consulting might look like in the future. That future, it turned out, was organisational network mapping. In his job, Valdis fielded a lot of calls from people trying to sell him system software. One vendor in particular was a repeat caller. This guy, says Krebs, said he had succession planning software. 'I said come back in two years. He persisted, telling me had an appointment right down the street and could come and see me that afternoon. So I said OK'. That random decision turned out to be rather life-changing. Like most random results, there was a tangent within the

---

[43] Karl. E. Weick, 'Improvisation as a Mindset for Organizational Analysis', Organisational Science.
[44] Mary Jo Hatch, 'Exploring the Empty Spaces of Organizing: How Improvisational Jazz Helps Redescribe Organizational Structure', Organization Studies.

randomness itself. The meeting the vendor wanted went as planned and Krebs did not change his view of the product. But as the vendor was leaving, they made software small talk. Valdis Krebs relates, 'I mentioned that I wanted to model organizations on a computer and he reaches in his pocket and pulls out a *New York Times*' piece on something called "NetMap" and it's about the guy I had taken classes from when I was a maths and computer science undergrad.'[44] The software to do what Krebs longed for – map people's relationships with each other at work – was there, and he had a connection to it. Galvanised, Krebs persuaded his boss to let him undertake a survey in the HR department, asking the simple question, 'Who do you work with to get things done?' After this, Krebs moved job and became, in his words, 'a data dog', compiling behavioural data in a highly technical company that specialised in building satellites. Many of the teams were actually proper rocket scientists. He noticed that the turnover amongst staff was high. People would arrive, be trained and then leave for competitors. He wondered if his data could shed light on how to change this. Up until now, pure 'data dog' analysis was statistics-led: you could see turnover rates, but you could not find out *why*. But Valdis was onto something. He now designed a system – 'Inflow' – to map the stories that people told him when he asked about their loyalty, retention and recruitment behaviours. As a result of this sophisticated blend of technology, human voice and experience, the bottlenecks and stuck patterns could be addressed differently and they began to shift. Network thinking was born. Krebs thought it had something to do with jazz.

Krebs' work came to the attention of the advertising and digital early adopter Esther Dyson. In 1996 she began to publish a newsletter. Given that platform, Krebs began to write what essentially were the results of his work in human resources and his new field of social network analysis, designed for the age

---

[45] See the *New York Times* report of Netmap's organisational structure mapping: '*Corporations Reshaped by Computer*', *7 January 1987*.

of connection: 'In today's business environment, companies that operate more like jazz ensembles than classical orchestras will fare better. Instead of one person controlling a piece's execution, teams and managers share responsibilities. Participants improvise. Instead of setting up boundaries and rules, each can look for the 'groove'. Sometimes it sounds quite messy. Good work groups, like good jazz groups, operate on the verge of chaos'.[45]

Like jazz, modern life is messy. Modern connected life is far from the neat boxes that productivity apps or some leadership gurus would have us believe. If we are going to survive and thrive, and *flourish*, in the Age of Overload, we are going to need to use our networks, manage our knowledge and time, and above all, go with the flow.

---

[46] Valdis Krebs' '*Visualising Human Networks*' was published in 'Release 1.0 Esther Dyson's Monthly Report' on 12 February 1996.

Conclusion
The fully connected future

Lotsa helping hands

My first MRI since completing radiotherapy and chemotherapy was clean . . .
YES. This gives me two months to take a deep breath and relax. Oh the joy. Such
a relief. I got so anxious I developed a twitch, noticeable only to me, on the left
side of my upper lip. I feared this was a sign of tumor regrowth, even if on the
wrong side of my body (my tumor is in the left side of my brain, meaning any
recurrence is likely to show signs on the right side of my body).

I tell you, I'm so cutting edge. It's exhausting being at the forefront of cancer
treatment fashion. One minute I'm infusing myself with the immunotherapy
that's turned President Carter's cancer around, the next I'm preparing to shave
the little hair I have left, in order to wear a bunch of electrodes on my head. For
years and years we've treated cancer with three weapons: surgery, radiotherapy,
chemotherapy. While the world's labs have been working away at diving deeper
inside our bodies to find answers to cancer cures, 78 year old Professor Yoram
Palti dreamt up electrotherapy while settling into retirement in Israel.

At a basic level, how it works is that I get to wear a backpack that feeds
electrodes attached to my head. These electrodes carry highly charged particles
that create an electric field and attack brain cancer cells. Specifically, they block
further division of cancerous cells in the brain. So this is proven to extend the
time between diagnosis and recurrence. This we want, as when recurrence

happens, it tends to narrow the time window to act. My neuro-oncologist said the medical community thought this was bizarre ... until they saw the data. Now it's thought that it will soon become the norm, alongside surgery, radio and chemo.

The online brain cancer community is charged/buzzing/literally electric about how to wear this contraption. Did I mention I'll need a special cooling pillow plus fan at night, as it generates heat? Oh, and this also means wigs are ruled out ...

I'm living in the moment. The one where patients like me move from being passive recipients of treatments designed to tackle conditions, delivered by saint doctors, to the one revolving around me. Us. We know the answer lies with me and my comrades, those of us dealt the bad hand. Let's document how we're doing, what we're doing, and how we're feeling. Let's feed those epidemiologists a banquet of data so rich they have to digest carefully. Let's make that data work and meantime, empower everyone to know what the best advice is, and who else is out there should they wish to connect.

I feel ... well. Excited and terrified in equal measure. This is a notable new chapter in the brave, mad, sane, cumbersome and confusing journey I'm choosing.

'GOOD FOR NOW' BLOG BY JESSICA MORRIS[1]

My friend Jessica suffered a seizure in upstate New York in January 2016 and has been documenting her Social Health approach to tackling her brain tumour ever since. Nine months earlier, as I started to write this book, my husband had major heart surgery. Social Health helped save his life. I watched him in the intensive care unit of one of the leading heart centres in the world, powerless. He lay surrounded by banks of machines, which blinked and beeped continuously, monitoring everything. He was surrounded by space, so that additional bedside surgery could be provided if necessary (it briefly was), and

---

[1] www.jessicamorrisnye.wordpress.com first published on the community website www. lotsahelpinghands.com.

he was connected, continuously, to one-to-one care by a nurse. In between, an intensive care monitoring supervision was overseen by medical staff, who gathered in huddles to consult each other about every minute development. He was visited by a surgeon who embodies the very essence of Social Health, someone who, through our family network, we knew, and who came to check on his progress. Iain Hutchison, a professor of oral maxillo facial surgery, has spent decades joining up mental and psychological attitudes to injury and disease together with the most cutting-edge technology available. He once sat on an aeroplane and spoke to a fellow passenger; when he discovered he was an aerospace engineer who had patented a device to detect early fissures in plane metal, Iain, who founded The Facial Surgery Research Foundation, immediately followed up to create a partnership using the technology to detect early and microscopically minute fissures in mouths which would develop into cancer.

It was Iain who used his sixth sense and instinct to know that I had pneumonia and sepsis when I rang him from Aldeburgh and explained what I felt. 'Go to hospital now', he said. When I demurred, saying the children needed dealing with his instincts were so strong he began shouting, 'Get in the fucking car!' Several years later, it was he who first spotted my husband Alaric's medical problems, again using instinct combined with deep medical knowledge of the symptoms being described.

After three tense days, my husband was ready to go to the 'high dependency unit', located a few floors down. As we were packing everything up, the last nurse to be on his watch, sitting at her architects' desk of a workstation on which she could chart everything, intervened. She needed to check something, she said. The emergency bedside intervention that had happened post-surgery had introduced new medicines and new tubes, and this meant that the sequence laid out might not, in fact, be the correct one after all.

I wanted to weep with gratitude and admiration.

Social Health is just pattern management of connection. It is a recognition that we humans need systems, patterns, trial, error, instinct, community and a sense of shared purpose in the suite of 'nutrients' that we put into the system we use to live and work by. When we do, marvellous life changing, life-securing and life-enhancing things happen. When we do not, information is degraded or lost, as it was in Cambridgeshire when Ian Huntley prowled outside his borders and took the lives of Jessica Chapman and Holly Wells. Or for the WHO officials who had become so entangled in their bureaucratic networks that they failed to heed the agile, nimble, on-the-ground calls from Médecins Sans Frontières in Guinea.

The global *lingua franca* now is not faith or a common language, but the signals, noise and systems of electric and wireless connection. Everything has been mapped, discovered and shared, or so at least it seems. Geography has been replaced by something both wonderful and worrying: geotagging. The new kid on the technology block is the Internet of Things. Now you can track your clothes, the content of your fridge, your field of cows or your cancer cells. It used to be that only mystics said everything was connected. But that is now literally true. You may not want to be found, seen, tracked or big data-ed. But that is no longer a choice you can really make. The choice you can make, however, is how to behave and how to introduce a healthy flow of ideas. It is ideas, after all, which *The Economist* notes are 'more powerful than blood or money'. Ideas are the pure currency of information. Without the right management or communication of that information, it stutters and falls.

How the connecting parts in society correlate and correspond is a critical component of Social Health. The police officer in one part of the country who suddenly makes a link with a crime he saw two counties away. The health charity that realises if it connects all the patient experience on which it has information, then it has a dataset that improves understanding of the disease it is researching. The multinational 'town hall' meeting culture, whereby employees connect and share their ideas and solutions to problems. A fully connected future is possible, but it is not yet here. The opportunity is to understand networks more and to use them differently – and more effectively.

Network structures themselves – fascinating things of beauty when you look at all their patterns, by the way – do not discriminate between beautiful art and dazzling digital innovation or terrorist networks and warmongering, any more than they distinguish Ebola from a common cold. Networks reproduce a myriad of patterns, replicating and amplifying using a series of hubs and nodes to pass sequences of information, from DNA and computer code to the most contagious of all network spreads, 'word of mouth'.

From the electronic tracking systems in an Amazon warehouse in Koblenz, Germany telling an 'Amabot' worker what to pick for the customer in Berlin, to the First Officer of an Airbus A380 on a long-haul flight across the Pacific, who is connected at all times to air traffic control on the ground in Panama. Or the entrepreneur in Mumbai using cookies to track visits to her merchandising website, connected by random 'chatter' intercepted by GCHQ in England concerning a 'cell' in Brussels. Or the art dealer uploading images in Naples to a museum in Qatar for a curator to review. Or a young 'Mooc' student taking a virtual class in a Harvard classroom from her living room in Rio de Janiero, who drinks from a can of soda that is connected to the Internet of Things, which in turn sends her an app message reminding her to restock when her supply gets low.

Our fully connected individual lives are in some ways easier to document, to assess and to modify than our communal or corporate lives, which are equally dominated by embedded and integrated 'operating systems' and cultures. Connectedness is taken for granted but can cause immense misconnection and miscommunication unless a human and electronic chain of intelligence and interconnection is fully joined up, fully connected. We are beginning to see a quantum shift in the patterns in policing, healthcare, anti-terrorism, health and safety, and education, in which new ways of collaborating and compiling information replace the old silos. But we have no national or global blueprints, just an emerging set of clustered patterns that have not yet been fully mapped. We may all be connected but not many of us are that joined-up.

I envisage a fully connected future that has absorbed technology and yet re-connected with the human who uses it. That may mean driverless cars, or it may mean devising better manual social systems to assist the elderly people who, we are told, are going to be major beneficiaries of this brave new technology. It cannot be one kind of outsourcing over the older 'other' – the human.

I also envisage a fully connected future where people, both collectively in organisations and individually, use a skillset made of knowledge and information from diverse sources they can trust, but combined with a use of instinct that is never ignored or sidelined for political or practical expediency. Where small-scale and intimate gatherings, which take place over extended periods, hold as much value as frenetic short-term meetings or large-scale conferences, all designed to do things fast and for top-down results rather than elongated, lateral as well as linear outcomes.

The fully connected future will be a well-travelled one. Staying put and staying at home cannot be a replacement, even as AI makes current face-to-face video technology look antiquated. It would be wonderful if, instead of trying to get everywhere fast, we travelled slow. The seas carry more computers and cars than they do people, but oceans cover more surface area of the planet than anything else. Let us return to the seas, on ships full of people learning, working and holidaying together, instead of just buckling up on the gas-guzzling 'dreamliners' of the skies.

Then there is coffee. Coffee will not be disappearing from our lives, but the coffee shop must transform back to its old self, a place of classless connection, of cultural exchange, of what Sandy Pentland rightly calls 'social physics'. And the gym – the Aristotlean centre of flourishing, of Arête. I write these final words sitting in the café in my local gym. The social centre is still an accidental, incidental one: the main action stays upstairs, with the equipment and the classes, or downstairs with the pool. When this book is published, I am going to ask to come and talk about it here. I want my gym to be a book fair, a library, just as I want the bank on the high street to stay open past closing time and give economists a chance to explain the business of finance to us, the citizen, the curious social soul, outside of transactional, siloed 'office hours'.

Finally, networks. We live, travel, speak, type and text on networks. Today we depend almost entirely on them. Modes of connection, means of connection, they are all networks forging ahead with the energy and momentum of the early steam engines, which hurtled along on shiny new nineteenth-century networks, the railroads. Our twenty-first-century networks are a series of interconnected carriages, each one connected to form a bigger, more co-ordinated whole. The members of a family who phone each other every day. A branch office that is part of a bigger corporate family. The global political family. Most of civil society and political society, as well as the corporate world, is organised in linked networks of interconnecting 'carriages'.

The fully connected future is not a dramatic one-stop set of idealistic flourishes but small steps, taken in concert, interlocking to reflect our individuality in a mass age.

Like the honeybee, or the softly fluttering crystals of a falling snowflake. Alone but shaped by structure and pattern, connected right until the end.

APPENDIX

Hexagon Thinking – six practical practices around Social Health

We are all so goal orientated it is not surprising that I am often asked for 'tips'. The very word makes me wince, because it somehow reduces what I hope are big, wide, open ideas, to cloistered, fast, siloed ones. However, human nature tends to want both the grandiose and the granular. So here are six main principles and practices to 'take away' and act on in the immediate future, if you want to rush out and get started on *doing something* about your own state of right connection, overload, or anything in between.

You know all about taking two steps forward and one back. Welcome to the real world. Think of the famous joke about a woman stopping a taxi driver in New York and asking for directions to the famous Carnegie Hall, to which he replied, 'Lady, you gotta practice. You gotta practice. You gotta practice.'[1] Achieving Social Health is all about a 'lifestyle not diet' approach. It is about using the principles of the Hexagon of Social Health: the 'top knot' of knowledge, networks and time being held in check by the 'coping mechanisms' of communication, management and sixth sense, and of designing your own system.

The first step in looking at changing from an unhealthy approach to a fully connected life to a more functional one is to admit trial and error, and start to practice. Behaviours that connect and flow, rather than staying in a silo, are what you must aim for. Think 'lifestyle', not 'diet'. You cannot know how your team is

---

[1] The origins of the 'How do I get to Carnegie Hall?' joke (answer: 'Practice') are unclear but attributed to violinist Mischa Elman, www.carnegiehall.org

going to respond to something until you try it. I had no idea I needed to ditch my fitness form at the gym until I had failed to follow it for weeks at a time, and yet realised I still had the motivation to stay with the machines: I needed to design my own system. So try to develop strategies and tactics that make you feel you are taking more steps forward than you are back, and congratulate yourself for being your own guinea pig, your own viable experiment.

It is probably a good idea to ask yourself what the exact driver is right now for wanting to get some Social Health strategy happening in your life – at home, work or both. Are you at breaking point and need some kind of emergency system? Or is this the case for the people who live with and/or work with you? This is a key distinction to make. The steps you take if you are in crisis, if you need to survive something – to make it through an obviously stressful time – will be short-term actions aimed at shoring up the basics. If, however, you can look longer ahead than the purely immediate future, you can horizon-scan and plan. Ask yourself which mode you are in right now. The tyranny of a short timeline often propels people into crisis: you have to pass an exam by a certain deadline, or your boss is demanding results within a period of time in which you cannot reasonably reach them. Or, as with diet and fitness, you want results sooner than your body can provide them on a sustainable basis. So organising goals in a realistic, sensible way, rather than one based on wishful thinking or on someone else's terms, will make the difference between being able to survive or thrive in terms of the changes you want to bring into effect.

Life in general swings on a modern fluctuating axis, something more lateral than linear. It runs from the large and grandiose, of course: a twenty-first birthday, a wedding, a launch, an election or a campaign. Big moments, big plans, big targets. But it also happens incrementally, in small steps. The management writers Chip and Dan Heath capture this beautifully in what they call the behaviours of either 'The Rider' or 'The Elephant'. One, the leader, thinks big, acts big and is often too far from the ground to see what their followers, the herd, see and feel. I call one the grandiose and the other the granular.

Back to the point on balance: you need both. I do not suggest only thinking small – I am all for big ideas. But remember you will only achieve them, gathering your herd of elephants (children, staff, pupils, whatever your group) along the way, if you connect with them on their terms and make those your terms too. Our bodies operate a series of infinitesimal actions to synchronise movement: eighty bones and around eight hundred muscles make up the human body. We do not acknowledge the movements but we would notice if they could not happen or were somehow impaired. When thinking about how to get things done at work, it is often better to look at the one or two things that we can do *today*, rather than aiming for the grandiose vision of an indistinct 'tomorrow'.

If we feel numb or disconnected, it is a stress-related sensation. Johann Hari's book, *Chasing the Scream*, is insistent, correctly in my view, that the central component of drug addiction is too much feeling in a person (the addict), which needs numbing and voiding.[2] To be fully connected in the Age of Overload is to survive and thrive in a fully present, fully feeling way. In practice, this means calling out a job that is not working well, a system that needs reversing, or a way of doing things that needs changing. The feelings must be listened to or they will not achieve change at all.

The next time you are in a meeting and someone says something idiotic, please pause for a moment and try and reach across to bridge the divide. See the world from their persepctive. I have had a lot of pracice at this with work colleagues, teenagers and one husband; this technique works, trust me. The idea of intimacy is terribly intrusive for people, especially as we often hide what we feel from ourselves. Having the courage to share (but without oversharing) is becoming more commonplace and neccessary. This is because, in order to trust people and build relationship capital, you need to give something of yourself. Generosity and reciprocity are drivers of change.

---

[2] Johann Hari, *Chasing the Scream: The First and Last Days of the War on Drugs*.

When I gave up smoking, hundreds of years ago, I was taught by an excellent teacher called Gillian Riley,[3] who made me realise that I was used to framing the choices I was making around smoking in terms of 'powerlessness'. She pointed out that despite feeling 'compelled' to smoke at certain times (I was a thirty-a-day young woman before I quit), there were times when I did *not* smoke. When I chose, through social convention, not to light up in a 'no smoking' cinema, for instance. It made me realise that how we behave socially is just that – a choice. People who lose their self control on social media and start trolling others are, despite their compulsions, choosing to let go. How you behave as a social soul is surely more of a choice than where you are born and your underlying health. Choice is a wealth: do not squander it. You can choose to make some changes and get into Social Health – or not.

One more thing: size matters. Forget the rush to build and have scale in your life. It really does not matter how many people follow you on Twitter or 'like' you on Facebook unless you are being purely transactional, not relational, in your approach. You may have *feelings* about this, of course, but the real deal lies in small Dunbar-Number-esque groups of approximately 150. If we hold in our minds that the number of countries in the world does not exceed 200, and the number of hours end-to-end in a week remains, obstinately, 168, then this kind of size for relationships makes (no pun intended) infinite sense.

Six principal practices of Social Health

1. The diary as a body

I cannot stress how significant the diary and schedule in your personal and professional life is likely to be, whether you feel overwhelmed by the Age of

---

[3] Gillian Riley's Skype consultations for both stopping smoking and eating less can be found on www. eatingless.com and her books include *Willpower* (Vermillion 2003) and *How to Stop Smoking and Stay Stopped for Good* (Vermillion 2007).

Overload or not. When we think of food in relation to fitness, we all understand that the first step is to control what you eat. Certainly having someone else in control (unless you happen to be a celebrity with a retinue of personal nutritionists) is something you recognise as wrong. Most people over the age of about six months are able to control and calibrate what they put in their mouths and stomachs. Not so the diary. A culture of diary outsourcing has grown up, which contributes massively to the way in which people lose control of their time and how they plan the movements of their day. If you do one thing immediately, do this: look at the patterns in your diary, look at what they mean to you, and decide some patterns that work better. An hour at the beginning or end of the day to manage your inbox, perhaps, or a two- or even three-day period in which to just think (yes!), are all ways of cleansing your palate of the overstuffed commitments that only cause bloat, blockage and overload.

2. Disconnection

It may seem strange, to advocate disconnection but this is exactly what I want you to consider. You may need the mental equivalent of a fast, of tuning out rather than burning out. Organisations that stay connected, lights on, ever-humming, such as hospitals and government departments, are often the ones that face periodic bouts of catastrophic disconnection. They never slow down, stand back and try to gain perspective. They find it hard to say 'We're not doing this right, we need to make some changes'. When they do, things improve: I'm thinking of the example of the hospital that consistently under-performed and ran overtime on scheduled operations. When they looked at the problem they realised embedding a form of disconnection was the answer; they needed to have an operating theatre permanently empty.[4] At first glance this seemed

---

[4] Gillian Tett refers to this in her book *The Silo Effect: Why Every Organisation Needs to Disrupt Itself to Survive.*

nonsensical, as if it would exacerbate the problem. But it did not. It focused minds on what to keep on schedule and allowed room to accommodate emergencies.

On a personal level, you and I are not personal computers; we need to switch off on a regular basis. Organised religion may have many flaws but a day of rest or Sabbath is not, in my view, one of them. I find a regular '*Techno Shabbat*', unplugged from technology, reconnecting to one kind of life as I disconnect from another, nothing short of refereshing and necessary. I immediately regret it when I override it and cheat. I have no religious faith, but I have faith in the importance of disconnection from the over-connected life. It is simply not possible to stay 'always on' and plugged in without feeling out of sync with our own psyches, bodies and minds. There is a danger that we are sold such a fully networked existence that we stay on, like computers and office lights, causing environmental mayhem. To connect one-sixth of the week with yourself, your family, your community, without the prop, benefit or accompaniement of technology is essential to surviving and thriving in the Age of Overload.

3. Diversity of thought

Surround yourself with people who think differently from you, who know different things, who are younger or come from a different background. This is not to say that you should invite conflict in to your life; argument and belligerence can lead to the opposite of consensus. But you know if there is too much like-mindedness, too much 'groupthink' and 'hivemind'. Use your Sixth Sense from the Hexagon of Social Health to read the body language in a room, to sense if colleagues are resisting something or have other ideas, and invite them to speak up and talk any glitches through. In other words, create jazz ensemble playing, not formal orchestras. How do you do this in general? Talk to different people. Notice different people. The waiter. The taxi driver. The intern. Read more widely so you notice the 'peripheral' ideas as well as the mainstream ones. Learn to think in a more diverse way yourself, as well as following the same pattern you take for granted. If you only recruit people with certain qualifications, think again. If you refuse to let your children play computer games that you do not understand and therefore disapprove of, try asking them to explain them to you. In other words, *be peripheral.* I can honestly say that, having worked my way up from the bottom, photocopying 800-page manuscripts and opening the post were good ways to watch, learn and listen. People think that being at the centre of the action is essential, but I have found that this can disconnect us from where the action really is, which is everywhere. This is why I talk to taxi drivers and waiting staff at cocktail receptions. I often recruit freelance staff by talking randomly to people. I try and notice things in the same way that network science notices: the edges, the borders and the links inbetween.

4. Design your honeycomb

Where and how you work could not be more essential. Remember how important it is to be productive, to feel essential, to connect with what you do. If you work somewhere you hate, either because of the job itself, or the location, or the journey, understand that this will impact your performance just as much as being on the wrong diet or having poor motivation in the gym. I only became even vaguely connected to exercise by ripping up the actual personal trainer-designed programme and personally designing my own. The same goes for work. Look at the pattern, shape and place of where and how you work. If you work in a really ugly building, or have a hideous commute, notice the way this affects you and design tactics to mitigate this. It could be downloading some great podcasts to listen to or it could be reading *The 4- Hour Work Week* by Tim Ferriss[5] and making sure you work productively and flexibly – to the satisfaction of your peers and bosses – elsewhere.

---

[5] Tim Ferriss, *The 4-Hour Work Week: Escape the 9–5, Live Anywhere, and Join the New Rich.* See also www.fourhourworkweek.com.

5. Social Six

In politics, a kitchen cabinet is not a piece of furniture. It is the very architecture of people and players you surround yourself with. It is the quantity and quality of your personal network who make up the people you can call on for advice, critical friendship, intelligence and mentoring. The network academic Zella King has designed a thought-provoking take on this, which she calls 'The Personal Boardroom'.[6] Interestingly, Zella believes that there are only six to twelve people in anyone's Personal Boardroom. I would call this having your 'Social Six' – that is six groups of people you know you are orbiting around in some way. This could look like:

(i)   **Close friends and Family**

(ii) **Wider friends and Family**

(iii) **Professional Priority**

People who you must keep top of mind and connected with over the next 3–6 months.

(iv) **Professional Social**

Those with whom you can be your 'blended self' - sharing trusted personal confidence and discussing professional matters. These are precious people for your productivity.

(v)   **Reconnect People**

Who lies buried in an email list who you last so saw long ago you can't remember but who remains relevant to your work today? Invite them to reconnect over a coffee. Get face-to-face!

(vi) **Wishlist People**

It takes courage to 'reach out' to someone you do not know and face rejection, but it can and must be done, as long as you do your research

---

[6] See www.personalboardroom.com.

and clearly state your 'reason why'. Start by identifying 6 people relevant who you are the best ambassador for your workplace to meet. In other words, be brave, but also keep it real.

SOCIAL SIX

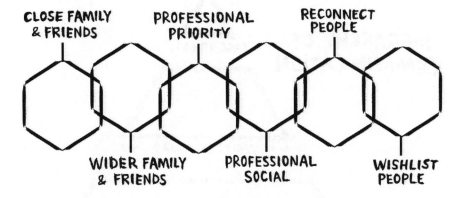

© Julia Hobsbawm 2017

Your Social Six will not only be individual, but it will change. These are the groups – ideally no more than 'Dunbar's Number' of 150 at a time (or even in total) – who are organised and downloaded from the various tangled networks in which these relationships normally reside: perhaps your Outlook, plus LinkedIn, as well as some from Yammer or another private group or public social network. Either way, they will fall into one of three categories, which are either active or dormant. 'Dormant ties' is another one of those appealing social network analysis terms and, like 'weak ties', conveys something counterintuitive about social network behaviour; we always think it is new people or greater numbers of relationships that are likely to yield success, be it personal or professional. After all, dating agencies pride themselves on just how *many* people you can 'swipe' in one go, taking it for granted that the more you can choose from, the better it is. That may be the case algorithmically but that is as far as it goes. Remember trust, the family ties and the kinship aspect of networks: keep your ties small. But where it comes to dormant ties, rekindle these. In practice, phone someone up you have not spoken to in a while. Arrange to have coffee to catch up. Keep in motion and progress your relationships, rather than let them lie inert on the tracks of an electronic network, disconnected from human hand–eye co-ordination.

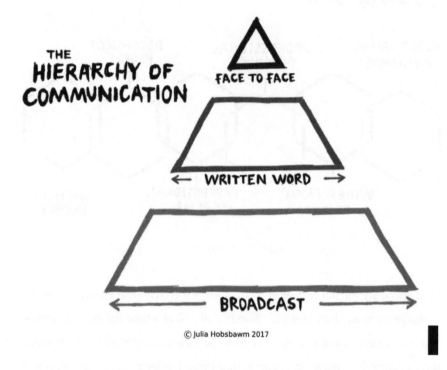

THE
HIERARCHY OF
COMMUNICATION

FACE TO FACE

← WRITTEN WORD →

← BROADCAST →

© Julia Hobsbawm 2017

Active ties speak more for themselves; you already know you are connected to them. They are in your social circle already, or they are people you interact with daily at work. What matters is that you pull, mentally or physically, these names from the bigger mass of connections you have, and either connect or reconnect. Who are the three groups that end up with either active or dormant ties? First of all, family. This could be literally just your family or a metaphor for those you regard first and foremost as a 'priority'. Second, friends. Again, this can be literal and social – some people do keep distinct groups, and yet by 'friends' I mean more of a blend like you see on Facebook: people you are friend*ly* with, on going-out-for-coffee terms with, as well as high school buddies you are lifelong pals with. In a work context, this group is intermediate: not necessarily an absolute priority but people you are connected with, wish to strengthen your ties to, and/or maintain this level of closeness with. Finally, the third group: colleagues. Once again, this does not have to be literal. This third group means that your ties with them – active or dormant – are less intimate than with the other two groups. In other words, you would not confide in them, or give them a piece of strong intelligence ahead of someone higher up on your network with whom you have strong ties going way back. This group can be the most important: you can help people in this group as much as they can help you; they may be distant because they are more junior, or because they have less influence than you do. They still know things, know people, have ideas, or they could be the opposite – people you wish you knew better, but at the very least you know 'of' them.

6. The knowledge dashboard

We know what we all need, really. To connect more face-to-face in a Facebook world; to spend time with people we trust and with whom we can build relationships, rather than in some kind of transactional or fleeting vortex in which the idea of 'networking' becomes a hideous chore rather than a matter of simply taking good care of yourself. We understand this, just as we know that we can do it with our physical fitness and mental wellbeing.

Understanding that there needs to be a pattern and process around how we treat our knowledge, networks and time is the vital first step. I spent many miserable years drowning in the possibility of diets and exercise options before I decided to design a pattern based on what I understood, knew and had learned. I was turning fifty by the time I created this pattern, but it made me realise the value of shape and design – hence what I call Hexagon Thinking itself.

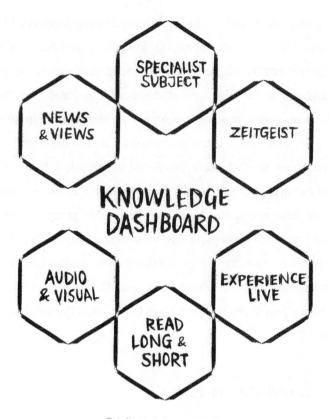

© Julia Hobsbawm 2017

This is especially true with knowledge. We count calories, we monitor our 'five-a-day' of fruit and vegetables (although this is a giant marketing construct rather than anything more scientific, as a healthy eating public campaign it has been tremendously effective).[7] I began to design a pattern around knowledge management which could be instrumental rather than theoretical. The 'Knowledge Dashboard' approach is the result. Instead of facing all the news, views, media platforms on a daily basis as a wall which can come crashing over

[7] The campaign to eat more fruit and vegetables – 5-a-day – was originally a marketing strategy devised in response to a World Health Organization paper in 1990 to try and combat heart disease. It was launched in 1991 by the Produce for Better Health Foundation, which collaborated with the National Cancer Institute.

you at any overwhelming moment, it divides information into six core types to allow you to check a more even spread on a daily or weekly basis. Like everything in Hexagon Thinking, the pattern is as important as the particular: you can create your own versions of the dashboard, if your own area of work or how you live makes it preferable. I hope, however, that it remains a useful guide.

- **News and views.** I know people who only look at the 'back pages' of a newspaper (or their digital equivalent) – i.e. the sports page. What is at the front does not seem to interest them. News and current affairs are to some extent the lifeblood of society. News pulses through it, whether we like it or not. Terror, globalisation, finance – they all happen with news. Please look at what is going on at home and abroad, and in the political ether. Not because I want to turn everyone into policymakers, but I want everyone to avoid myopia. Remember: tuneout is the new burnout.

- **Specialist subject.** This is the easy one. We all generally stay on top of our specialist subjects. Trade publishing of journals, websites and blogs continues to flourish relative to other media because we know how to stay smart and up to speed with these. You cannot be taken seriously if you do not read up on your subject, even though knowledge is now so limitless that you will only ever scratch the surface.

- **Zeitgeist.** I confess that I have virtually no interest in sport. I can be quite a bore about why I think football competitions incubate unhealthy nationalism, and I find the rules of cricket literally indecipherable. However, I recognise that everyone has their passions, their subjects which ignite them. The key to connecting fully with someone is to notice what theirs are. Not to fake interest but to be in with a chance of finding some common ground – or connection, in the absence of it (after all, remember how opposites attract).

- **Watch and listen.** If you remember the Communications Hierarchy that was outlined at the beginning of Part Two, you'll perhaps be relieved that just as there are only really three core forms of communication for humans – face-to-face, written or social media broadcast (it is the language and images in between that are infinite) – the same is true with actual forms of information. The first is anything we watch or hear. These mediums – principally TV and radio, but equally mobile video, podcast, cinema or talking books – matter because they are a different way to ingest information. You do not only drink soup: that would deliver nutrients to your body one way and one way alone. The experience of watching a news programme, or listening to some zeitgeist-enhancing culture – these are different dimensions and should be part of your regular information 'diet'.

- **Read, long and short.** The pace and dimension of words has also changed. Reading a signposted 'long read' in a news medium such as *The Guardian* or *The New Yorker* may take thirty minutes or more, and occupies a different bit of headspace and pace than a Twitter feed or a Buzzfeed news scroll on a mobile device. The two need to be taken in tandem. Remember: fruit *and* vegetables; cardio *and* weights.

- **Sharing, seeing, live.** Finally, the face-to-face of information – seeing something live, sharing it. I can never quite forget a blistering live lecture by Simon Schama on portraiture, or watching Maya Angelou, America's late Poet Laureate, reading *Still I Rise* to 3,000 women in Lewisham, South London in the 1980s, or hearing Andrew Solomon talk about difference and exclusion at the Hay Festival.

Having this blend of information, a *Knowledge Dashboard* which at least attempts to organise what the former US Secretary of State Donald Rumseld called 'known unknowns', makes navigating the Age of Overload that little bit more manageable. That bit more connected. Maybe even – with a bit of luck – fully connected.

POSTSCRIPT

A view from the bridge

Something else happened in 1964, the year I was born and the year of 'Moore's Law' and the doubling of computer power which was to last for fifty years. One of the biggest achievements in modern industrial engineering was finalised and its very construction serves as a metaphor for modern Social Health. The Forth Bridge in Fife was built by a large workforce of thousands. From working class secretaries to middle-class accountants, from industrial engineers to workmen, together they forged alliances over the six long years it took to build the one of the biggest suspension bridges anywhere in the world in a tiny corner of Scotland.

Apart from the project itself, which was clearly absorbing and well-run, this group, thrown together by the accident of work, had a diversity of background and skill, disposition and age, which went against the natural choice many people make to stick with their own – *homophilly* as it is termed by sociologists. Their experience mirrors that of well-run units that, in the main, deliver very productively, such as army units. Contrast this with the groupthink of some social services or police departments, seen in my earlier examples. How much diversity of thought is there? It is another key to Social Health.

The Forth Bridge became necessary due to the relentless march of modernity: a ferry crossing had taken day trippers and commuters over the water for centuries. But it became overrun in just a few short years by the volume of cars which had been ushered in by the new prosperity of the 1950s.

The current bridge master and chief engineer said of the bridge, 'It's just like a rope bridge over the Andes, except it is made of steel'.[1] The ancient and the modern. The very basis of good health. If we think about structure as being core to Social Health, about a marriage between attitude and behaviour, between mindset and action, between hardware and software, and if we learn from where Social Health happens, not just in the world of health and fitness but in the wider worlds of business, engineering, education and the home, we can begin to see what a fully connected future might look like. A future we can look forward to and be fully engaged in constructing.

---

[1] Barry Colford, Bridge Master, quoted in 'The Other Forth Bridge – 50 Years of the Remarkable Road Crossing', Steven Brocklehurst, BBC Scotland News, 5 September 2014.

BIBLIOGRAPHY

Books

Allen, David (2001), *Getting Things Done: The Art of Stress-Free Productivity*. New York: Penguin.

Auletta, Ken (2010), *Googled*. London: Virgin Books.

Baker, Wayne E. (1994), *Networking Smart*. New York: McGraw-Hill.

Ball, Philip (2005), *Critical Mass: How One Thing Leads to Another*. London: Arrow Books.

Balmond, Cecil with Smith, Jannuzzi (2007), *Informal*. New York: Prestel.

Barabási, Albert-László (2002), *Linked: The New Science of Networks*. Cambridge, MA: Perseus Publishing.

Barabási, Albert-László (2011), *Bursts: The Hidden Patterns Behind Everything We Do, From Your E-mail to Bloody Crusades*. New York: Plume.

Barton, Allen H., Bogdan Denitch and Charles Kadushin (Eds) (1973), *Opinion-Making Elites in Yugoslavia*. New York: Praeger.

Batty, Michael (2013), *The New Science of Cities*. Cambridge, MA: MIT Press.

Baumeister, Roy F. and John Tierney (2012), *Willpower: Rediscovering Our Greatest Strengths*. London: Allen Lane.

Borgatti, Stephen P., Martin G. Everett and Jeffrey C. Johnson (2013), *Analysing Social Networks*. London: SAGE Publications Ltd.

Brooks, David (2011), *The Social Animal: A Story of How Success Happens*. London: Short Books.

Browne, John, Tommy Stadlen and Robin Nuttall (2016), *Connect: How Companies Succeed By Engaging Radically with Society*. London: W. H. Allen.

Brynjolfsson, Eric and Robin McAfee (2014), *The Second Machine Age: Work, Progress, and Prosperity in a Time of Brilliant Technologies*. New York and London: W. W. Norton & Co.

Burt, Ronald S. (2005), *Brokerage and Closure: An Introduction to Social Capital*. Oxford: Oxford University Press.

Burt, Ronald S. (2011), *Neighbor Networks: Competitive Advantage Local and Personal*. Oxford: Oxford University Press.

Cain, Susan (2013), *Quiet: Growing Up as an Introvert in a World That Can't Stop Talking*. London: Penguin.

Cairncross, Frances (1997), *The Death of Distance: How the Communications Revolution Will Change Our Lives*. London: Orion.

Carswell, Douglas (2012), *The End of Politics and the Birth of iDemocracy*. London: Biteback Publishing.

Castells, Manuel (2010), *The Rise of the Networked Society*. Oxford: Wiley Blackwell.

Chaline, Eric (2015), *The Temple of Perfection: A History of the Gym*. London: Reaktion Books.

Christakis, Nicholas A. and James H. Fowler (2009), *Connected: The Surprising Power of Our Social Networks and How They Shape Our Lives*. New York: Little, Brown and Co.

Cialdini, Robert B. (2001), *Influence: The Psychology of Persuasion*. Boston, MA: Allyn and Bacon.

Collins, Jim (2001), *Good to Great: Why Some Companies Make the Leap and Others Don't*. New York: HarperCollins.

Collins, J. C. and Porras, J. I. (1997), *Built to Last*. New York: HarperCollins.

Colvile, Robert (2016), *The Great Acceleration: How the World is Getting Faster, Faster*. London: Bloomsbury Publishing.

Covey, S. R. (2004), *The 7 Habits of Highly Effective People*. London: Simon & Schuster Ltd.

Crawford, Matthew (2015), *The World Beyond Your Head: How to Flourish in an Age of Distraction*. London: Penguin Random House.

Cross, Rob and Andrew Parker (2004), *The Hidden Power of Social Networks: Understanding How Work* Really *Gets Done in Organisations*, Boston, MA: Harvard Business School Press.

De Botton, Alan (2009), *The Pleasures and Sorrows of Work*. London: Penguin.

Dunbar, Robin (2010), *How Many Friends Does One Person Need? Dunbar's Number and Other Evolutionary Quirks*. London: Faber & Faber.

Dunbar, Robin (2012), *The Science of Love and Betrayal*. London: Faber & Faber.

Durkheim, Emile (1897 [2002]), *Suicide: A Study in Sociology*. London: Routledge.

Easley, David and Jon Kleinberg (2010), *Networks, Crowds, and Markets: Reasoning About a Highly Connected World*. New York: Cambridge University Press.

Egan, Gerard (1973), *Face to Face: The Small-Group Experience and Interpersonal Growth*. Belmont, CA: Wadsworth Publishing Company.

Enders, Giulia (2014), *Gut: The Inside Story of Our Body's Most Under-Rated Organ*. London: Scribe Publications.

Ferguson, Niall (1998), *The House of Rothschild: Money's Prophets, 1798–1848*. New York: Viking Penguin.

Ferguson, Niall (2014), *The Great Degeneration: How Institutions Decay and Economies Die*. London: Penguin Books.

Ferrante, Elena (2012), *My Brilliant Friend*. New York: Europa Editions.

Ferris, Joshua (2008), *Then We Came to the End*. London: Penguin.

Ferriss, Tim (2011), *The 4-Hour Work Week: Escape the 9–5, Live Anywhere, and Join the New Rich* (2nd edn). London: Vermilion.

Festinger, Leon (1957), *A Theory of Cognitive Dissonance*. Stanford, CA: Stanford University Press.

Field, Ophelia (2008), *The Kit-Cat Club*. London: Harper Perennial.

Flaherty, G. Michael (2011), *The Textures of Time: Agency and Temporal Experience*. Philadelphia, PA: Temple University Press.

Fletcher, Tom (2016), *Naked Diplomacy: Power and Statecraft in the Digital Age*. London: William Collins.

Floridi, Luciano (2014), *The 4th Revolution: How the Infosphere is Reshaping Human Reality*. Oxford: Oxford University Press.

Floridi, Luciano (Ed.) (2015), *The Onlife Manifesto: Being Human in a Hyperconnected Era*. London: Springer Open.

Furnham, Adrian (1998), *The Psychology of Managerial Incompetence: A Sceptic's Dictionary of Modern Organizational Issues*. London: Whurr Publishers.

Gansky, Lisa (2010), *The Mesh: Why the Future of Business Is Sharing*. New York: Portfolio Penguin.

Garton Ash, Timothy (2016), *Free Speech: Ten Principles for a Connected World*. London: Atlantic Books.

Gatrell, Vic (2013), *The First Bohemians: Life and Art in London's Golden Age*. London: Penguin.

Gawande, A. (2015), *Being Mortal*. London: Wellcome Collection.

Gerber, M. E. (1995), *The E-Myth Revisited*. New York: HarperCollins.

Gill, A. A. (2002), *A. A. Gill is Away*. London: Orion Publishing.

Gill, A. A. (2008), *Breakfast at the Wolseley*, London: Quadrille.

Gill, A. A. (2013), *To America With Love*. London: Simon & Schuster.

Gladwell, Malcolm (2001), *The Tipping Point: How Little Things Can Make a Big Difference*. London: Abacus.

Gladwell, M. (2008), *Outliers: The Story of Success*. London: Allen Lane.

Gladwell, M. (2009), *What the Dog Saw and Other Adventures*. London: Allen Lane.

Gleick, James (2011), *The Information: A History, a Theory, a Flood*. London: Fourth Estate.

Godin, Seth (2002), *Permission Marketing: How To Turn Your Ideas Into Marketing Epidemics*. London: Simon & Schuster.

Godin, S. (2002), *Unleashing the Ideavirus*. London: Simon & Schuster.

Goffman, Erving (1969), *The Presentation of Self in Everyday Life*. London: Allen Lane.

Goyal, Sanjeev (2007), *Connections: An Introduction to the Economics of Networks*. Woodstock, Oxon: Princeton University Press.

Grant, Adam (2013), *Give and Take: A Revolutionary Approach to Success*. London: Weidenfeld & Nicholson.

Gratton, Lynda (2011), *The Shift: The Future of Work is Already Here*. London: Collins.

Gratton, Lynda and A. Scott (2016), *The 100-Year Life: Living and Working in an Age of Longevity*. London: Bloomsbury Information.

Hagel III, John, John Seely Brown and Lang Davison (2010), *The Power of Pull: How Small Moves, Smartly Made, Can Set Big Things in Motion*: New York: Basic Books.

Halpern, David (2005), *Social Capital*. Cambridge: Polity Press.

Halpern, David (2015), *Inside the Nudge Unit: How Small Changes Can Make a Big Difference*. London: W. H. Allen.

Handy, Charles (1993), *Understanding Organizations*. New York: Oxford University Press.

Handy, Charles (2015), *The Second Curve: Thoughts on Reinventing Society*. London: Random House.

Haralambos, Michael, Martin Holborn, Steve Chapman and Stephen Moore (2008), *Sociology: Themes and Perspectives*. London: Collins.

Harari, Yuval N. (2011), *Sapiens: A Brief History of Humankind*. London: Vintage.

Harford, Tim (2011), *Adapt: Why Success Always Starts with Failure*. London: Little, Brown.

Hari, Johann (2015), *Chasing the Scream: The First and Last Days of the War on Drugs*.
    London: Bloomsbury Circus.
Harkin, James (2011), *Niche: Why the Market No Longer Favours the Mainstream*. London:
    Little, Brown.
Heath, Chip and Dan Heath (2010), *Switch: How to Change Things When Change Is Hard*.
    New York: Broadway Books.
Heath, Chip and Dan Heath (2013), *Decisive: How to Make Better Decisions*. London:
    Random House Books.
Heffernan, Margaret (2011), *Wilful Blindness: Why We Ignore the Obvious at Our Peril*.
    London: Simon & Schuster.
Heffernan, Margaret (2015), *Beyond Measure: The Big Impact of Small Changes*. London:
    Simon & Schuster.
Hertz, Noreena (2013), *Eyes Wide Open: How to Make Smart Decisions in a Confusing
    World*. London: William Collins.
Hilton, Steve (2015), *More Human: Designing a World Where People Come First*. London:
    W. H. Allen.
Hoffman, Reid and Ben Casnocha (2012), *The Start-Up of You: Adapt to the Future, Invest
    In Yourself, and Transform Your Career*. London: Random House Business Books.
Holmes, A. M. (2012), *May We Be Forgiven*. New York: Viking.
Honoré, Carl (2013), *The Slow Fix*. London: Collins.
Horner, Avril and Ann Rowe (Eds) (2015), *Living on Paper: Letters from Iris Murdoch
    1934–1995*. London: Chatto & Windus.
Howell, David (2014), *Old Links and New Ties: Power and Persuasion in an Age of
    Networks*. London: I.B. Tauris.
Ibarra, Herminia (2015), *Act Like a Leader, Think Like a Leader*. Boston, MA: Harvard
    Business School Publishing.
James, Oliver (2013), *Office Politics: How to Thrive in a World of Lying, Backstabbing and
    Dirty Tricks*. London: Vermillion.
Jenkins, Henry, Sam Ford and Joshua Green (2013), *Spreadable Media: Creating Value and
    Meaning in a Networked Culture*. New York and London: New York University Press.
Johnson, Steven (2002), *Emergence*. London: Penguin Books.
Johnson, Steven (2010), *Where Good Ideas Come From*. London: Allen Lane.
Johnson, Steven (2012), *Future Perfect: The Case for Progress in a Networked Age*. London:
    Allen Lane.
Judt, Tony (2010), *Ill Fares the Land*. London: Allen Lane.
Kadushin, Charles (2012), *Understanding Social Networks: Theories, Concepts, and
    Findings*. New York: Oxford University Press.
Kahneman, Daniel (2012), *Thinking, Fast and Slow*. London: Penguin Books.
Katz, Bruce and Jennifer Bradley (2013), *The Metropolitan Revolution: How Cities
    and Metros Are Fixing Our Broken Politics and Fragile Economy*. Washington, DC:
    The Brookings Institution.
Keen, Andrew (2012), *Digital Vertigo: How Today's Online Social Revolution is Dividing,
    Diminishing, and Disorienting Us*. London: Constable.
Keen, Andrew (2015), *The Internet is not the Answer*. New York: Atlantic Monthly Press.

Khanna, Parag (2016), *Connectography: Mapping the Global Network Revolution*. London: Weidenfeld & Nicolson.

Krznaric, Roman (2014), *Empathy*. London: Rider.

Lanier, Jaron (2011), *You Are Not a Gadget*. London: Penguin Books.

Leadbeater, Charles (2009), *We-Think: Mass Innovation, Not Mass Production* (2nd edn). London: Profile Books.

Leader, Darian and David Corfield (2008), *Why Do People Get Ill?* London: Penguin Books.

Levine, Caroline (2015), *Forms: Whole, Rhythm, Hierarchy, Network*. Princeton, NJ: Princeton University Press.

Levitin, Daniel (2014), *The Organized Mind: Thinking Straight in the Age of Information Overload*. New York: Penguin Group.

Lewis, Michael (2015), *Flash Boys*. New York: Penguin.

Lieberman, Matthew D. (2013), *Social: Why Our Brains are Wired to Connect*. Oxford: Oxford University Press.

Lipnack, J. and J. Stamps (1986), *The Networking Book*. New York and London: Routledge & Kegan Paul.

Lipnack, Jessica and Jeffrey Stamps (1994), *The Age of The Network: Organising Principles for the 21st Century*. New York: John Wiley & Sons.

Lomax, Alan (1978), *Folk Song Style and Culture*. New Brunswick, NJ: Transaction Publishers.

Mason, Paul (2015), *PostCapitalism*. London: Allen Lane.

McGonigal, Jane (2011), *Reality is Broken: Why Games Make Us Better and How They Can Change the World*. London: Jonathan Cape.

McLuhan, Marshall (1969), *Counterblast*. London: McLelland and Stewart.

McRae, Hamish (2010), *What Works: The Secrets of the World's Best Organisations and Communities*. London: HarperPress.

Mike, S. (2015), *Social Class in the 21st Century*. London: Pelican.

Mind Gym (2009), *The Mind Gym: Relationships*. London: Sphere.

Moreno, Jacob (1934), *Who Shall Survive? A New Approach to the Problem of Human Interrelations*. Washington, DC: Nervous and Mental Disease Publishing Co.

Mrs Moneypenny and Heather McGregor (2012), *Mrs Moneypenny's Careers Advice For Ambitious Women*. London: Portfolio Penguin.

Mulgan, Geoff (1991), *Communication and Control: Networks and the New Economies of Communication*. New York: Guilford Press.

Mulgan, Geoff (1998), *Connexity*. Boston, MA: Harvard Business School Press.

Mulgan, Geoff (2013), *The Locust and the Bee: Predators and Creators in Capitalism's Future*. Woodstock, Oxon: Princeton University Press.

Munro, Alice (2009), *Too Much Happiness*. London: Vintage.

Newman, Mark, Albert-László Barabási and Duncan J. Watts (2006), *The Structure and Dynamics of Networks*. Princeton, NJ: Princeton University Press.

Nussbaum, Martha C. (2001), *Upheavals of Thought: The Intelligence of Emotion*. Cambridge: Cambridge University Press.

Nye, Joseph. S. Jr (2011), *The Future of Power*. New York: PublicAffairs.

O'Malley, Michael (2010), *The Wisdom of Bees*. London: Penguin Books.

Pariser, Eli (2011), *The Filter Bubble: What the Internet Is Hiding from You*. London: Viking.

Park, Benjamin (1880), ed: *Appleton's cyclopaedia of applied mechanics: a dictionary of Mechanical engineering and the Mechanical arts*. New York, D. Appleton and company.

Parker, Tony (1963), *The Unknown Citizen*. London: Hutchinson.

Parker, Tony (1985), *The People of Providence*. London: Penguin.

Paul, Lalline (2014), *The Bees*. London: Fourth Estate.

Pentland, Alex (2014), *Social Physics: How Good Ideas Spread – Lessons from a New Science*. New York, Penguin Press.

Peters, Tom (1994), *The Tom Peters Seminar: Crazy Times Call for Crazy Organizations*. London: Macmillan.

Pink, Daniel H. (2011), *Drive: The Surprising Truth About What Motivates Us*. Edinburgh: Canongate Books.

Pinker, Susan (2015), *The Village Effect: Why Face-to-Face Contact Matters*. London: Atlantic Books.

Prell, Christina (2012), *Social Network Analysis: History, Theory and Methodology*. London: SAGE Publications.

Pryke, Stephen (2012), *Social Network Analysis in Construction*. Chichester: Wiley-Blackwell.

Putnam, Robert D. (2001), *Bowling Alone: The Collapse and Revival of American Community*. New York: Simon & Schuster.

Quammen, D. (2014), *Ebola: The Natural and Human History*. London: The Bodley Head.

Rainie, Lee and Barry Wellman (2012), *Networked: The New Social Operating System*. Cambridge, MA: MIT Press.

Richardson, Ian, Andrew Kakabadse and Nada Kakabadse (2011), *Bilderberg People: Elite Power and Consensus in World Affairs*. Abingdon: Routledge.

Riley, Gillian (2003) *Willpower* (Vermillion).

Riley, Gillian (2007) *How to Stop Smoking and Stay Stopped for Good* (Vermillion).

Robbs, George (2002), *British Culture and the First World War*. London: Palgrave Macmillan.

Robertson, Ivan and Cary Cooper (2011), *Well-Being: Productivity and Happiness at Work*. Basingstoke: Palgrave Macmillan.

Rosenberg, Howard and Charles S. Feldman (2008), *No Time to Think: The Menace and Media Speed and the 24-hour News Cycle*. New York: Continuum.

Ross, Lee and Richard E. Nisbett (2011), *The Person and the Situation: Perspectives of Social Psychology*. London: Pinter and Martin.

Ryckman, Pamela (2013), *Stiletto Network: Inside the Women's Power Circles That Are Changing the Face of Business*. New York: Amacom.

Sandel, Michael (2013), *What Money Can't Buy: The Moral Limits of Markets*. London: Penguin.

Scarlett, Hilary (2016), *Neuroscience for Organizational Change: An Evidence-Based Practical Guide to Managing Change*. London: Kogan Page.

Schama, S. (2010), *Scribble, Scribble, Scribble: Writings on Ice Cream, Obama, Churchill and My Mother*. London: The Bodley Head.

Schmidt, Eric and Jared Cohen (2013), *The New Digital Age: Reshaping the Future of People, Nations and Business*. London: John Murray.

Scott, Laurence (2015), *The Four-Dimensional Human: Ways of Being in the Digital World*. London: Heinemann.

Sennett, Richard (2012), *Together: The Rituals, Pleasures and Politics of Co-operation*. London: Allen Lane.

Shirky, Clay (2009), *Here Comes Everybody*. London: Penguin Books.

Shirky, Clay (2010), *Cognitive Surplus: Creativity and Generosity in a Connected Age*. London: Allen Lane.

Siegel, Lee (2008), *Against the Machine: Being Human in the Age of the Electronic Mob*. London: Serpent's Tail.

Sills, David L. (Ed.) (1968), *International Encyclopedia of the Social Sciences*. New York: Crowell Collier and Macmillan.

Skyrme, David J. (1999), *Knowledge Networking: Creating the Collaborative Enterprise*. Oxford: Butterworth Heinemann.

Sontag, Susan (1978), *Illness as Metaphor*. Toronto: McGraw-Hill Ryerson.

St. George, Andrew (2013), *Royal Navy Way of Leadership*. London: Random House.

Standage, Tom (2013), *Writing on the Wall: Social Media, the First 2,000 Years*. London: Bloomsbury Publishing.

Stewart, Thomas (1997), *Intellectual Capital: The New Wealth of Organizations*. New York: Doubleday/Currency.

Surowiecki, J. (2005), *The Wisdom of Crowds*. London: Abacus.

Susskind, Richard and Daniel Susskind (2015), *The Future of the Professions: How Technology Will Transform the Work of Human Experts*. Oxford: Oxford University Press.

Taleb, Nassim Nicholas (2008), *The Black Swan: The Impact of the Highly Improbable*. London: Penguin.

Taleb, Nassim Nicholas (2012), *Antifragile: How to Live in a World We Don't Understand*. London: Allen Lane.

Tett, Gillian (2016), *The Silo Effect: Why Every Organisation Needs to Disrupt Itself to Survive*. London: Abacus.

Thaler, Richard H. (2016), *Misbehaving: The Making of Behavioural Economics*. London: Penguin Books.

Thaler, Richard H. and Cass R. Sunstein (2009), *Nudge*. London: Penguin Books.

Tharp, Twyla (2006), *The Creative Habit: Learn It and Use It for Life*. New York: Simon & Schuster.

Toffler, Alvin (1970), *Future Shock*, London: Bodley Head.

Trentmann, Frank (2016), *Empire of Things: How We Became Consumers, from the Fifteenth Century to the Twenty-First*. London: Allen Lane.

Turkle, Sherry (2011), *Alone Together: Why We Expect More from Technology and Less from Each Other*. New York: Basic Books.

Turkle, Sherry (2015), *Reclaiming Conversation: The Power of Talk in A Digital Age*. New York: Penguin Press.

Trollope, Anthony (1864/5 [1986]), *Can You Forgive Her?* London: Penguin Books.

Wajcman, Judy (2015), *Pressed for Time: The Acceleration of Life in Digital Capitalism.* London: University of Chicago Press.

Wallman, James (2015), *Stuffocation: Living More with Less.* London: Penguin Books.

Warren, P., J. Davies and E. Simperl (2011), *Context and Semantics for Knowledge Management.* Berlin: Springer.

Wasserman, S. and K. Faust (1994), *Social Network Analysis.* Cambridge: Cambridge University Press.

Watts, Duncan (2004), *Six Degrees: The Science of a Connected Age.* London: Vintage.

Westen, Drew (2007), *The Political Brain: The Role of Emotion in Deciding the Fate of the Nation.* New York: Perseus Book Group.

Williams-Ellis, Clough (1971), *Architect Errant.* London: Constable.

Wolff, Michael (2015), *Television Is the New Television: The Unexpected Triumph of Old Media in the Digital Age.* New York: Portfolio Penguin.

Wu, Timothy (2010), *The Master Switch: The Rise and Fall of Information Empires.* London: Atlantic Books.

Zborowski, M. and E. Herzog (1962), *Life is With People: The Culture of the Shtetl.* New York: Schocken Books.

Articles and Papers

Adler, Paul S. and Charles Heckscher (2005), 'Towards Collaborative Community', University of Southern California.

Adler, Paul and Seok-Woo Kwon (2009), 'Social Capital: The Good, the Bad and the Ugly', USC Marshall School of Business, Marshall Research Paper Series, Working Paper MKY 03-09.

Alter, Alexandra (2013), 'The New Explosion in Audio Books: How They Re-emerged as a Rare Bright Spot in the Publishing Business', *Wall Street Journal*, 1 August.

An, W. and L. Doan (2015), 'Health Surveillance through Social Networks', *Social Networks*, 42: 8–17.

Asch, Solomon E. (1955), 'Opinions and Social Pressure', *Scientific American*, 193(5).

Ball, Philip (2013), How honeycombs can build Themselves *Nature* 17 July.

Ballantine, Matt (2016) 'Who shares wins'-Leading Edge Forum June

Bar–Yam, Yaneer: Transition to extinction: Pandemics in a connected world. 3rd July 2016 www.medium.com

Bar–Yam, Yaneer: How community response stopped Ebola 11 July 2016 www.medium.com

Baumeister, Roy E., Ellen Bratslavsky, Mark Muraven and Dianne M. Tice (1998), 'Ego Depletion: Is the Active Self a Limited Resource?', *Journal of Personality and Social Psychology*, 74: 1252–65.

Benton, R. A. (2016), 'Uniters or Dividers? Voluntary Organizations and Social Capital Acquisition', *Social Networks*, 44: 209–18.

Bian, Y., X. Hunag and L. Zhang (2015), 'Information and Favouritism: The Network Effect on Wage Income in China', *Social Networks*, 40: 129–38.

Bilbao-Osorio, Benat, Soumitra Dutta and Bruno Lanvin (Eds) (2014), 'The Global Information Technology Report 2014: Rewards and Risks of Big Data', Insight Report, World Economic Forum.

Billings, Molly (1997), 'The Influenza Pandemic of 1918', *University of Standford*. Available from: www.virus.stanford.edu

Bohn, A., C. Buchta, K. Hornik and P. Mair (2014), 'Making Friends and Communicating on Facebook: Implications for the Access to Social Capital', *Social Networks*, 37: 29–41.

Brashears, M. E. and E. Quintane (2015), 'The Microstructures of Network Recall: How Social Networks Are Encoded and Represented in Human Memory', *Social Networks*, 41: 113–26.

Brynjolfsson, Erik and Andrew McAfee (2015), 'Will Humans Go the Way of Horses? Labor in the Second Machine Age', *Foreign Affairs*, July/August 2015.

Burt, Ronald S. (2001), 'Structural Holes Versus Network Closure as Social Capital', in *Social Capital, Theory and Research*, edited by Nan Lin, Karen S. Cook and R. S. Burt. New York: Aldine de Gruyter.

Burt, Ronald S. (2015), 'Time as a Contingency Factor in Network Advantage', *Strategic Leadership Research Papers*, University of Chicago Booth.

Burt, Ronald S. and Jennifer Merluzzi (2013), 'Embedded Brokerage: Hubs Versus Locals', preprint of chapter from *Research in Sociology of Organisations*, edited by Stephen P. Borgatti, Daniel J. Brass, Daniel S. Halgin, Giuseppe Labianca and Ajay Mehra. Chicago, IL: Chicago Booth.

Canning, David and Esra Bennathan (n.d.), 'The Social Rate of Return on Infrastructure Investments', in *Infrastructure and Growth: A Multicountry Panel Study*, World Bank, RPO 680–9.

Christakis, Nicholas (2007), 'The Spread of Obesity in a Large Social Network over 32 Years', *New England Journal of Medicine*, 357: 370–9.

Cholle, Francis P. (2011), 'What Is Intuition and How Do We Use It?', *Psychology Today*, 31 August 2011.

Colen, B. D. (2015), 'An Indictment of Ebola Response', *Harvard Gazette*, 22 November. Available from: www.news.harvard.edu

Collins, Andrea, Dimitris Potoglou and Andy Fryers (2016), 'Reducing the Impact of Visitor Travel: Reflections on Hay Festival, Hay-on-wye, Wales'. *Cardiff University Study* Available from: www.hayfestival.com

Cross, Rob, Andrew Parker, Laurence Prusak and Stephen P. Borgatti (2001), 'Knowing What We Know: Supporting Knowledge Creation and Sharing in Social Networks', *Organizational Dynamics*, 30(2): 100–20.

Cross, Rob and Robert Thomas (2011), 'A Smarter Way to Network: Successful Executives Connect with Select People and Get More out of Them', *Harvard Business Review*, July–August.

d'Ancona, Matthew (2015), 'Forget History, in the New Politics Only the Now Matters', *The Guardian*, 10 August 2015.

Dasgupta, Partha and Ismail Serageldin (Eds) (1999), *Social Capital: A Multifaceted Perspective*. Washington, DC: The World Bank.

Deming, David J. (2015), 'The Growing Importance of Social Skills in the Labor Market',
    National Bureau of Economic Research Working Paper 21473.
Dell Women's Entrepreneur Network (2014), 'The Gender Global Entrepreneurship and
    Development Index (GEDI)', Global Entrepreneurship and Development Institute.
Desmarais, B. A., V. G. Moscardelli, B. F. Schaffner and M. S. Kowal (2015), 'Measuring
    Legislative Collaboration: The Senate Press Events Network', Social Networks, 40: 43–54.
Dobbs, Richard, Anu Madgavkar, Dominic Barton, Eric Labaye, James Manyika, Charles
    Roxburgh, Susan Lund and Siddarth Madhav (2012), The World at Work: Jobs, Pay and
    Skills for 3.5 Billion People. McKinsey Global Institute.
Dunbar, Robin. I. M., V. Arnaboldi, M. Conti and A. Passarella (2015), 'The Structure of
    Online Social Networks Mirrors Those in the Offline World', Social Networks, 43: 39–47.
Edwards, Luke (2016), 'What is Elon Musk's 700mph Hyperloop? The Subsonic Train
    Explained', Pocket-lint, 10 May. Available from: www.pocket-lint.com
Esman, Milton J. (2003), 'Social Capital and Empowerment', Cornell University. Available
    from: www.siteresources.worldbank.org
Fang, Lily and Sterling Huang (2011), 'Gender and Connections among Wall Street
    Analysts', INSEAD Faculty & Research Working Paper.
Farrar, Jeremy, (2016), The Future of Global Health. They Festival www.nayfestival.com.
Fischer, M. and P. Sciarini (2015), 'Unpacking Reputational Power: Intended and Unintended
    Determinants of the Assessment of Actors' Power', Social Networks, 42: 60–71.
Fowler, James H. and Nicholas A. Christakis (2009), 'Dynamic Spread of Happiness in a
    Large Social Network: Longitudinal Analysis of the Framlingham Heart Study Social
    Network', British Medical Journal, 338(7685): 23–7.
Gaudeul, A. and C. Giannetti (2013), 'The Role of Reciprocation in Social Network
    Formation, with an Application to LiveJournal', Social Networks, 35: 317–30.
Gërxhani, K., J. Brandts and A. Schram (2013), 'The Emergence of Employer Information
    Networks in an Experimental Labour Market', Social Networks, 35: 541–60.
Gladstone, Rick (2015), 'Liberian Leader Concedes Errors in Response to Ebola', The New
    York Times, 11 March.
Gladwell, Malcolm (1999), 'Six Degrees of Louis Weisberg', The New Yorker, Annals of
    Society, 11 January.
Glover, Bill (2010), 'Cabot Strait Cable and 1857–58 Atlantic Cables'. Available from:
    www.atlantic-cable.com//
Granovetter, Mark S. (1973), 'The Strength of Weak Ties', American Journal of Sociology,
    78(6): 1360–80.
Hartmans, Ruud and Luc Kamperman (2009), 'People Organise Their Own Flow',
    Boss Magazine, Issue 36.
Hatch, Mary Jo (1999), 'Exploring the Empty Spaces of Organizing: How Improvisational
    Jazz Helps Redescribe Organizational Structure', Organization Studies, 20(1): 75–100.
Health and Safety Executive (2016), 'Work-related Stress, Anxiety and Depression Statistics
    in Great Britain 2016'. Available from: www.hse.gov.uk
Hedström, P. and F. Collet (2013), 'Old Friends and New Acquaintances: Tie Formation
    Mechanisms in an Interorganizational Network Generated by Employee Mobility',
    Social Networks, 35: 288–99.

Holt-Lunstad, J., T. B. Smith and J. B. Layton (2010), 'Social Relationships and Mortality Risk: A Meta-Analytic Review', *PLoS Medicine* 7(7).

Husslage, B., P. Borm, T. Burg, H. Hamers and R. Lindelauf (2015), 'Ranking Terrorists in Networks: A Sensitivity Analysis of Al Qaeda's 9/11 Attack', *Social Networks*, 42: 1–7.

Ibarra, Herminia (2004), ' "Men and Women of the Corporation" and "The Change Masters": Practical Theories for Changing Times', *The Academy of Management Executive (1993–2005)*, 18(2): 108–11.

Ibarra, Herminia and Mark Hunter (2006), 'How Leaders Create and Use Networks', *Harvard Business Review*, Article ref No 1727.

Jones, Diana (2006) *Sociometry and Social Network Analysis: Applications and Implications*, ANZPA Journal, 15 December 2006.

Joseph Banks, the plant collector who made the exotic everyday in British gardens, Kew Magazine, 2009. Available at: www.kew.org.

Kantor, Jodi and David Streitfeld (2015), 'Inside Amazon: Wrestling Big Ideas in a Bruising Workplace', *New York Times*, 15 August.

Kelland, Kate (2016), 'Doctoring WHO. The World Health Organization's Critical Challenge: Healing Itself', *Reuters*, 8 February.

Kellaway, Lucy (2015), 'A Blast of Common Sense Frees Staff from Appraisals', *Financial Times*, 26 July.

Kendall, Sue (2014), 'Mapping the History of Wellbeing', *OECD Insights: Debate the Issues*, 2 October.

Krantz, Matt (2015), 'Google's 16% Leap Lifts Nasdaq to New High', *USA Today*, 17 July.

Krebs, Valdis (1996), 'Visualizing Human Networks', *Release 1.0 Esther Dyson's Monthly Report*, 12 (February): 2–96.

Lim, Chaeyoon and Robert D. Putnam (2010), 'Religion, Social Networks, and Life Satisfaction', *American Sociological Review*, 75(6): 914–33.

Linge, Nigel, 'The Trans-Atlantic Telegraph Cable: 150th Anniversary Celebration, 1858–2008, www.cntr.salford.ac.uk

Lu, Y., D. Ruan and G. Lai (2013), 'Social Capital and Economic Integration of Migrants in Urban China', *Social Networks*, 35: 357–69.

McClurg, S. D. and D. Lazer (2014), 'Editorial: Political Networks', *Social Networks*, 36: 1–4.

McKissack, Ian J. (1971), 'Conformity in Ghana', *British Journal of Clinical Psychology*, 10(1).

McKnight, Jenna (2016), 'Architects for Society Designs Low-Cost Hexagonal Shelters for Refugees', *dezeen*, 14 April.

Medeiros, João (2014), 'How Geographic Profiling Helps Find Serial Killers', *Wired*, 10 November. *American Cancer*.

Mendes, Elizabeth (2015), 'Personalised Medicine: Redefining Cancer and Its Treatment'. *American Cancer Society* Available from: www.cancer.orgpersonalized-medicine-redefining-cancer-and-its-treatment. Accessed 8 December 2016.

Morris, Alex (2014), 'Tales from the Millennials' Sexual Revolution', *Rolling Stone*, 31 March.

Morris, Jessica (2016), 'Living with Uncertainty'. Available from: www.jessicamorrisnyc. wordpress.com.

Mullin, Benjamin (2016), 'Buzzfeed undergoes company-wide reorganisation, separating entertainment from news', 23 August. *Poynter* www.poynter.org

NCD Risk Factor Collaboration (2016), 'Trends in Adult Body-Mass Index in 200 Countries from 1975 to 2014: A Pooled Analysis of 1698 Population-Based Measurement Studies with 19.2 Million Participants', *The Lancet*, 387: 1377–96.

Niekamp, A., L. A. G. Mercken, C. J. P. A. Hoebe and N. H. T. M. Dukers-Muifrers (2013), 'Sexual Affiliation Network of Swingers, Heterosexuals Practicing Risk Behaviours That Potentiate the Spread of Sexually Transmitted Infections: A Two-Mode Approach', *Social Networks*, 35: 223–36.

Obergfell, Ralf (2016), 'Experience: I Was Out to Sea When the Tsunami Struck', *Guardian Weekend*, 23 January.

OECD (2015), 'The Future of Productivity', Preliminary Version, Corresponding Authors: Muge Adalet McGowan, Dan Andrews, Chiara Criscuolo, Giuseppe Nicoletti. Available www.oecd.org

Office for National Statistics (2014), 'National Well-Being'. Available from: www.ons.gov.uk.

Owen-Smith, J., N. C. Cotton-Nessler and H. Buhr (2015), 'Network Effects on Organisational Decision-Making: Blended Social Mechanisms and IPO Withdrawal', *Social Networks*, 41: 1–17.

Parsfield, M., D. Morris, M. Bola, M. Knapp, A. Park, M. Yoshioka and G. Marcus (2015), 'Community Capital', Community Capital: The Value of Connected Communities RSA Available from www.thersa.org

Penny, Laurie (2016), 'Fighting Words: Yes, Most Moaning Millennials are Middle Class. But That's Exactly What Should Worry This Government', *The New Statesman*, 18–31 March.

Pentland, Alex (Sandy) (2010), 'To Signal is Human: Real-Time Data Mining Unmasks the Power of Imitation, Kitch and Charisma in Our Face-to-Face Social Networks', *American Scientist*, 98: 204–11.

Perry, Keith (2014), 'Stampede as Kate Bush tickets sell out in 15 minutes', *The Telegraph*, 28 March.

Prosser, David (2015), 'How Freelancers Are Taking Over the World', *Forbes*, 24 June.

Randall, Chris, Ann Corp and Abigail Self (2014), 'Measuring National Well-Being: Life in the UK, 2014', *Office for National Statistics*.

Reagans, R. and B. McEvily (2003), 'Network Structure and Knowledge Transfer', *Administrative Science Quarterly*, 48: 240–67.

Reagans, Ray and Ezra W. Zuckerman (2001), 'Networks, Diversity, and Productivity: The Social Capital of Corporate R&D Teams', *Organization Science*, 12(4): 502–17.

Rivers, I. and N. Noret (2010), ' "I h8 u": Findings from a Five-Year Study of Text and Email Bullying', *British Educational Research Journal*, 36(4): 643–71.

Rogers, Paul, Rudy Puryear and James Root (2013), 'Infobesity: The Enemy of Good Decision', *Bain Insights*, 11 June. Available from: www.bain.com

Rutledge, Pamela (2011), 'Social Networks: What Maslow Misses', *Psychology Today*, 8 November. Available from: www.psychologytoday.com

Sabatini, Fabio and Francesco Sarrancino (2013), 'Will Facebook Save or Destroy Social Capital? An Empirical Investigation into the Effect of Online Interactions on Trust and Networks', *University of Rome*.

Sankar, C. P., K. Asokan and K. S. Kumar (2015), 'Exploratory Social Network Analysis of Affiliation Networks of Indian Listed Companies', *Social Networks*, 43: 113–20.

Schawbel, Dan (2015), 'The Top 10 Workplace Trends for 2015', Forbes.

Schweer, Margaret, Dimitris Assimakopoulos, Rob Cross and Robert J. Thomas, '*Building a Well-Networked Organisation*', 21 December 2011.

Schweinberger, M., M. Petrescu-Prahova and D. Q. Vu (2014), 'Disaster Response on September 11, 2001 through the Lens of Statistical Network Analysis', *Social Networks*, 37: 42–55.

Shafak, Elif (2015), 'As Storytellers, We Speak for Pluralism and Democracy', *The Guardian*, 21 March.

Shipilov, A., G. Labianca, V. Kalnysh and Y. Kalnysh (2014), 'Network-Building Behavioural Tendencies, Range, and Promotion Speed', *Social Networks*, 39: 71–83.

Siem, Brooke (2016), 'Abbye "Pudgy" Stockton is the Reason Why Women Lift Weights', Barbend, 6 April *Barbend*. Available from: www.barbend.com

Silverman, Lauren (2013), 'Young Adults with Autism Can Thrive in High-Tech Jobs', *NPR Morning Edition*, 22 April.

Sloan Management Review. '*Building a well-Networked organisation*' Margaret Schweer, Dimitris Assimakopoulos, Rob Cross and Robert J. Thomas, 21 December 2011.

Smith, Aaron (2016), 'Gig Work, Online Selling and Home Sharing', *Pew Research Centre*, 17 November.

Smith, Craig (2016), 'By the Numbers: 41 Impressive Tinder Statistics', 29 May *expandedramblings*, See: www.expandedramblings.com.

Smith, Emily Esfahani (2013), 'Social Connections Make a Better Brain', *The Atlantic*, 29 October. www.theatlantic.com

Stern, Corey (2015), 'The 21 Biggest Family-Owned Businesses in the World', *Business Insider*, 14 July.

Stewart, James B. (2016), 'Facebook has 50 Minutes of Your Time Each Day. It Wants More', *New York Times*, 5 May.

St. George, Andrew (2013), 'Leadership Lessons from the Royal Navy', *McKinsey Quarterly*, January.

Sutherland, Rory (2015), 'The Most Important Test That HS2 Doesn't Pass', *The Spectator*, 21 November.

The 2016 Doloitte Millennial Survey: winning over the next generation of leasers.

The Royal Society (2011), 'Knowledge, Networks and Nations: Global Scientific Collaboration in the 21st Century', The Royal Society, Policy Document 3/11.

Thielman, Sam (2016), 'Facebook Fires Trending Team, and Algorithm without Humans Goes Crazy', *The Guardian*, 29 August.

Tinti, Peter (2014), 'The Toxic Politics of Ebola', *Foreignpolicy*, 6 October.

Trentmann, Frank (2016), 'The transatlantic cables built in the mid-19th century shrank time and space', — *History Today*, 16 September.

Uzzi, Brian (1997), 'Social Structure and Competition in Interfirm Networks: The Paradox of Embeddedness', *Administrative Science Quarterly*, 42(1): 35–67.

Vanhoutte, Bram (2011), 'Social Capital and Well-Being in Belgium (Flanders): Identifying the Role of Networks and Context', *Katholieke Universiteit Leuven, Faculteit Sociale Wetenschappen*.

Vanhoutte, Bram and Marc Hooghe (2012), 'The Influence of Social Structure, Networks and Community on Party Choice in the Flemish Region of Belgium: A Multilevel Analysis', *Acta Politica*, 1–28.

Warwick, Josh and Philip Allen (2014), 'Meet the 21-Year Old YouTuber Who Made Millions Playing Video Games', *The Telegraph*, 16 October.

Watts, Duncan J. and Stephen H. Strogatz (1998), 'Collective Dynamics of "Small-World" Networks', *Nature*, 393: 440–2.

Weare, C., W. E. Loges and N. Oztas (2007), 'Email Effects on the Structure of Local Associations: A Social Network Analysis', *Social Science Quarterly*, 88(1): 222–43.

Weick, Karl. E. (1998), 'Improvisation as a Mindset for Organizational Analysis', *Organizational Science*, 9(5).

Weisberg, Jacob (2016), 'Hopelessly Hooked', *New York Review of Books*, 25 February–9 March.

Wellcome Trust (2013), 'House of Commons Science and Technology Committee: Antimicrobial Resistance – Response by *Wellcome Trust*'.

Wolf, Christopher (2015), 'What If I Told You . . . Gen-Z Matters More Than Millennials', Emerging Theme Radar Report, 2 December. *Goldman Sachs*.

World Economic Forum in collaboration with Boton Consulting Group (2015), 'Managing the Risk and Impact of Future Epidemics: Options for Public–Private Co-Operation', *World Economic Forum, Industry Agenda*.

World Economic Forum (2016), 'The Internet of Things is Here'. Available from: www.weforum.org

World Health Organization (2014), 'Antimicrobial Resistance: Global Report of Surveillance', *World Health Organisation*.

Zack, Michael H. (2000), 'Jazz Improvisation and Organizing: Once More from the Top', *Organization Science*, 11(2): 227–34.

ACKNOWLEDGEMENTS

Each person listed here has allowed me to transform pieces of a complex, changing jigsaw in my head over a decade of thinking about modern connectedness into words on the page. I feel indebted to them all. Anything I get right, I owe to them. Any errors and omissions, I have only myself to blame.

Family

Alaric Bamping, my husband, who always holds the fort, holds my interest, and holds my hand. Roman, Anoushka and Wolfie, who repeatedly asked 'Mum, how's the book going?'. Andy Hobsbawm, who I turn to first for all new technology intelligence and who has been my protective big brother for over half a century; Marlene, my mum, who read every word early and fully connects to the world even at the grand old age of 85; The entire original Schwarz clan and its descendent cousins and spouses who are not just family but friends: Wal, Dot, Habie, Ben, Tanya, Niall, Zac, Laura, and along the family tree Charlotte, Isabel, Patsy. And to to the memory of my late father, Eric Hobsbawm, because I would be lying if I said I wasn't, deep down, writing this in part for him and my other family members who influence me after death as much as they did when they were alive, especially my grandmother Lily Schwarz, the finest salonniere in all of St John's Wood and before that, Vienna.

Personal Trainers

Toby Mundy, my agent, who helped me bring this project to fruition with his perpetual verve, kindness and clarity. Gratitude and admiration in equal measure to the Bloomsbury Set: Ian Hallsworth my editor; Alexandra Pringle and Nigel Newton who first met the idea with such enthusiasm; Jude Drake, Vicky Beddow, Maria Hammershoy, Giles Herman, Heather Cushing, Merv Honeywood: great publishers and editors are, in fact, alive and well. Others who painstakingly talked through aspects of the book in detail, reading drafts, taking a polite literary scalpel at crucial moments, who wear their intelligence lightly, and who coach diplomatically: Stephen Barber, Margaret Bluman, Helen Brocklebank, Pamela Dow, Giles Gibbons, Martin Harris, Roman Hobsbawm Bamping, Henry Mason, Matt Peacock, Judy Piatkus, Wendell Steavenson, Alice Sherwood, Andrew St George, Stefan Stern, Frank Trentmann, Rachael Ward and James Woudhuysen.

Early Adopters

Many of the ideas in this book were shaped by conversations over several years with people who may not even realise how influential they have been on my thinking. I would like to thank them here. Matt Ballantine, Mitch Besser, Richard Carvalho, Louise Casey, Caroline Corby, Finn Craig, Brendan Finegan, Emma Gilpin-Jacobs, Elsbeth Johnson, Jude Kelly, Gemma Lines, Caroline Michel, Heather "Mrs Moneypenny" McGregor, Ben Moss, Gwyn Miles, Adrian Monck, Harry Ritchie, Julia Neuberger, Cliff Oswick, Matthew Rycroft, Anya Stiglitz, Jack Stoerger and Richard Straub.

Giant Shoulders

There is a particular group of writers, academics and thinkers whose intellectual shoulders so many of us stand on and who personally provided me with encouragement and succinct contribution to this book exactly when it counted: Matthew d'Ancona, Yasmin Alibhai-Brown, Bronwen Maddox, Niall Ferguson, Misha Glenny, Lynda Gratton, Andrew Keen, Charles Handy, Herminia Ibarra, Dambisa Moyo, Simon Schama, Nassim Nicholas Taleb, Marc Ventresca and Barry Wellman.

Keep Fit Class

The following people always give me an expresso shot of energy, wisdom, friendship. Their support has bolstered me in particular for this book. Decca Aitkenhead, Sarah Benton, Jane Brien, Colin Byrne, James Caplin, Caitlin Davies, William Eccleshare, Liz De Planta, Sarah Dudney, Liesel Evans, Angela Ferreira, Esther Freud, Adam Gemmell, Viv Groskop, Charles and Liz Handy, Stephen Hargrave, Lennie Goodings, Kirsty Lang, Fiona Legg, Sophie Levey, Kimberly Quinn, Rachel Johnson, Sarah McTavish, Fiona McMorrough, Jessica Morris, Sanjay Nazerali, Sally Osman, Shyama Pereira, Ed Pilkington, Sophie Radice, Hannah Rothschild, Jenni Russell, Natalia Schiffrin, Saskia Sissons, Harriet Spicer, Luke Syson, Suzanna Taverne, Brigitte Trafford, Claire Fox, Julia Llewellyn Smith. And of course, everyone at Editorial Intelligence. There is never a dull moment with Charlie Burgess, Hayden Brown, Andrew Davidson, Stephen Fleming, Harvey Goldsmith, Tommy Helsby, Laura Musins, Geraldine Sharpe-Newton, Fiona Thorne, and Peter York.

Special Thanks

To Antonia Jennings for preliminary research; to my 'Reader Zero' John Bamping for his; to Ravi Veriah Jacques for help on permissions and final research; To the estates, publishers and agencies who have given their permission to reproduce quotes: Ed Victor Ltd (Iris Murdoch); Europa Editions (Elena Ferrante) The Sunday Times Magazine (Tanya Gold); The New York Review of Books (Jacob Weisberg); Barbara Hogenson Agency (Carl Sandberg); The Estate of Corine McLuhan (Marshall McLuhan); BBC Radio 4 'Thought for the Day' (Lucy Winkett); Namoi Feil those Validation Method' I write about at the beginning of Chapter 4 for 'The Social Soul' and Valdis Krebs for telling me his story in Chapter 6 'Networks and Networkers, Jessica Morris for allowing me to reproduce from her blog 'Good for Now'; To Herminia Ibarra for permission to reproduce her 'How Connective is your Network?' Illustration and to Theo Borgvin-Weiss for the illustrations of The Hexagon of Social Health, The Hierarchy of Communication, the Social Six and The Knowledge Dashboard.

Lastly

To Helena Kennedy QC at Mansfield College, University of Oxford, for inviting me to talk about the ideas in the book before anywhere else, and to Jane Buswell in the Principal's Lodge, Mansfield, where I retreated to write; to Kirsten Lass of BBC Radio 4 for giving the chance to air some of my ideas, and to colleagues and students at Cass Business School, London, and the University of Suffolk. Final thanks to the staff at The Laboratory Spa and Gym in Muswell Hill, North London, where I did much writing and editing, head down and headphones on, and especially Kasia and Sarah-Jane who would arrive at my table unprompted with – what else – a strong cup of coffee.

INDEX